'This is Churchill in his slippers, off guard. But how little history would tell us if its great figures were shown only in their public attitudes!' George Malcolm Thomson, *Daily Express*

'The world should be grateful . . . that the full story of Churchill as a human being with frailties at times in proportions to his strengths, should be brought out by so sensitive and knowledge-able a companion.' Herbert Black, *Boston Globe*

'The most magnificent portrait of Winston, his strength and his weakness, yet drawn.' Edward Weeks, *Atlantic*

'Will prove to be a valuable contribution to the history of our times.' *British Medical Journal*

'It is a book of high quality and unflagging interest, a priceless witness to the history of our time.' *Daily Express*

'Lord Moran's eloquent and amazingly forth-right chapters will undoubtedly change many a reader's opinions of some wartime leaders, but they can only add to Winston Churchill's stature . . . He emerges from this book clothed in greatness of spirit . . .' Henry C. Wolfe, *Chicago Tribune*

'Delightful literary style . . . the precious intimate record, by the perfect chronicler.' Katherine Gauss Jackson, *Harper's*

'As a contribution to history it is of the first importance . . . it adds very greatly to our knowledge of one of the foremost figures of modern times.' Sir Charles Petrie, *Illustrated London News*

'Humour, urbanity, penetrating analysing of the motives which moved men on important occasions . . . love and sympathy for the man who was his patient – all these are present in this book.' Barrie Pitt, *Book Society*

# CHURCHILL
# AT WAR 1940–45

## LORD MORAN

Introduction by his son John,
the present Lord Moran

**ROBINSON**
London

Constable & Robinson Ltd
3 The Lanchesters
162 Fulham Palace Road
London W6 9ER
www.constablerobinson.com

First published in the UK as
*Churchill: The Struggle for Survival 1940–1965*
by Constable and Company, 1966

This abridged and revised edition published by Robinson,
an imprint of Constable & Robinson Ltd, 2002

A copy of the British Library Cataloguing in
Publication Data is available from the British Library

ISBN 1-84119-608-8

Printed and bound in the EU

10 9 8 7 6 5 4 3 2 1

To
*DOROTHY*
who has been given back to me
and to

*JOHN & GEOFFREY*

who in their different ways
are not unlike her

# Contents

# Acknowledgements

I wish to express my thanks to Mr Richard Church for his help in keeping this book within manageable proportions. I am grateful to Professor Terence Spencer of Birmingham University for his valuable advice while I was writing this book. I have been able to turn to him whenever a doubtful point arose.

Mr Henry Laughlin of Houghton, Mifflin Co., of Boston, U.S.A., has followed my story as it unfolded, and I have found his sustained interest heartening. Mr Craig Wylie has read the text and has given me the benefit of his careful judgment. I have, too, been fortunate in my London publisher, Mr Ben Glazebrook of Constable and Co. He has met me at every point and has made things easy for me. And here may I pay tribute to Mr Denis Hamilton's warm encouragement.

I have to thank the late Professor Una Ellis-Fermor and Professor Muriel Bradbrook for criticism and counsel. I have come to rely on the frank criticism of my son, John Wilson: at every stage he has helped me to settle points of difficulty.

I would like to thank my wife and Miss Marian Dean for the time and care they have given to correcting the proofs.

In expressing my thanks to publishers for allowing me to make quotations, I wish to underline my debt to Cassell and Co. for permission to use words from Sir Winston's books.

When I put down my pen, I wish to be sure that I have reported faithfully those who have talked to me about him. I trust that in checking those conversations I have forgotten no one.

*Made by Lord Moran in the original edition*

The present Lord Moran expresses his thanks to Lady Soames for permission to quote in his Introduction a passage from *Clementine Churchill: the revised and updated biography* by her daughter, Mary Soames.

# Introduction

by Lord Moran's son John,
the present Lord Moran

When my father's publisher, Ben Glazebrook, asked me to write an introduction to this book I was not sure that I was the right person to do this, as I am far from impartial about my father. I was fond of him and I admired him. When I was quite young we used to go for long walks together round the Inner Circle in Regent's Park. He treated me as a grown-up and told me all about his plans. Later on he often talked or wrote to me about the putting together of his two books, *The Anatomy of Courage* and his book on Churchill, *The Struggle for Survival*. As I am one of the few survivors of those who were consulted about the Churchill book as it took shape, I thought I should agree to Ben's request.

I am glad that Constable & Robinson are bringing out a new edition of that part of the original book which deals with the war years. It now includes new passages from my father's papers which were not included in the original edition. I hope that a new generation of readers will find his account as absorbing as did those who first read it in 1966.

My father began to look after Mr Churchill as he then was, in May 1940. Churchill had, after long years in the political wilderness, become Prime Minister just two weeks before. He faced a situation that looked almost hopeless. France had been overrun, the British Expeditionary Force was about to be driven out of continental Europe, the victorious Wehrmacht and Luftwaffe expected to be launched any day on an early invasion leading to the crushing of a weakly-defended island. Some members of the Cabinet and even of the military staffs were known to feel that there was no alternative but to sue for peace. The weight of responsibility carried by the First Minister of the Crown was immense. But Churchill had reached sixty-five, the age at which men in England now qualify as old-age pensioners.

It was not surprising that some of his colleagues thought that Churchill should have a regular medical adviser. His close associates, Lord Beaverbrook and Brendan Bracken, recommended my father, whose patients they had been. So he was called in. He thought his attendance would be brief – 'I do not like the job, and I don't think the arrangement can last.' But last it did, till Churchill's death twenty-five years later. My father regarded it as a privileged duty to look after the nation's leader at such a time, as his contribution to the war effort, and he would take no fee for it.[1]

My father put the care of the Prime Minister before anything else, making himself available at any time of the day or night. He came to know Churchill very well indeed and, while being aware of his faults, regarded him with affection and admiration, realising that he had been brought into close contact with one of the most remarkable men of our time, or indeed of British history. He did slightly disapprove of the brandy and cigars atmosphere that Churchill enjoyed with his cronies and he was never part of that way of life. But this did not prevent him from having a deep respect for Churchill, and the two men formed a close association which lasted for a quarter of a century.

That Churchill was kept going until he was over ninety, despite a heart attack, a number of strokes and three attacks of pneumonia,

---

[1] Churchill, the most generous of men, was uncomfortable about this. In 1945 he suggested that my father should be paid a stipend from public funds. This was put to him by Sir Edward Bridges but he turned it down, telling Churchill that he didn't want any reward. It was his war job and 'payment would spoil the flavour of it for me'. After the war, in 1949, Churchill finally persuaded my father to accept some recompense for his services. This took the form of covenants in favour of my brother and myself of £300 a year each, for which we were both very grateful, and later a covenant for my mother of £500 a year, which helped what my father's biographer described as my parents' tight financial position.

suggests that my father was an effective physician and performed a service which was of real value to the country. For the years covered in the present book Churchill was all the time working under great stress. My father also knew when to call in the right expert. As one of Churchill's secretaries, Anthony Montague Browne, wrote, he was a 'specialist of specialists'[1]. But there were also times when he had to make up his mind alone, for example when he had to decide what to do when Churchill had a heart attack in Washington in 1941, described on pages 17–18 of this edition, when he knew that to insist on the normal treatment of six weeks' complete rest would be catastrophic for our country, since it would mean 'publishing to the world . . . that the P.M. was an invalid with a crippled heart and a doubtful future', whereas if he did nothing and Churchill had another and more serious attack he himself would be accused of killing him by not insisting on rest. He decided to take the risk. His biographer, a professor of medicine, had no doubt that his decision to sit tight and tell no one was 'brave and correct'.[2] He was again responsible for what should be done when an exhausted Churchill was seriously ill at Carthage at the end of 1943.

In these cases and in others he was alive to the political and general background, not merely to the immediate clinical problems. As Churchill's daughter Mary later wrote:

'Lord Moran understood Winston thoroughly, and he was indeed fortunate he had as his doctor a man who understood not only the medical considerations and risks to his patient, but one who was also fully aware of the implications with regard to the office he held, of his condition at any time. Lord Moran moreover understood the relationships between, and with, Winston's colleagues, and where one could expect loyalty, understanding, and total discretion – and where one could not.'[3]

---

[1] *Sunday Express*, 22 May 1966.
[2] *Churchill's Doctor: A biography of Lord Moran* by Richard Lovell, p. 165.
[3] *Clementine Churchill: the revised and updated biography* by her daughter, Mary Soames, Chapter 26, page 470.

During the war and after it my father thought it his primary task to keep his patient going. In this he succeeded, but at some cost to himself. He had risen gradually to the summit of his profession. After serving as Medical Officer with the First Battalion of the Royal Fusiliers during the First World War he had in 1920 become Dean of St Mary's Hospital Medical School. At that time it was generally described as a dump. Its buildings were out of date or derelict and it had a substantial overdraft. He transformed it into one of the finest medical schools in the country; rebuilt it, obtaining large contributions from those he knew, notably Lords Revelstoke and Beaverbrook, and himself took charge of the selection of students, aiming at people of all-round ability on the pattern of Rhodes scholars, though he was accused of favouring good rugby players. I once heard St Mary's students singing cheerfully at a Christmas concert:

'In good King Charles's golden days

When rugger meant promotion.'

He was Dean of the Medical School for twenty-five years. The history of St Mary's describes him as 'The Great Dean'.

From 1938 he had been treasurer of the Royal College of Physicians and was to become its President in April 1941, being re-elected annually thereafter for ten years, often after close contests with the conservative Lord Horder. This was a critical time for the medical profession as the College, under his leadership, was to be much involved in the creation of the National Health service and the role of consultants in it. In effect he was taking part in a revolution in the organisation of medicine in the United Kingdom. This kept him very busy and it was not always easy to keep things under control when he was constantly swept off without notice to Teheran, Cairo, Moscow, Casablanca, Ottawa, Potsdam, Yalta or Washington.

Normally, having reached this eminence in the profession, my father should have expected to have, as a consultant, a large practice which would have provided him with a substantial income. In fact, his constant absences when away with Churchill on his numerous wartime journeys resulted in the disappearance of his practice, for general practitioners who bring patients to consultants expect them to be available whenever they want them. So, towards the end of the war, my father appeared to be living largely on air.

From his own point of view, however, there was another, and much more important, side to the case. He had always wanted to write. He once recalled what happened when he left school at the age of sixteen:

'The day after my return home my father summoned me to his study and asked me what I wanted to do for a living. "I want to write books," I replied. "I have no money," my father said, "and writing is a precarious business. You had better write as a hobby and follow me into medicine."'

This he did, devoting most of his working life to medicine and medical education.

But his original ambition was never extinguished. When, after his return from France at the end of the First World War, he read that a committee had been set up to consider shell-shock which included no-one who had actually been in the trenches, he was outraged and wrote a letter to *The Times* which turned into a long essay on courage. He was warned that as an unknown person he should keep any letter short but he took no notice and wrote an immensely long letter. My mother took it down to Printing House Square on her bicycle. After a few days *The Times* printed it – on the centre page where it took up a column and a half. A young professional soldier called Goschen took note and resolved that if ever he was in a position to do so he would get hold of its writer. Some years later he became Commandant of the Royal Military Academy at Woolwich. He asked my father to speak to his students. This led to his lecturing regularly to the Staff College and to the writing of his first book.

The structure of my father's two books is fundamentally the same. He wrote in the Preface to the first edition of *The Anatomy of Courage*:

'In a sense I have made two books: one, which was scribbled down in an army note book during the last war, is an epitaph of a battalion of the professional army of 1914 . . . I have altered nothing . . . even when it has not worn well with time . . . I wrote to fill the day and to save myself from the awful sameness of those years of trench warfare.

The other I have written when I could . . . I am writing now in a bomber by a port-hole through which if I stand I can see far below me the Libyan desert. It was written for the soldier and the sailor . . .'

The two books have become one – the first is only used to illustrate the second – yet there still hangs around the whole a kind of dual nature.

This weaving together of notes made at the time with later reflections is as true of the Churchill book as it was of the earlier book. One of the few critics who understood the way he worked was John Rowan Wilson, who wrote:

'Lord Moran has always taken his writing seriously, as anyone can tell from his earlier book The Anatomy of Courage. He has a feeling for words and a sense of style – he is also a tireless observer of his fellow men. His relationship with Churchill placed him in a unique position to make use of these gifts. He was to be, as it were, a fly on the ceiling in the corridors of power. He observed; he listened; he recorded, and then afterwards he wrote, not merely as a painstaking recorder of events, but creatively, arranging and interpreting the facts from an extremely individual point of view.'[1]

The earlier book was taking shape when my father first met Churchill and was to be published in 1945. But from 1941 onwards he was also writing about Churchill. Given his lifelong determination to write, and having been brought into close and regular association with a fascinating and complex personality of historic importance, my father, being the man he was, inevitably came to write about him. When he looked in to see Churchill, he would jot down immediately afterwards anything interesting Churchill had said.

In 1940 he did not see much of Churchill. There is nothing in

[1] *World Medicine*, 5 July 1966.

this book about the Battle of Britain. But after 1941 he began to see him frequently and to accompany him on his many wartime journeys, often at first on risky journeys in an unheated bomber. On these occasions he was not only able to observe and record Churchill's reactions. He met all the great actors in the alliance against Hitler – Roosevelt and Stalin, Smuts, Harry Hopkins, Marshall, Alan Brooke, Portal, Alexander, Montgomery, Norman Brook and many others. These also he observed and what they said was noted down. The historian J. H. Plumb wrote:

'A very convincing picture of Churchill emerges . . . Nor is it only Churchill who emerges as a full and rich human character . . . Lord Moran met, with Churchill, all the great men of the western Alliance, watched them, and pinned them down in his pages. Whether he is discussing Stalin or Bernard Baruch, he always has something new, something wise, something memorable to say.'[1]

These contemporary notes were the equivalent of scribblings in the army notebooks. To them were added my father's reflections, on the many aspects of Winston Churchill, on the problems he faced in the war and how he overcame them.

The publication of the first edition of the Churchill book in 1966 gave rise to a prolonged controversy, mostly conducted in the correspondence columns of *The Times*, about the propriety of a doctor writing about a patient and the publication of private conversations. *The Lancet* attacked him but he was supported by the *British Medical Journal*. He was censured by the British Medical Association, of which he was surprised to find himself a member. He was also attacked by Churchill's son, Randolph. Now himself over eighty, he had to defend himself against their accusations. It was at times hard going, particularly when he was rung up by the press when he was fast asleep in the small hours and told that so-and-so had a letter in *The Times* that morning and what did he have to say about it. My father's defence was that it was permissible to write about a great

[1] *Saturday Review*, 23 May 1966.

historical figure after his death, and that he had told Churchill what he proposed to do. This was confirmed by the greatly respected surgeon Sir Herbert Seddon who had twice treated Churchill. He wrote to *The Times* saying that he had evidence that my father's book was written with Sir Winston's knowledge and consent and this satisfied him that no ethical problem had arisen.

The attacks on my father would have been more understandable if he had used his close relationship with Churchill to paint a generally critical picture of him. But this was not so. His considered assessment of him is contained in the paragraph on pages 132–3 of this edition, beginning 'What his critics are apt to forget is that you cannot measure inspiration . . .' and ending, 'gradually I have come to think of him as invincible.'

It was argued that the book had been published too soon after Churchill's death. The fact was that my father was an old man and wanted to see the book, into which he had put so much, in print in his own lifetime. He also wished, generously, to deal with any criticisms himself rather than leaving it to me.

That controversy, stormy though it was, took place nearly forty years ago and may now perhaps be allowed to rest.

Of more concern today is, perhaps, how reliable my father's account is. In writing this book, as in his earlier book, he frequently referred to 'my diary'. This has caused a certain amount of difficulty and misunderstanding. It has, not unreasonably, suggested to some people, including some of those who have written about Churchill, that throughout the twenty-five years that he looked after Churchill he kept a full diary with entries for each day, from which passages were extracted to go in the book. The title of the American edition (for which he was not responsible), *Churchill: Taken from the Diaries of Lord Moran*, reinforced that impression.

In fact he did not keep a diary of that sort, except for very short periods. What he did was explained by Professor Lovell in the preface to his 1992 biography of my father, *Churchill's Doctor*. In that he wrote:

'In his two books . . . Lord Moran alluded to his diary. But he indicated in the prefaces to both books that he did not keep a diary in the ordinary sense of the word. In the First World War he scribbled in army notebooks, on the backs of orders and odd sheets of paper and in his Churchill years on the backs of envelopes and other scraps of paper. The scribblings in the army notebooks, and the elaboration of his thoughts in other notebooks, formed the basis for *The Anatomy of Courage*. In his Churchill years, the earliest orderings of his thoughts from his jottings (some of which, often barely legible, were also scattered through the family papers) appeared in diary form in closely written loose-leaf manuscript books, which overflowed into collections of separate pages. Judging by varied use of past, present and future tenses, and references under some dates to events that had not yet happened, these manuscript books cannot be regarded literally as a diary. Finally, in regard to the notion of a diary, the closest diary-like records from the Second World War onwards were unquestionably the letters written by Lord Moran to his family, many of which they kept.'

Dick Lovell had a greater knowledge of my father's papers than anyone else. But I suspect that his book, published by the Royal Society of Medicine, was not widely read outside the medical profession. So many people were unaware that 'my diary' was, in effect, shorthand for the notes my father jotted down at the time and which formed the basis of both his books.

My father's Churchill book duly became for historians an indispensable source for the last twenty-five years of Churchill's life. But the rather haphazard way in which the contemporary passages were assembled and the constant revision and rewriting to which the text was subjected over a period of years sometimes made it difficult to determine what was written at the time and what was added later.

In 1994 doubt was thrown on the reliability of my father's account by Martin Gilbert, who had continued the official life of Churchill begun by Randolph Churchill. In a book entitled *In Search of Churchill* he wrote:

'Perhaps the most disturbing discovery I have made on sources for Churchill's life came after I had finished the eighth and final volume of the biography, in which a major source, for me as for all historians of his last twenty years, was the voluminous diary kept by Churchill's doctor, Lord Moran. Throughout the period of my researches the diary was closed to historians. Then, after the completion of an authorised life of the doctor, it was brought to a leading medical library in London. I asked for the diary entry for a single date .. To my dismay, not merely for myself but for historical truth I was told ... that there was no entry for that day at all, even though an entry under that exact date appears in the published book. Even the entries that did exist, I was told, were "not a diary in the accepted sense of the word". The mind boggles at how much misinformation may have crept into history books, mine included, by such routes.'

Gilbert does not appear to have read Lovell's biography of my father with its explanation of 'my diary'. He appears to have believed that there was, in the Wellcome Library, a 'voluminous diary' which formed the basis of my father's book. On learning that there was not, he appears to have concluded that the published account was suspect. But I do not for a moment think that it is.

In November 2001 I had a letter from an Oxford historian who had written about Churchill saying that he had used my father's account 'with admiration and gratitude' but that Gilbert's piece 'necessarily makes me wonder' and had made others wonder too. He asked if he could see my father's papers in the Wellcome Library. I suggested that to begin with he should read Professor Lovell's book, about which he did not know. Having found it in the Bodleian he wrote to me saying, 'What a rich book it is! And indispensable to the "Churchillian".' He continued, 'How your father worked on his famous book becomes admirably clear. It is, as I myself had suspected, the product of experience and reflection and any amount of revision ... everything that is good and enlightening other than, for the most part, the exact chronicle for which incautious readers mistake it.'

It seems to me a pity that Professor Lovell's book was not more generally known among historians who were writing about Churchill. Some of them, and not only Gilbert, have tended to refer to my father in somewhat disparaging terms, while still quoting extensively from his account. One recent example is Lord Jenkins's *Churchill*. In describing the occasion in 1943 when Churchill, exhausted after the Teheran conference, fell seriously ill at Carthage with pneumonia and heart trouble (auricular fibrillation), his account begins by saying, 'Moran then began a relentless but wise process of telegraphing for medical assistance from all directions.'[1] He then quoted a story about Jock Colville being asked by a new junior private secretary what he should do if Churchill became ill when he was on solitary duty, and replying, 'You telephone Lord Moran and he will send for a real doctor.'

Thus Lord Jenkins contrives to suggest that my father panicked and that he didn't really know his job. In fact he was the man responsible for looking after the nation's leader in the middle of a war in what he described as a 'God-forsaken spot – no nurses, no milk, not even a chemist'. What he did was to telegraph to Cairo for two nurses and a pathologist and to Tunis for a portable X-ray apparatus. Until the nurses arrived he himself shared the night watches with Churchill's detective. He arranged for three specialists to join him – a cardiologist, a lung specialist and an expert on the new drug M & B. Dealing, as he was, with a 68-year-old Prime Minister in a remote location in the desert, this seems only common prudence. It was the Cabinet in London who were, as he put it, in a complete dither, urging my father to agree that they should send out any specialists he cared to name. He maintained that no one, 'not even a Prime Minister, could properly be treated by a committee'. He told Martin, the principal private secretary, to thank the Cabinet, but to tell them it was not necessary to send out any doctors. 'I could see that he did not think that I was wise'. But he already had what he needed and he was not afraid of taking the blame if things went wrong. Jenkins conceded that 'Moran was quite right to take matters seriously'. If so, why begin by jeering

---

[1] Jenkins, Lord, *Churchill* p. 726.

at him and quoting a malicious remark attributed to Jock Colville?

Elsewhere in his book Lord Jenkins accepts that 'the surrounding evidence suggests that, whatever may be thought of the medical ethics of his clinical revelations, he was mostly accurate in substance',[1] though in another part of the book he makes the curious assertion that my father 'was so anxious to give himself a central role that he was not only an indiscreet but sometimes an unreliable witness of events'[2]. He says nothing to support this view. The doubters seem to forget that, after all, my father was there and they, for the most part, were not.

Some of the criticisms were valid. Lord Normanbrook, for example, pointed out that in seven places in his account my father had described Roosevelt in 1943 as appearing to be a very sick man and as showing 'all the symptoms of hardening of the arteries of the brain' which might have impaired his judgement.[3] He quotes with approval a late passage in the book in which my father wrote, 'When we look back we see that Winston was often right in his clashes with the President . . . If he was at first taken in by Stalin, he woke to the Russian designs before most people. Roosevelt never did.' Normanbrook consequently found it strange that in his Preface to the original edition my father should have suggested that the deterioration in Churchill's relations with Roosevelt was due to his own exhaustion of mind and body. Clearly what he wrote at the time was right and what he said in the Preface was not. I think the explanation was that when he wrote the Preface he was eighty-two, had had a coronary thrombosis and was under intense pressure to finish the book. This time it was he who was exhausted and writing in a hurry.

I have no doubt that my father sometimes got confused about dates. He had no research assistants, not even a secretary. He wrote the whole book himself, and his constant revisions may well have caused discrepancies. But I have equally no doubt that in the main

---

[1] Jenkins, Lord, *Churchill* p. 871.
[2] Ibid, p. 674.
[3] Normanbrook, Lord in *Action This Day*, pp. 34–7.

his account was a truthful and accurate one by an observer who saw an aspect of Churchill that no one else saw. This is not just my own, perhaps prejudiced, view. It was substantially what respected critics concluded when they read the first edition of the book in 1966.

Lord Blake, the biographer of Disraeli, wrote:

'It is an absorbing character study, a unique portrait of one of the greatest figures of our time delineated by a man who might have made his fortune as a writer if he had not devoted himself to medicine. It certainly cannot be argued that any disservice has been done to Sir Winston's reputation. On the contrary, he emerges as an even greater figure than one had realized. He also emerges as a rather different one, more complicated, more sensitive, more apprehensive, more worried – altogether less of the English bulldog, the tough extrovert, the John Bull, than most of us imagined . . . Above all, he was an artist'.[1]

Cyril Connolly wrote in the *Sunday Times*, 'How good a Boswell is Lord Moran? I would say first-rate . . . The test is that all his observations of others seem both just and penetrating, and his memory, his mental filing-system, his recording of dialogue most exact.'[2]

John Grigg wrote:

'Of Churchill himself, the description is marvellously vivid and convincing . . . We are shown as never before (and perhaps never again) the intimate working of his prodigious nature; the grandeur and pettiness; the vast comprehension and strange blindness; the industry, intuition and willpower which made him a formidable leader, and the flashes of generosity and gaiety which made him a lovable man. . . It is only fair to say that Lord Moran has produced the literary masterpiece which it was his ambition to produce.'[3]

---

[1] *Belfast Telegraph*, 23 May 1966.
[2] *Sunday Times*, 22 May 1966.
[3] *Guardian*, 23 May 1966.

Critics in the United States were, without exception, enthusi-astic. Frank Freidal of Harvard was typical in describing it as 'irre-sistible reading . . . not only fascinating, but also of great importance'.[1]

This new edition contains the first half of the original book, essentially the record of Churchill as my father saw him during the war years of 1941 to 1945, but not the gradual decline after the war or his not very successful second spell as Prime Minister.

What will it mean to a new generation of readers? It is, I believe, a highly individual picture of an extraordinary man who held the destiny of Great Britain in his hands in some of the most dangerous and critical years of our history. It also gives a vivid picture of the wartime conferences between Churchill, Roosevelt and Stalin, of the strains and stresses of the great wartime alliance, of how it was kept together, and of the notable personalities who took part in it.

Finally, as many of the critics noted, my father could write. Like Churchill, he loved words, as did his father before him, and he was able to produce some memorable passages. I was myself enormously impressed when, in old age, he wrote the final paragraphs of the original book:

'For fourteen days he was not seen to move. His strength left him slowly, as if he were loath to give up life. On the night of the twenty-fourth of January it appeared that a crisis was at hand. His breathing became shallow and laboured, and at eight o'clock in the morning it ceased. Mary, sitting by his side, looked up at me. I got up and bent over the bed, but he had gone.

He was taken at night to Westminster, to the Hall of William Rufus, and there for three days he lay in state, while the people gathered in crowds that stretched over Lambeth Bridge to the far side of the river, to do honour to the man they loved for his valour. On the fourth day he was borne on a gun-carriage to St Paul's. There followed a long line of men in arms, marching to sorrowful music. With all the panoply of Church and State, and in the presence of his Queen, he was carried to

[1] Department of History, Harvard University.

an appointed place hard by the tombs of Nelson and Wellington, under the great dome, while with solemn music and the beating of drums the nation saluted the man who had saved them and saved their honour.

The village stations on the way to Bladon were crowded with his countrymen, and at Bladon in a country churchyard, in the stillness of a winter evening, in the presence of his family and a few friends, Winston Churchill was committed to English earth, which in his finest hour he had held inviolate.'

# This star of England

*May 1940–February 1945*

Small time, but in that small most greatly lived
This star of England: fortune made his sword.

HENRY V

# PART ONE

# The Riddle of the War

# CHAPTER ONE

# The New War

*May 24, 1940*

Winston Churchill is 65. He has just been appointed Prime Minister, and I have become his doctor, not because he wanted one, but because certain members of the Cabinet, who realized how essential he has become, have decided that somebody ought to keep an eye on his health.

It was in these rather ambiguous circumstances that I made my way this morning to Admiralty House,[1] wondering how he would receive me. Though it was noon, I found him in bed reading a document. He went on reading while I stood by the bedside. After what seemed quite a long time, he put down his papers and said impatiently:

'I don't know why they are making such a fuss. There's nothing wrong with me.'

He picked up the papers and resumed his reading. At last he pushed his bed-rest away and, throwing back the bed-clothes, said abruptly:

'I suffer from dyspepsia, and this is the treatment.'

With that he proceeded to demonstrate to me some breathing exercises. His big white belly was moving up and down when there was a knock on the door, and the P.M. grabbed at the sheet as Mrs Hill came into the room.

---

[1] Mr Churchill continued to live for some weeks after he became Prime Minister in the rooms he had occupied as First Lord of the Admiralty.

Soon after I took my leave. I do not like the job, and I do not think the arrangement can last.

*

The next entry in my diary is dated January, 1941. One day in that month, when I called at the Annexe[1] at Storey's Gate, the man at the door said that Mrs Churchill wanted to see me before I saw the Prime Minister. She said that he was going to Scapa.[2]

'When?'

'Today at noon. There is a blizzard there, and Winston has a heavy cold. You must stop him.'

I went to his room and said my piece. He became very red in the face, and throwing off the bed-clothes, shouted, 'What damned nonsense! Of course I am going.'

I went back to Mrs Churchill to report progress. 'Well,' she said shortly, 'if you cannot stop him, the least you can do is to go with him.' I had nothing with me, but the P.M. lent me a greatcoat with a broad astrakhan collar. He said it would keep out the wind. The purpose of the visit was ostensibly to bid farewell to Lord Halifax, who was about to take up his office as our Ambassador in Washington. But I suspect that the Prime Minister's real purpose was to have a look at the Fleet at Scapa. Facing sheets of driving snow and sleet which caught the breath, I found it difficult to share his enthusiasm. As for Lord Halifax, even in those Arctic surroundings, he had the aspect of an Italian primitive.

On the return journey, Tom Johnston[3] dined us at the Station Hotel at Glasgow, and I sat next to Harry Hopkins,[4] an unkempt figure. After a time he got up and, turning to the P.M., said:

'I suppose you wish to know what I am going to say to President Roosevelt on my return. Well, I'm going to quote you one verse from that Book of Books in the truth of which Mr Johnston's

[1] Fortified Office of the Ministry of Defence (see also p. 94).
[2] The naval base in the Orkney islands used by the Home Fleet in both world wars.
[3] Tom Johnston, Secretary of State for Scotland, 1941–5.
[4] Harry Hopkins, President Roosevelt's closest adviser and confidant.

mother and my own Scottish mother were brought up: "Whither thou goest, I will go; and where thou lodgest, I will lodge: thy people shall be my people, and thy God my God.'" Then he added very quietly: 'Even to the end.'

I was surprised to find the P.M. in tears. He knew what it meant. Even to us the words seemed like a rope thrown to a drowning man.

*

There is no other entry in my diary until December, 1941. There is nothing about the great events which happened during those months, when England stood alone and the Prime Minister touched the peak of his achievement. He did not talk to me about them, though I visited him regularly. When I entered his room, he would put down his papers reluctantly. 'Cannot you see,' he seemed to say, 'that I am very busy and want to get on with my work?' He was fit and well and did not need me. He grudged every second that was taken from his work. My visits became shorter and shorter – a few perfunctory questions and I was out of his room.

*

*December 12, 1941*
Mr Churchill has been panting to meet the President ever since he heard of Pearl Harbour,[1] so today we are bound for Washington. This morning, about noon, he pulled himself out of a launch and was piped aboard the *Duke of York* as she lay at anchor at Greenock; his feeling for a naval occasion had been partly met by a yachting cap over a double-breasted blue reefer coat. I gave him time to be received on the quarter-deck before I followed, and sensed at once the ordered peace of a great battleship.

[1] On December 7, 1941, Japanese aircraft, launched from aircraft-carriers, attacked Pearl Harbour, the headquarters of the American Pacific Fleet, in the Hawaiian islands. This act of pure aggression brought the United States into the war.

*December 20, 1941*

Since we left the protection of the Clyde, we have been battened down for eight days, listening to the dull pounding of the great seas on the ship's ribs. Everyone here takes whatever comes as it comes, save Lord Beaverbrook,[1] whose undisciplined spirit chafes at the confinement. He hates the hours we spend round the table when lunching or dining. The P.M. does the talking, of course, and Max does his best to listen. It is not easy for him; his life has not prepared him for this sort of thing. The people he gathers round him at Cherkley are not interested in books; their conversation is earthy and full of the frailty of man. Max never seems to tire of the shabby drama of some men's lives, their infidelities and their passions: that is what he means by good talk. Winston, on the other hand, speaks as he writes. There are brilliant descriptive passages that fall on Max's ears as prosy stuff, interminably long-winded; he often wonders if it will ever come to an end. Besides, Max does not like playing second fiddle to anyone. At Cherkley he is king.

Winston for his part is too much taken up with his own thoughts to notice Max's fretting. If Max is particularly argumentative – well, what of that? It is just Max's way. Moreover, the astute little man is at pains to hide his feelings. If he is restless as he endures this tribulation, at any rate he keeps a close guard on his tongue when the P.M. is present. He knows – no one better – that Winston is his only friend in politics, and he intends to keep that friend, even if it means playing the part of patient listener, a role for which he is not equipped by nature. You can see his grey face, devoid of colour, sourly surveying his plate for a long time. Suddenly the P.M. will pause in the monologue:

'What do you say, Max? Don't you agree?'

'Oh, yaas,' Max hurriedly chimes in.

Chimes is, of course, the least appropriate verb I could have hit upon. It is rather as if he were trying to spit out something which has an unpleasant taste.

The P.M. is not affected, as Max is, by being sealed below decks.

---

[1] Max Beaverbrook, then Minister of Supply.

Tonight he embarked on a long *post-mortem* on Dakar.[1] When he had done, someone asked how, just before Dakar, the Vichy ships from Toulon had succeeded in passing through the Straits of Gibraltar under the nose of our Navy. It was, the P.M. said, because three things had gone wrong; that all three should happen together was an extraordinary coincidence. First, a warning message came to the Foreign Office, but it came during a raid and the deciphering people had retired to their dug-out. On their return after the 'All Clear' they dealt with priority stuff, and this message was not marked 'priority.' Secondly, an officer at the Admiralty with whom rested the decision whether to wake the First Lord or not did not do so, and action which could have been taken at 2 a.m. was not taken until 11 a.m.

Max pushed back his chair and stretched out his legs; his whole aspect gave an impression of a spent runner. 'Thirdly,' Winston went on, 'the man in command at Gibraltar did nothing.'

Max pulled himself together.

'And the Prime Minister,' he said in a loud voice, 'accepted blame and criticism for all this himself and blamed no one.'

The Prime Minister required no encouragement to continue. He began to talk about Stalin and his demand for Lithuania. Winston would never be a party to countries being given over to Communism. This was not entirely new to his audience, and they settled down to hear more. Harriman,[2] however, intervened. At this juncture, Max permitted himself a noisy yawn. Harriman paused. It was fatal. He had lost his chance. 'De Gaulle,' the P.M. broke in, 'has perhaps done his best, but it amounts to very little.'

Poor Max! After all, their styles of conversation have a good

---

[1] The French naval base on the coast of Senegal in French West Africa. In September Free French forces, led by General de Gaulle and supported by the Royal Navy, attempted a landing at Dakar in an effort to secure the base against the Axis. The attempt failed, and Churchill was severely criticized by the Press for having been easily persuaded by de Gaulle to back the expedition.

[2] Averell Harriman, Roosevelt's special representative in the United Kingdom.

deal in common. Both of them mean the same thing by the word 'conversation.' They bat, and the other fellows field. Max is very sensitive to his audience: he talks to impress them; pretty women put him on his mettle, but they are not expected to contribute to the talk. Winston talks to amuse himself; he has no thought of impressing anybody. He requires no help, least of all from women. His subjects come from the past; some are set pieces, such as the Boer War or the charge of the 21st Lancers at Omdurman.

Max is only concerned with the bare drama of events. He is a miser about words. But Winston feasts on the sound of his adjectives; he likes to use four or five words all with the same meaning, as an old man shows you his orchids; not to show them off, but just because he loves them. The people in his stories do not come to life; they are interred in a great sepulchre of words. His incidents soon lose their sharp edges; they do not linger in the memory. So it happens that his audience, tired by the long day, only wait for the chance to slip off to bed, leaving Winston still talking to those who have hesitated to get up and go.

To say that the P.M. does not seem any the worse for wear from the tedious days below deck is an understatement. He is a different man since America came into the war. The Winston I knew in London frightened me. I used to watch him as he went to his room with swift paces, the head thrust forward, scowling at the ground, the sombre countenance clouded, the features set and resolute, the jowl clamped down as if he had something between his teeth and did not mean to let go. I could see that he was carrying the weight of the world, and wondered how long he could go on like that and what could be done about it. And now – in a night, it seems – a younger man has taken his place. All day he keeps to his cabin, dictating for the President a memorandum on the conduct of the war. But the tired, dull look has gone from his eye; his face lights up as you enter the cabin. A month ago, if you had broken in on his work, he would have bitten off your head. And at night he is gay and voluble, sometimes even playful.

The P.M., I suppose, must have known that if America stayed

out there could only be one ending to this business. And now suddenly the war is as good as won and England is safe; to be Prime Minister of England in a great war, to be able to direct the Cabinet, the Army, the Navy, the Air Force, the House of Commons, England herself, is beyond even his dreams. He loves every minute of it.

But there are moments when the old craving for adventure stirs in him. It is not at all his idea of war to see it through in the security of Whitehall; he wants to see for himself what is happening at the Front. It is not unreasonable, he will pout, to want to go into things there. Whereas for Max there is no comfort in a sniff of danger. If he makes himself fly the Atlantic, he fears for his life, although, he says, he prefers 'one night of terror' to 'a week of boredom' in a ship. When there is nothing else to worry about, he will imagine he has some new disease that is bound to kill him in the end. For years he has kept a book in which he enters with meticulous accuracy every fluctuation in his health.

The P.M. knows, of course, that there will be stupid people who will say that he ought to stay in London at the centre of things, but he scarcely gives them a thought. His plan is simple. First, he decides what he would like to do, and then he experiences no difficulty in finding good reasons for doing it.

Besides, this trip requires no excuse. When Winston told me this he got so excited that he began to lisp:

'We were at dinner at Chequers on Sunday when I lifted the lid of the pocket wireless which Harriman gave me. The nine o'clock news had started. At the end there was something about the Japanese attacking American shipping. It wasn't very clear, and I didn't realize what had happened when Sawyers[1] came into the room. He said: "It's quite true. We heard it ourselves outside. The Japs have attacked the Americans."'

Since that moment it has never been out of his mind that America's entry into the war might mean a change in her strategy:

'They may concentrate upon Japan and leave us to deal with

[1] Churchill's valet.

Germany. They have already stopped the stream of supplies that we were getting.'

*Washington, December 22, 1941*

After nine days' racket I cannot get the sound of the great seas out of my head. Before we anchored in Chesapeake Bay the P.M. was talking about steaming up the Potomac to Washington. Now he was like a child in his impatience to meet the President. He spoke as if every minute counted. It was absurd to waste time; he must fly. Portal,[1] Harriman, Max and I came with him. The rest of the party followed by train.

Our Lockheed was over the lights of Washington in three-quarters of an hour. It gave me a sense of security; we were a long way from the war and the London black-out. On landing I let the P.M. have a start before I got out. Looking around, I noticed a man propped against a big car, a little way off. The P.M. called me and introduced me. It was President Roosevelt. Even in the half-light I was struck by the size of his head. I suppose that is why Winston thinks of him as majestic and statuesque, for he has no legs to speak of since his paralysis. He said warmly that he was very glad to welcome me. I was a doctor, and he immediately began to speak of the casualties at Pearl Harbour, many of them with very bad burns. He made me feel that I had known him for a long time. Halifax took me in his car to the Mayflower Hotel, while Max went with the P.M. to the White House.

It was nearly midnight and I had gone to my room when a page brought a message from the P.M. to say that he wanted to see me at the White House. I went in one of the President's cars, but when we arrived at the gate the guards ran out from the lodge and flashed their torches on the driver's pass. They looked at me doubtfully before they allowed the car to enter the grounds. A black servant opened the door with a friendly smile.

I was taken up some stairs to the P.M.'s bedroom, which I found deserted. It smelt of cigar smoke and I tried to open the window.

[1] Air Marshal Portal, Chief of Air Staff.

The crumpled bed-clothes were thrown back, and the floor was strewn with newspapers, English and American, just as the P.M. had thrown them away when he had glanced at the headlines; it would have been the first thing he would have done when they took him to his room, for he always wants to know what the papers are saying about him. I had plenty of time to catch up with the news, for it was an hour and a half before the P.M. came out of the President's room. He looked at me blankly; he had forgotten that he had sent for me.

'I am sorry I have kept you waiting.'

'Is there anything wrong?' I asked.

'The pulse is regular,' he said with a whimsical smile.

He wanted to know if he could take a sleeping pill. He must have a good night. No; there was nothing else he needed. Already his thoughts were back in the President's room. When I left him I said he could take two reds,[1] for I could see he was bottling up his excitement. Max took me down in the lift.

'I have never seen that fellow in better form. He conducted the conversation for two hours with great skill.'

Max, too, was agog; he lives on his nerves. The P.M. had been able to interest the President in a landing in North Africa. Indeed, according to Max, the President was very forthcoming; he said he would like to send three American divisions to Ulster. That had gone down well.

*December 23, 1941*

I told the P.M. what Max had said. Winston was full of Pearl Harbour.

'Well,' he said, 'when heads of states become gangsters, something has got to be done.'

*December 24, 1941*

This evening, as the light began to fail, 30,000 people gathered round a Christmas tree in the grounds of the White House. They

---

[1] Barbiturate sleeping pills.

sang hymns; then there was a sermon, and then speeches by the P.M. and the President. Winston spoke with emotion:

'Let the children have their night of fun and laughter. Let the gifts of Father Christmas delight their play. Let us grown-ups share to the full in their unstinted pleasures before we turn again to the stern task and the formidable years that lie before us, resolved that, by our sacrifice and daring, these same children shall not be robbed of their inheritance or denied their right to live in a free and decent world. And so, in God's mercy, a happy Christmas to you all.'

When the P.M. came in from the balcony he told me that he had had palpitations during the ceremony; he made me take his pulse.

'What is it, Charles?'

'Oh, it's all right.'

'But what is it?' he persisted.

'A hundred and five.'

He was a little taken aback.

'It has all been very moving,' he lisped with excitement. 'This is a new war, with Russia victorious, Japan in, and America in up to the neck.'

Afterwards Harry Hopkins, who is living in the White House, took me to his bedroom. His lips are blanched as if he had been bleeding internally, his skin yellow like stretched parchment and his eyelids contracted to a slit so that you can just see his eyes moving about restlessly, as if he was in pain. He looks like a Methodist minister, but he brought me whisky and oysters, with which I was toying diplomatically when Mrs Roosevelt burst in with a lot of parcels. We talked about the ceremony, and Harry was full of praise for the P.M.'s speech. I saw Winston later and told him that Harry had said it was interesting to hear two great orators with such different methods.

'I don't know about oratory,' the P.M. retorted, 'but I do know what is in people's minds and how to speak to them.'

Does he know what is in people's minds? Though he may have learnt by long experience the feel of an audience, he knows nothing of their lives, their hopes and aspirations. When he speaks it is to express his ideas; he says a piece. In England, outside the House of Commons, all audiences are much the same to him; they differ only in size. Whereas Roosevelt, if Hopkins is right, when he is preparing a speech, wastes little time in turning phrases; he tries to say what is in his mind in the shortest and simplest words. All the time he gives to that particular speech is spent in working out what each individual in his audience will think about it: he always thinks of individuals, never of a crowd. His whole purpose in speaking is to try to bring them over to his point of view.

Since 1940 we do not think of the P.M. as handicapped by living apart from the people. His countrymen have come to feel that he is saying what they would like to say for themselves if they knew how. He still says a piece, but for perhaps the first time in his life he seems to see things through the eyes of the average man. He still says what he is feeling at the moment, but now it turns out that he is speaking for the nation.

*December 25, 1941*

The President took the P.M. to church this morning.

'It is good for Winston,' he said, 'to sing hymns with the Methodies.'

Winston thought so too.

'I am glad I went,' he said to me. 'It's the first time my mind has been at rest for a long time. Besides, I like singing hymns.'

The P.M. is going to Ottawa in a few days, and he wants me to go with him:

'Of course, Charles, I am not afraid of being ill, but I must keep fit for my job.'

He made a little affectionate gesture. He is full of the address which he is to make to Congress tomorrow. He showed me a quotation from the 112th Psalm, which the aged Lord Selborne had sent him:

'He shall not be afraid of evil tidings: his heart is fixed, trusting in the Lord.'

He likes the words and is going to use them. I was reading the psalm when he said:

'Come along, Charles. We will go to the President.'

He led the way to a small room, where the President was making cocktails for his English visitors, the three Chiefs of Staff, Martin[1] and myself. The P.M. took the Bible from me and read his quotation to the President, who liked it. Then at eight o'clock we went down to a room where there was a plan for the dinner table. It was a family party, all members of one of the two branches of the Roosevelt family, but there must have been forty or fifty names on the plan. Everybody stood in a circle and Mrs Roosevelt went round and shook hands. We then went in to dinner. The President said there would be no speeches, but he just wanted to remind us that the King and Queen had dined there two and a half years ago, and this had been a beginning of the coming together of the two English-speaking races, which would go on after the war. He then proposed the health of Sir John Dill,[2] whose birthday it was, and 'absent relatives.' When dinner was over we saw a film, a history of the war up to the present time.

The P.M. was silent and preoccupied. Perhaps he was turning over in his mind tomorrow's speech to Congress. It was a tremendous occasion, he told me; he could remember nothing quite like it in his time. The two democracies were to be joined together and he had been chosen to give out the banns. In what mood, he wondered, would he find the Senate? He knew, of course, that some of the senators were not at all friendly to the British. Would they perhaps show it? This morning he decided that what he was going to say to them was all wrong. At any rate, he had to finish his speech before he went to bed. He yawned wearily. He would be glad when it was all over. It must be getting late. He got up and asked the President to excuse him. 'I must prepare for tomorrow,' he said. It would take him, he thought, until about two o'clock. Smiling vaguely at the company, he withdrew.

[1] John Martin, Principal Private Secretary to Churchill.
[2] Sir John Dill, Head of British Joint Staff Mission to Washington.

When he had gone, we resumed our seats, and sheets of music were given to each of us. Then a fellow in a uniform like a bandmaster's came in and conducted while we sang carols, beginning with 'O Come, All Ye Faithful.' At the end they wheeled away the President in his chair after he had waved 'Good night' to us. He had been like a schoolboy, jolly and carefree. It was difficult to believe that this was the man who was taking his nation into a vast conflict in which, until Pearl Harbour a few days ago, she had no thought of being engaged.

*December 26, 1941*

After breakfast I went to the White House to pay my daily visit to the P.M. Martin said he was buried in his speech, so I did not ask to see him. He went on working at it until they told him he would be late for Congress. Then we set off from the back entrance of the White House, dashing through the streets with the siren wailing and two G-men on each of the running boards, their pockets bulging with revolvers, ready to jump off in a second if anything happened. A few people lining the streets waved and cheered, though without fervour. At the Capitol I was about to walk up the stairs when the P.M. caught sight of me and called me into the lift. He took me with him to a small room to wait for his call. There he sat arranging his thoughts as he gazed at the floor. Once he got up and paced rapidly up and down the room, mumbling to himself; then he stopped, and, looking down at me, he said, with his eyes popping:

'Do you realize we are making history?'

They came for him and I slipped into my seat. The P.M. began effectively and at once got on terms with his audience:

'I cannot help reflecting that if my father had been American and my mother British, instead of the other way round, I might have got here on my own.'

When the laughter was dying down, it would break out again, and this, coming right at the beginning, convinced him that he had got a grip on things. There was great cheering when he mentioned China and a loud shout when, speaking of the Japanese, he said with passion:

'What sort of people do they think we are?'

At this, Congress rose as one man and stood cheering as if they would never stop. They think of Japan just as we think of Germany. But when the P.M. said: 'If we had kept together after the last war, if we had taken common measures for our safety, this renewal of the curse need never have fallen upon us,' there was less applause, and when he went on: 'Five or six years ago it would have been easy, without shedding a drop of blood, for the United States and Great Britain to have insisted on fulfilment of the disarmament clauses of the treaties which Germany signed after the Great War,' Congress listened in silence. Nor did he seem to touch his hearers when he vituperated Hitler and Mussolini, any more than people at home like this side of his oratory. Nevertheless, taken as a whole, it was Winston at his best.

There was a great scene at the end. The Senators and Congressmen stood cheering and waving their papers till he went out.

I met him in the small room where he had awaited the summons to address the American people. He was sweating freely, but he said it was a great weight off his chest. He laughed with one of the Senators, almost noisily, so that people looked round.

On my return to the White House I found him pacing up and down the garden. He said he had been doubtful about his speech overnight; he had not liked it. When he awoke he thought it was all right, but before he got up he was sure it would be just right.

'I hit the target all the time,' he said.

'Yes; but they listened in silence when you said, "If we had acted together after the last war . . ." I don't think they would have taken that at all, even a few months ago.'

He went on to express concern that he never met anyone but the President. He ought, he said, to see some of the other members of the Administration. Men like Cordell Hull,[1] he realized, resent everything being done at the White House, behind closed doors, between the President and the P.M., without so much as a word to

---

[1] Cordell Hull, Secretary of State in President Roosevelt's Administration.

them. He was afraid that when he left they would do their best to undo what he had done. He is thinking about giving a dinner at the Embassy to these people when he returns from Ottawa.

*December 27, 1941*
The P.M. seems so preoccupied with his mission of good fellowship to America in general and to the President in particular that I decided not to bother him by calling this morning. When I got back to the hotel at ten o'clock, after a stroll through the streets, I found an urgent message. I was wanted at the White House. Would I go at once. I took a taxi.

'I am glad you have come,' the P.M. began.

He was in bed and looked worried.

'It was hot last night and I got up to open the window. It was very stiff. I had to use considerable force and I noticed all at once that I was short of breath. I had a dull pain over my heart. It went down my left arm. It didn't last very long, but it has never happened before. What is it? Is my heart all right? I thought of sending for you, but it passed off.'

There was not much to be found when I examined his heart. Indeed, the time I spent listening to his chest was given to some quick thinking. I knew that when I took the stethoscope out of my ears he would ask me pointed questions, and I had no doubt that whether the electro-cardiograph showed evidence of a coronary thrombosis or not, his symptoms were those of coronary insufficiency. The textbook treatment for this is at least six weeks in bed. That would mean publishing to the world – and the American newspapers would see to this – that the P.M. was an invalid with a crippled heart and a doubtful future. And this at a moment when America has just come into the war, and there is no one but Winston to take her by the hand. I felt that the effect of announcing that the P.M. had had a heart attack could only be disastrous. I knew, too, the consequences to one of his imaginative temperament of the feeling that his heart was affected. His work would suffer. On the other hand, if I did nothing and he had another and severer attack – perhaps a fatal seizure – the world would undoubtedly say that I had killed him through not insisting on rest. These thoughts went racing through my head while I was listening to his heart. I took my stethoscope out of my ears. Then I replaced it and listened again. Right or wrong, it seemed plain that I must sit tight on what had happened, whatever the consequences.

'Well,' he asked, looking full at me, 'is my heart all right?'

'There is nothing serious,' I answered. 'You have been overdoing things.'

'Now, Charles, you're not going to tell me to rest. I can't. I won't. Nobody else can do this job. I must. What actually happened when I opened the window?' he demanded. 'My idea is that I strained one of my chest muscles. I used great force. I don't believe it was my heart at all.'

He waited for me to answer.

'Your circulation was a bit sluggish. It is nothing serious. You needn't rest in the sense of lying up, but you mustn't do more than you can help in the way of exertion for a little while.'

There was a knock at the door. It was Harry Hopkins. I slipped away. I went and sat in a corner of the secretaries' room, picking up a newspaper, so that they would not talk to me. I began to think things out more deliberately. I did not like it, but I determined to tell no one. When we get back to England, I shall take him to Parkinson, who will hold his tongue.

*December 28, 1941*

When Max heard the P.M. speak against Marshall's[1] proposal of one supreme commander of the Allied forces, he began to concoct one of those little schemes in which he is an adept. He went to Harry Hopkins and they arranged a meeting between Marshall and the Prime Minister. This took place today, and Winston was soon won over by Marshall's arguments. Two days ago the P.M. was sure that the plan was neither workable nor desirable. Now his doubts are dispelled; it has become plain to him that it is a trump card.

I wish Winston would be more sensible about things. The pace

---

[1] General George Marshall, Chief of Staff of the U.S. Army.

here is prodigious. Usually when he has an important speech on the stocks he lives with it for forty-eight hours. During that time he is on edge, his temper is short and he is best left to himself. But these historic pronouncements to Congress and to the Parliament at Ottawa have to be ground out in odd moments when he is not needed in conference and when he is not closeted with the President. Sometimes the night is nearly over before he goes to bed. It is true that he seems to revel in every moment of the long day, but little things, straws in the wind, warn me that a price must be paid for flouting Nature. I dread Ottawa.

We left the White House this evening by the back entrance. The President and Harry Hopkins came to the door to see us off. The P.M. asked me to drive with him in his car to the station. As we drove out of the grounds he opened the window of the car. He was short of breath.

'There seems no air,' he said, 'in this car. Is it a stuffy night, Charles?'

And then he put his hand on my knee.

'It is a great comfort to have you with me,' he said.

He has used these words twice in four days; the first time was before the heart attack. This is something new; it has not happened before.

*December 29, 1941*
On our arrival at Ottawa, the big fur-hatted Canadian Mounted Police kept back with difficulty the vast, enthusiastic crowds which pushed good-humouredly towards the P.M. and soon enveloped him. The atmosphere of Ottawa after Washington is like Belfast after Dublin. We drove to Government House through streets banked with snow. After a hot bath, Winston seemed his usual self, and we lunched with the Canadian Cabinet, a ceremony that lasted for two hours. There was still dinner at Government House to be got through, and then a reception. However, so far nothing untoward has happened. Whenever we are alone, he keeps asking me to take his pulse. I get out of it somehow, but once, when I found him lifting something heavy, I did expostulate. At this he broke out:

'Now, Charles, you are making me heart-minded. I shall soon think of nothing else. I couldn't do my work if I kept thinking of my heart.'

The next time he asked me to take his pulse I refused point-blank.

'You're all right. Forget your damned heart.'

He won't get through his speech tomorrow if this goes on.

*December 31, 1941*

Winston's speech, particularly his attack on Vichy, roused the Canadians, though it was not up to the Washington standard. At one point he talked in his variation of the French tongue. And then he told them how he had warned the French Government that Britain would fight on alone whatever France did, and how Weygand had gone to the French Cabinet and said:

'In three weeks England will have her neck wrung like a chicken.'

The P.M. paused.

'Some chicken. Some neck!' He spat out his contempt.

Gust after gust of delighted laughter ended in applause, which went on for a long time.

At night we dined with Mackenzie King.[1] I got there early. He had been my patient in London, and did not hesitate to speak his mind. I found him restive about the P.M. He said that there were many men winning the war and confessed that he was 'rather put off by a strain of violence in the Prime Minister.' I argued that it is no more than a certain lack of restraint, but it was plain that this was no passing mood.

Wilson[2]: 'You have known Winston for a long time?'

Mackenzie King: 'Yes; I have. I first met him when he was going round Canada on a lecture tour.'

Wilson: 'That can't have been long after the Boer War.'

Mackenzie King: 'No. I found him at his hotel drinking cham-pagne at eleven o'clock in the morning.'

---

[1] Mackenzie King, Prime Minister of Canada.
[2] Sir Charles Wilson became Lord Moran in 1943.

'The great thing in politics,' said our host later, 'is to avoid mistakes.' I could almost see the P.M. sniffing as Mackenzie King, looking at us through his pince-nez, which were tethered to a button-hole by a long black ribbon, made this pronouncement. King had never been a man to take risks, and this prudent outlook no doubt accounts for some lack of fervour on the P.M.'s part. The two men are, of course, quite friendly, but the P.M. is not really interested in Mackenzie King. He takes him for granted.

I cannot help noticing Winston's indifference to him after the wooing of the President at the White House. There the P.M. and the President seemed to talk for most of the day, and for the first time I have seen Winston content to listen. You could almost feel the importance he attaches to bringing the President along with him, and in that good cause he has become a very model of restraint and self-discipline; it is surely a new Winston who is sitting there quite silent. And when he does say anything it is always something likely to fall pleasantly on the President's ear. But here, in Ottawa, he does not seem to bother.

We go back to Washington tomorrow.

*January 1, 1942*
I sometimes wonder if the P.M. feels the full weight of the decisions he has to make. I have not been present at the meetings, but I cannot help being there in spirit. It is as if Winston has a family of twelve children and there is not enough food for all of them – some of them must starve to death. He has to decide which.

But these decisions are at least taken when everyone who counts is here in Washington. The Americans are worried about what will happen after we disperse. It was to decide this that the P.M. came to Washington: he wanted to show the President how to run the war. It has not worked out quite like that. On the 29th, the day after we left Washington for Ottawa, the Chiefs of Staff of both countries met. The discussion was heated until they at last decided that there should be two committees, one in London, the other in Washington. There was no hope of agreement on any other basis. But this did not suit the President. He wanted one committee in

Washington, and after what Hopkins calls 'a hell of a row' he got what he wanted.

It is, of course, an unequal contest. Our Chiefs of Staff miss Brooke,[1] whom we had left in London picking up the threads. The peace-loving Dill is no substitute. What he lacks is the he-man stuff. That is why he is no longer C.I.G.S. And Winston is only half-hearted in their support; he is just now possessed with one idea to the exclusion of all others. He feels he must bring the President into the war with his heart set on victory. If that can be done, nothing else matters. Nor is Max very helpful. He has not much use for our sailors and soldiers, and likes showing off to the Americans his influence with the P.M. But after all Marshall remains the key to the situation. The P.M. has a feeling that in his quiet, unprovocative way he means business, and that if we are too obstinate he might take a strong line. And neither the P.M. nor the President can contemplate going forward without Marshall.

*Florida, January 5, 1942*
The P.M. decided to come here because he did not want to tax the hospitality of the President, who likes to get away over the weekend to Hyde Park.[2] It was a thoughtful move to give the White House a respite, and we are seeing Winston in a new role.

General Marshall brought us in his own plane from Washington to Florida. The air here is balmy after the bitter cold of Ottawa – oranges and pineapples grow here. And the blue ocean is so warm that Winston basks half-submerged in the water like a hippopotamus in a swamp.

*Florida, January 9, 1942*
The P.M. was on his best behaviour in Washington. Now he is suffering from a sharp reaction. He does not like making important decisions, especially when he finds himself lined up with the

[1] General Sir Alan Brooke became Chief of the Imperial General Staff late in 1941.
[2] Birthplace and family home of President Roosevelt, a small town on the east side of the Hudson River, some eighty miles north of New York.

Americans against his own Chiefs of Staff, and the strain mounts when they are interspersed by important pronouncements that will be read, sentence by sentence, over the world. Nor has he yet forgotten what he calls his 'pump,' though he has given up feeling his pulse. At any rate, he has had plenty of time here to work off steam.

Nothing seems to be right. Perhaps it is the close atmosphere; anyway, the P.M. is in a belligerent mood. He told us that he had sent a stiff telegram to Curtin, the Prime Minister of Australia. The situation in Malaya was making Australia jumpy about invasion. Curtin was not satisfied with the air position. He had renewed his representations to London in blunt terms. The P.M. fulminated in his reply. London had not made a fuss when it was bombed. Why should Australia? At one moment he took the line that Curtin and his Government did not represent the people of Australia. At another that the Australians came of bad stock. He was impatient with people who had nothing better to do than to criticize him.

The significance of this outburst was not lost on me. I did not worry about the Australians. I knew that he had been persuaded to tone down the cable before it was sent. Besides, he liked them as men and respected them as fighting soldiers. But this was a bulletin, signed by himself, which said more plainly than bulletins usually do what it meant: that this particular patient needed rest. He was just hitting out blindly, like a child in a temper. But I knew that he had not the slightest intention of taking his doctor's advice.

The P.M. was still glowering at his plate. He had not yet come to the end of his grievances. It had been suggested to him that the Archbishop of York[1] should be the new Archbishop of Canterbury; yet he, the Archbishop, went about talking of Christian revolution and stuff of that kind. Winston sniffed; he would take his time about the appointment. He was much worried about Singapore. Wavell's telegram was depressing. Winston recalled Wavell's warning, while crossing the Atlantic, not to dissipate our strength defending Malaya. He wanted to concentrate on Singapore. The new position was that reinforcements were needed but they would do no more

[1] Archbishop Temple.

than replace what had been lost. He spoke of submarines being adequate to prevent Japanese landings on the West Coast. But is not the position quite different? Our screen of aerodromes around Singapore, in Malaya, have been lost. Singapore might be like Gibraltar: ours but not usable by our own fleet. The probable truth is we never anticipated losing command of the sea. The P.M. was much incensed by an article in *Life* magazine arguing that the position of Singapore was due to our conference. It was, the P.M. asserted, purely a question of equipment. There was not enough to go round. But was the explanation so simple? The P.M. admitted he had never gone into the military position there as he had done in Libya, in particular the Battle of El Alamein. He got very hot under the collar against two or three people in the House of Commons who had criticized the Singapore preparations or the lack of them . . . These oddments represented no one in the House, yet they were fully reported in the foreign press. He was going to give it to them hot on his return.

The news from London did not help matters. The *Queen Elizabeth* and the *Valiant* had been put out of action, and we had lost command of the Mediterranean. To get him in a sunnier mood, I asked him about Hess, whereupon the P.M., throwing off his ill humour, launched out into a description of Hess's motives.[1] He said Hess was an intimate of Hitler, dined with him and was his Deputy Führer. When war broke out, the Generals became more important and Hess felt this change in his position, though his devotion to Hitler was no less than it was before. He heard Hitler say that he (Hitler) wished England no harm, or some such expression, but that if she resisted her punishment would be terrible. It occurred to Hess on hearing this that he would fly to England and put this before the King, then he would return to Hitler having performed a great service and so restore his position. He chose the Duke of Hamilton because he had met him at the Olympic Games and he

[1] Rudolph Hess, deputy to Hitler, flew alone from Augsburg and landed in Scotland on May 10, 1941. He was treated as a prisoner of war. When he was freed after the war, Lord Moran was sent by Mr Attlee to Nuremberg to report on Hess's sanity.

had read that he was Steward to the King: no doubt his position in relation to the King was similar to Hess's position to Hitler. This would put things right and put an end to the usurpation of power by the Churchill clique. The Duke of Hamilton, Winston said with a chuckle, compared this to going to a restaurant with one's wife and being accosted by a brazen harlot . . . There was around Hitler a school boy atmosphere. Perhaps that accounted for the Russian war; he, Hitler, would deliver Europe from the scourge of Bolshevism. The P.M. said there had never been any suggestion by Hess that his object was to square England before Germany took on the Russian war (which is Stalin's idea of Hess's mission). Hess's value was that from time to time he revealed what Hitler thought.

The P.M. said he had met Ribbentrop a lot when he was in London.[1] He was a commercial traveller (i.e. travelling salesman) for champagne, who had got mixed up in 'high crime and misdemeanours' and was wondering what would be the end of it all . . .The P.M. had not met the other German leaders.

Somebody mentioned Max. Max, according to Winston, was a genius, a little dynamic man. Someone asked the P.M. if the Philippines would have to surrender. He smiled.

'That depends on the strength of the forces defending and of the forces attacking.'

Attempts to pump the P.M. never get anywhere: if he is going to be indiscreet, he does not want anyone's help.

During luncheon with Madame Balsan[2] she said, 'Winston looks very well. This is due to Sir Charles. He is President of the Royal College of Physicians but he has given up everything to do this'. I think the P.M. was rather surprised at this pronouncement. It had never been put like this before. Perhaps he took this too much for granted. When we left, Winston mused a little, and then said half to himself: 'Wealth, taste and leisure can do these things, but they do not bring happiness.'

Tomorrow we go back to Washington.

---

[1] Joachim von Ribbentrop, German Foreign Minister.
[2] Former Duchess of Marlborough, later married to M. Jacques Balsan.

*January 14, 1942*

The Americans have got their way and the war will be run from Washington, but they will not be wise to push us so unceremoniously in the future. Our people are very unhappy about the decision, and the most they will agree to is to try it out for a month. They were, however, brought back to good humour by the final figures of the production estimates. Harry gave me some figures which meant something even to me: 100,000 aircraft in 1943 for 45,000 in 1942, and 75,000 tanks in 1943 for 45,000 in 1942. The P.M. gives Max most of the credit; Harry hands it to the President. I would bracket them together: to set a seemingly impossible target requires a particular cast of mind, and they have both got that kind of mind. I think Winston, more than anyone here, visualizes in detail what this programme means to the actual conduct of the war. He is drunk with the figures.

*January 15, 1942*

To Bermuda this morning by air. I was strolling in the garden of Government House when I learnt that there was a conference going on indoors to decide whether we should return by air or by the ship. At that moment the P.M. came up to me and, putting his arm through mine, said:

'We are returning by air. They are fixing up the details now. But we cannot all go in the flying-boat. I am sure, Charles, you won't mind returning in the ship.'

I was completely taken by surprise, but as he spoke I knew I must not give way. There flashed through my mind the mishap at the White House when he tried to open the bedroom window. I had kept this to myself, and if I let him go alone and anything happened to him in the air I alone was responsible. It would be my doing. Apart from this, my own position would become impossible. I had been the target of a good deal of criticism because I had come on this journey while President of the College.[1] I had always met this criticism by arguing that looking after the Prime Minister's

[1] The Royal College of Physicians.

health was even more important than doing my job as President. But if he should cross the Atlantic alone, and I follow by sea a week or so later, what would become of my argument? I disengaged my arm and made for the house. I heard the P.M. say something soothingly, but I took no notice. I found the Chiefs of Staff in a room in conference. I broke into their discussion without ceremony. 'I believe,' I said, 'it has been decided to return by air, and that it is suggested the Prime Minister fly and I come by sea.' I made it plain that I could not agree. And with that I withdrew. I hated to be so abrupt, but I could not go into a long rigmarole with these people.

*January 16, 1942*
We left Bermuda today in a flying-boat, R.M.A. *Berwick*. In mid-Atlantic they brought the P.M. a bulletin. He read it and, leaning towards me, put his hand on my knee.

'Do you realize we are fifteen hundred miles from anywhere?'

'Heaven is as near by sea as by land,' I reminded him.

'Who said that?' he asked.

'I think it was Sir Humphrey Gilbert.'

He looked at the bulletin again. We have still nine hours to go, but we have enough fuel for fifteen.

*

I learnt afterwards that we were fortunate that night. We lost our way and turned north only just in time to avoid the German batteries outside Brest. In another five minutes we should have been over them. Then, when we approached the English coast from Brest, we were mistaken for an enemy bomber, and fighter aircraft came out to intercept us. However, they missed us.

# CHAPTER TWO

# Lord Beaverbrook Resigns

*January 17, 1942*

As the train carried the Prime Minister towards London, he sat for a time with his white hands laid out on his thighs, his head poked forward, absorbed in thought. The five weeks that he had been out of the country had not been wasted, he felt; the close friendship he had established with President Roosevelt had smoothed out every difficulty.

'I have done a good job of work with the President,' he said yesterday. 'We got on together. I think we shall soon see dividends. I am sure, Charles, the House will be pleased with what I have to tell them.'

When, however, he picked up a pile of morning papers, he was pained to find that the country did not share his satisfaction. On the contrary, public opinion seemed to be baffled by the way things had gone wrong; the nation was frankly puzzled and worried. He put down the *Manchester Guardian* with an angry gesture.

'There seems to be plenty of snarling,' he said in a tired voice.

*January 27, 1942*

It has been an uneasy ten days since we landed, and I know the P.M. feels that, if there must be a debate in the House of Commons, it is a good thing to get it over. He told me that when he rose today he knew at once that he had a critical House.

He began by admitting that there had been many blunders. As far as military secrecy would permit, he believed in telling the

House everything, for it had always been his policy to discount future calamities by describing the immediate outlook in the darkest terms. It seemed that the blacker he painted the picture, the more their hearts went out to this courageous man. He, at any rate, told them the truth: they had not forgotten Baldwin.[1] The P.M. somehow made them feel that they were partners in that heroic struggle, though taking, himself, the fullest personal responsibility for whatever went wrong:

'If we have handled our resources wrongly, no one is so much to blame as I.'

Besides, his main theme struck the House as reasonable. Caught unprepared, we had only just managed to keep our heads above water. We could not be armed everywhere:

'If we had started to scatter our forces over these immense areas in the Far East we should have been ruined.'

The House was silent, but reconciled to the hard truth of the Prime Minister's argument. He told me that he felt they were with him as he drew towards the end: he had spoken for nearly two hours:

'Although I feel the broadening swell of victory and liberation bearing us and all the tortured peoples onwards safely to the final goal, I must confess to feeling the weight of the war upon me even more than in the tremendous summer days of 1940.'

*January 29, 1942*
As the P.M. prepared for bed tonight, his feeling of relief at the rout of his critics was expressed rather more freely:

'H— is a silly bastard. There are about half a dozen of them; they make a noise out of all proportion to their importance. The House knows this, but unfortunately people abroad take them too seriously; they do a lot of harm. You know how they voted? Four hundred and sixty-four to one.'

His voice rose as if he would like to annihilate his detractors. The wind fell as quickly as it had risen. After all, the majority was only what he had expected.

[1] Stanley Baldwin, Prime Minister, 1923–4, 1924–9, 1935–7.

*January 30, 1942*

This morning there was a message from the President, whose
birthday it is, which gave the P.M. great pleasure. 'It is fun,' it said,
'to be in the same decade with you.'

*

It would appear from my diary that the Prime Minister's
Parliamentary triumph was only a momentary gleam in a dark
winter. February in particular dealt him some hard blows.
Something more than a vote of confidence was required to put the
Government on its feet. The country needed a tonic, and the only
tonic that would do any lasting good was a resounding victory. What
the country got was the disaster of Singapore.[1] Political tension
grew, and with it a demand for a strengthening of the Government.

My diary records:

'The P.M. hates being told what to do, though he knows that
he will have to bow to the storm. But if he must change his
Ministers, he is determined that he will do it in his own way. I
think, from what I hear, that he has decided to make a change that
has long been in his mind. He wants Lord Beaverbrook to organize
production. Nothing "that dynamic little man" does – and he is
pretty erratic at times – can shake the P.M.'s faith in his genius.'

The political figures with whom Winston Churchill had grown
up in politics, John Morley, Arthur Balfour, Asquith and Lord
Rosebery, were all dead; Max was almost the last of those who had
lived with him through the shocks and strains of the First World
War, when the members of his present Cabinet were quite
unknown. It comforted the P.M. to talk to Max and to compare
their troubles with those they had had to overcome in the First

---

[1] The fall of Singapore on February 15, 1942, was described by Churchill
as 'the worst disaster and largest capitulation in British History.' Despite
the rapid advance of the Japanese in the Malayan peninsula, it was thought
that the island could hold out indefinitely. However, the defences, built in
1921, were designed only to meet an attack from the sea. The defence of
the besieged island became impossible when the Japanese cut the water
supply, which came from Johore on the mainland.

World War. It had long been in his mind to combine the Ministries of Aircraft Production and of Supply in one Ministry of War Production. Max was to be the Minister; there, surely, he would have abundant scope for his genius.

The Ministers of the various departments concerned took a rather different view of the Prime Minister's proposal. They were frankly horrified by the thought of having to work under or with Lord Beaverbrook. Max was quite aware of their hostility and – this influenced him more – of his own limitations. By his own peculiar methods, he knew he could get a tremendous drive in any department that he took over. But it did not last. At every turn he seemed to upset those with whom he had to work, and though he could bluff through, he was never sure that he was right. And so, when he found that no one had any confidence in his judgment or wanted to work under him, he seemed to lose faith in himself.

How easy it would be in a vast undertaking of this kind to make a single error of judgment which might have catastrophic consequences! Beaverbrook's vivid imagination already pictured the glee of his enemies at his public exposure and downfall. A profound dejection of spirit took possession of him; his attacks of asthma grew more frequent and more severe; his distaste for office became an obsession. And yet he could not bring himself to say 'No' to the Prime Minister. On February 4 he was appointed Minister of War Production.

The fall of Singapore on February 15 stupefied the Prime Minister. He had begun to talk about Malaya when he was in Florida, and I recall how one day in the middle of January I found him in a positively spectacular temper. He had just learnt from Wavell[1] that the defences of Singapore – the work of many years – were built only to meet attacks from the sea. Many of the guns could only fire seaward. It had never entered his head, he complained, that the rear of the fortress was quite unprotected against an attack from the land.

'Why didn't they tell me about this? Oh, no; it is my own fault.

[1] General Sir Archibald Wavell, Allied Supreme Commander in the Far East except the Pacific.

I ought to have known. I could have asked. I cannot understand it. Did no one realize the position?'

There was another and more crucial question, to which the Prime Minister could find no answer. How came 100,000 men (half of them of our own race) to hold up their hands to inferior numbers of Japanese? Though his mind had been gradually prepared for its fall, the surrender of the fortress stunned him. He felt it was a disgrace. It left a scar on his mind. One evening, months later, when he was sitting in his bathroom enveloped in a towel, he stopped drying himself and gloomily surveyed the floor: 'I cannot get over Singapore,' he said sadly.

Winston's dejection over the surrender of 100,000 men was the result of one of those hunches that came to him in which he appeared to stumble on the truth before it was seen by others: he knew that the surrender of Singapore was something more than a reverse. I think he wondered if it were a portent.

It is the will to fight that counts in war. That, in some measures, was missing at Singapore. Wavell, after visiting the garrison, had reported to the Prime Minister on February 11, 1942:

'Morale of some troops is not good, and none is as high as I should like to see.'

Singapore was a symptom of a malady which broke out during the war in various places from time to time. When the chance came, I asked some of the soldiers at the top how far the infection had spread. There was a discussion about the comparative merits of the soldier in the two wars that was not reassuring. I was left to turn over in my mind the social implications to a nation of a decay in its martial spirit.

Meanwhile, things were far from well with the newly appointed Minister of War Production. Lord Beaverbrook did not give up his search for a way out of his dilemma. He was still stalling, and day after day he used all his astuteness to block any attempt by the Prime Minister to bring things to a head. At last the P.M. reached the end of his patience. He sent to Lord Beaverbrook a proof of the White Paper defining the Ministry of War Production with a note. He had given time and thought to a plan that would be agreeable to Lord Beaverbrook and to those with whom he would have to work. There followed an abrupt intimation that this was the Prime Minister's last word. The letter ended with a sad warning. If Lord Beaverbrook insisted on resigning at a time when everything was at stake, he ought to realize that it would do grave hurt to his country and to his own name.

This letter left Lord Beaverbrook no way out. There was nothing for it but to accept the Prime Minister's plans, and on February 10 the White Paper was presented to the House by the P.M. Then, in the third week of February, when everything seemed settled, Lord Beaverbrook resigned. He persisted that he was a sick man, but that was no reason why he and the Prime Minister should not part friends.

February 26, 1942.

My dear Winston,

I am leaving this Office today and going to the place I came from. And now I must tell you about twenty-one months of high adventure, the like of which has never been known.

All the time, everything that has been done by me has been due to your holding me up.

You took a great chance in putting me in, and you stood to be shot at by a section of Members for keeping me here.

It was little enough I gave you, compared with what you gave me. I owe my reputation to you. The confidence of the public really comes from you. And my courage was sustained by you. These benefits give me a right to a place in your list of lieutenants who served you when you brought salvation to our people in the hour of disaster.

In leaving, then, I send this letter of gratitude and devotion to the leader of the nation, the saviour of our people, and the symbol of resistance in the free world.

Yours affectionately

Max.

The P.M. showed me the letter – 'a very nice letter' – saying: 'I like him very much.' With a stroke of the pen, Max had won back all the lost ground. Soon after it was noticed that Lord Beaverbrook's health had taken a sharp turn for the better.

That Beaverbrook was determined to resign is plain, but the motive for his going is more open to doubt. Six days after Mr Churchill became Prime Minister, I wrote to Lord Beaverbrook congratulating him on his appointment as Minister of Aircraft Production. He replied briefly the same day:

May 16, 1940.

Dear Wilson,

I am disappointed that you, a doctor, did not reproach me for taking this monstrous risk with my health.

Although I do not need anybody to tell me I am a fool for bending my old shoulders to this burden, I know it very well myself.

With kindest regards,

Yours sincerely,

Beaverbrook.

Only Lord Beaverbrook would embark on his stupendous task in that mood. And yet I wonder if it was as simple as this. Could it be that he was staking out a claim in advance that if he wanted to throw in his hand at any time the state of his health must be accepted as a reasonable and proper explanation for his resignation?

Nearly a year went by, and then in the spring of 1941 I find in my diary a copy of a long letter to Max,[1] bearing the date, April 18, 1941. Max said his job was finished. I said it had only begun. I told him plainly that I had made it clear to the P.M. that there was no health reason why he should not go on doing his job.

Max replied the next day. It is a strange letter.[2] To justify his resignation, he sets out his infirmities – he was quite unrepentant – but those who know him will pay more attention to a postscript

[1] See Appendix 2.
[2] See Appendix 2.

in which he complains that the P.M. did not ask his advice and looked upon him as a quarrelsome fellow.

But nothing happened. Six months later, his resignation was again in the air. This time his health was not mentioned. Lord Beaverbrook said that he did not think we were helping Russia enough. Unless more vigorous steps were taken, he would have to reconsider his position. To this threat of resignation, the Prime Minister dryly replied: 'We shall all have to reconsider our position.'

However, four months later, Russia appeared to have dropped out of the picture: in February, 1942, Beaverbrook blamed his asthma for his resignation. Woodrow Wyatt, in his book, *Distinguished for Talent*,[1] suggests another explanation:

> 'Singapore, to the shame of Britain, fell on the 15th February. It was the blackest hour of the war. Churchill's prestige was on the recoil and the country was turning against him.
>
> 'Beaverbrook . . . chose this exact moment to make a resignation that for once he would not withdraw. It took effect on the 19th February, four days after the fall of Singapore. He estimated that Churchill would be driven from power by a dispirited and resentful country. He thought himself the automatic next choice . . .
>
> 'He believed the country would demand him.'

As his doctor, I had been familiar with Lord Beaverbrook's asthma for many years, and I did not accept it then as an adequate explanation of his resignation. It is true that his attacks became more frequent and more severe in times of strain, but he did not allow them to interfere with anything in which he was interested. It may be that after the fall of Singapore, as Wyatt suggests, Lord Beaverbrook caught a brief glimpse of himself as First Minister of the Crown. But there is no reason to think that this was at the back of his mind when he was on the point of resigning in the spring of 1941, and again in the autumn. Looking back, I still believe that it was his own profound mistrust of himself that haunted him in

[1] Woodrow Wyatt, *Distinguished for Talent*, Hutchinson, 1958.

office. If he found that he was not up to his job, he must get out of it before he made some disastrous mistake.

In a sense, he was the architect of his own misfortunes. With all his astuteness, his uncanny skill in probing motives, he could never understand the mind of the average Englishman. And the average Englishman could not understand him.

When Max had disposed of himself in this fashion, I hoped the P.M. would be left in peace, but my diary in March of that year is full of imprecations on the head of Franklin Roosevelt, of all men. I was concerned with his views of India only in so far as they contributed to the burden the Prime Minister bore in the spring of 1942, for I could not help noticing that a difference of opinion with the President or Max Beaverbrook took more out of him than a major disaster in the field.

The dispute began during the visit to Washington after Pearl Harbour, when the friendly atmosphere of the White House was sharply broken one day after Roosevelt had given his views on India's future. There was a violent explosion, and we had Mr Churchill's own word that the President did not venture again to raise the subject when they met. But in his correspondence Roosevelt did not exercise the same self-denying ordinance.

The P.M. looked with pride on the story of our Indian Empire – Henry Lawrence and Clive and Dalhousie were men after his own heart – whereas the President, whose feelings went back to the American War of Independence, saw only a subject people in the grip of a conqueror, a lamentable example of British imperialism.

The issue was simple. The Prime Minister was willing to summon a Constituent Assembly and ready to grant full independence to India if the Assembly should demand it, *after the war*. But any attempt, however well meant, to solve the problem during the war would, he feared, lead to unrest and bloodshed. With the Japanese at the gates of India, he dreaded the effect on the Indian Army of opening up an issue which must divide Moslem from Hindu.

The President, however, was not convinced. He could not

understand why, if we were willing to allow India to secede from the Empire after the war, we should deny self-government to them during the war. He wanted to set up a nationalist government immediately.

In the light of events, Mr Churchill has been proved right. He was prepared to resign if he could not get his way. What the President proposed was, Winston felt, an act of madness. He did not feel that it was an issue that could be left to public opinion in the United States; it was not for them to decide, and if his colleagues had thought otherwise, the P.M. makes it plain that he would not have hesitated to lay down a personal burden 'which at times seemed more than a man could bear.'

His views about the future of India were another matter. His India was the land he knew as a subaltern. He could not conceive of an India without the British. How often on our travels did he come back in his talk to the religious massacres which he felt must happen when we left the country. He was a prophet of woe:

'I prophesy that in our lifetime the "softy" English people at home will let India in for a war in which the casualties will exceed those in the present conflict up to now.'

He was speaking not long after Pearl Harbour.

It may be that at this time the Prime Minister was suffering from a kind of rebound after the excitement and exhilaration which he had felt when America came into the war. Certainly he had expected some easing of the tension, whereas when in March he looked glumly around, he could see nothing but a deterioration of the whole position.

Perhaps, even then, something of the old crusading fire had already left him. At least he was more ready to make concessions to expediency than he had been. In Washington, in January, the Prime Minister was roused by Stalin's demand for the Baltic States. 'If that were done,' he said hotly, 'it would dishonour our cause.' As time passed his spirit became more chastened. 'Under the pressure of events, I did not feel that this moral position could be physically maintained. In a deadly struggle it is not right to assume more burdens than those who are fighting for a great cause can bear.' And he told Stalin in March that he had urged President Roosevelt to support Russia's claim to the Baltic States at the Peace Conference.

And yet these irritants, each of which could drive him into a frenzy for a short time, hardly counted when set against the persistent erosion of the submarine threat. I find this note in my diary:

'The P.M. tells me that 640,000 tons of merchant shipping have been sunk in the last two months in what he calls "American waters." I have been finding out that wherever he goes he carries in his head the monthly figures of all sinkings, though he never talks about them. He is always careful to consume his own smoke; nothing he says could discourage anyone. When I say the P.M. never talks, I am not quite accurate. There are times – this does not happen very often – when I fancy I serve as a safety-valve. Occasionally, too, I may pick up by chance a stray hint of what is going on in his head. One day when things at sea were at their worst, I happened to go to the Map-room. There I found the P.M. He was standing with his back to me, staring at the huge chart with the little black beetles representing German submarines. "Terrible," he muttered. I was about to retreat when he whipped round and brushed past me with his head down. I am not sure he saw me. He knows that we may lose the war at sea in a few months and that he can do nothing about it. I wish to God I could put out the fires that seem to be consuming him.'

# CHAPTER THREE

# The American Bid for a Second Front

It was not, however, the Battle of the Atlantic, but the invasion of France which, in the spring of 1942, was growing in the Prime Minister's mind like a canker. When the Americans came into the war after Pearl Harbour they began to plan for the day when the Allied armies would land again upon the French shore. It was General Marshall's conviction that only in that way could the war be won. Mr Churchill was as sure that only by the premature invasion of France could the war be lost. To postpone that evil day, all his arts, all his eloquence, all his great experience were spent.

Why did Winston so much dread this particular operation? He feared the casualties. It was the carnage on the first day of the Battle of the Somme which led the P.M. to invent a monster tank of his own. He told me this before we left London for Washington:

'The War Office,' Winston began, 'is always said to be preparing for the last war. I certainly entered this war with a mentality born in the last war. I had a waterproof suit made so that I might keep dry in the communication trenches. I wanted to be prepared for those visits to the front line which,' the P.M. added with a mischievous smirk, 'I felt my position as First Lord of the Admiralty entitled me to make. What I had learned in the last war was deeply rooted in my mind – the terrible losses in an assault on a prepared position. But I still believed that the Siegfried Line facing us could be broken with the increased fire power of this war without those losses.

'This was the way I planned to do it. In the last war the tanks went overland. In this war they would have to plough through the surface of the ground. In the next war,' Winston added with a grin, 'they will be underground. So I evolved a plan in which a tank of great length,' and here the P.M.'s eyes dilated, 'weighing sixty or seventy-five tons, ploughed a way six feet deep by six feet wide, giving the troops cover to attack through this communication trench. There were to have been eighty or ninety of these tanks,' Winston added reflectively, 'but it all came to nothing.'

The whole episode was pure Winston. On the one hand, the never-failing fertility of ideas and the astonishing capacity to impose them on others:

'It passed the Cabinet,' he said. 'It was demonstrated to Gamelin and Georges. All were impressed.'

On the other hand, the unscientific approach to a problem. The P.M. admitted that he had not followed the development of tanks between the two wars. He did not know that the tank he invented was already obsolete. de Gaulle's conception of tank warfare, outlined in his book, *La France et Son armée*, published in 1938, and adopted by the Germans in the invasion of France, was quite new to Churchill in 1940.

Winston's service with a battalion in France in the First World War had not weaned him from the great game of playing at soldiers. But it must be his kind of war. He shrank back from the bloody immobility of Continental warfare. His imagination was staggered by the thought of what might happen if things went wrong in an invasion of France or Belgium.

President Roosevelt was impressed at that time by the P.M.'s knowledge of military matters; his dread of a frontal attack on the French coast appeared reasonable. Roosevelt was a humane man, and the P.M.'s picture of the probable fate of the cross-Channel operation appalled him. However, he had complete confidence in his Chief of Staff, and Marshall was convinced that there was only one way to shorten the war – to invade France. Full of that conviction, he set out to educate the President.

Early in April, Roosevelt, with the zeal of a convert, sent Hopkins and Marshall to London to say that his heart and mind were in this plan for landing on the French coast.

Brooke and Marshall, who now met, had a good deal in common. They both came of virile stock. Brooke's ancestors, the 'Fighting Brookes,' had taken part as soldiers in the settlement of Ulster in the reign of Queen Elizabeth, while a forebear of Marshall's, an Irish Captain of Horse, fought for Charles I against Cromwell.

However, the acquisitive instinct, common enough among full-blooded men, had no part in their lives. Their one ambition was to lead armies in the field, but they would not lift a finger to bring this about. They were both selfless men with a fine contempt for the pressures of the mob.

Brooke, who had a feeling for character, decided in Washington that Marshall was 'a great gentleman and a great administrator,' while Marshall, in his own slow and rather cautious manner, came to much the same conclusion about Brooke. When, however, the two men first met in London, neither impressed the other.

To Brooke it was inexplicable that Marshall would cross the Atlantic to advocate the early invasion of France without first priming himself by a prolonged study of all the relevant factors. And yet when he asked Marshall on the eighth day of the Conference, 'Do we go west, south or east after landing?' he found that the American had not begun to think of it. As for Marshall, he decided that Brooke 'lacked Dill's brains.'

Even if Brooke was not impressed by Marshall's ability, he could not help liking him; he felt he could trust him – and that went a long way with the C.I.G.S. In truth, it was impossible not to trust Marshall the moment you looked into his plain, home-spun countenance. It was indeed an unusual face. With his long upper lip and craggy features, Marshall looked more like a painting by Dobson than a modern staff officer. He was a man of simple faith, and yet we owe it to this man of God, as we shall see, that Stalin got his own way at Teheran, with all the mournful consequences that have followed in the world. In such fashion do we see the imp of history grinning at our impotence.

Marshall was a man of strong convictions; he did not find it easy to give way. It appeared inevitable that there would be a prolonged tussle between these two obstinate men, whereas, in fact, the mission from Washington seemed to get almost at once what they wanted, and it was decided that a force of forty-eight divisions should take part in the invasion of France.

I was puzzled at the time by the manner in which the P.M. agreed with Marshall, almost, as it were, without a fight. It was not like him. I made this note in my diary:

> 'The P.M. is an experienced and tenacious campaigner, and he may have decided that the time has not yet come to take the field as an out-and-out opponent of a Second Front in France. Anyway, 1943 seems a long way off, and a good deal may happen in the meanwhile.'

From what the P.M. said to me then, I know that he was still fearful that the President might be driven by public clamour to concentrate on the war with Japan. It was not a time for argument. Winston put it like this: 'I had to work by influence and diplomacy in order to secure agreed and harmonious action with our cherished ally.'

Whatever may be the truth, we know that the Americans left London in great heart; they were satisfied that there was complete agreement, and that the question of a Second Front had been settled once and for all. However, if the P.M. had yielded too quickly, he soon made amends. In the first days of June he sent a cable to the President impressing on him that we must never let TORCH (the invasion of North Africa) pass from our minds, while Mountbatten was sent to Washington to explain that certain difficulties had arisen in the planning of an invasion of France.

The P.M. did not doubt that he could convince the President of the folly of such an invasion at the present time, if only he could talk with him. He determined to make such an opportunity without more delay.

# CHAPTER FOUR

# In Which the Full Size of the Prime Minister is Seen

That was how we came to leave London for Washington on June 17, travelling comfortably in a flying-boat for twenty-eight hours before we came down on the Potomac River.

*June 18, 1942*
The P.M. is always a little apprehensive in the air and our 'narrow squeak' flying back from Bermuda has not helped matters. He asked me whether I minded flying. But before I could answer, I saw that he was thinking of something else. Last night, when we were making our way along the quay at Stranraer to the launch which took us to the flying-boat, I heard him humming: 'We're here because we're here.' I wondered if he was whistling to keep up his spirits. All the same, he is in good shape.[1]

Once installed in the White House, the P.M. lost not a moment in beginning his campaign. It was not an easy task which he had set himself. Those whom the President trusted, Hopkins, Marshall and the rest, were of one mind: there was only one way to shorten the war, and that was to set up a Second Front in France. No one but Winston could have hoped for a hearing in such circumstances.

*June 21, 1942*
Went to the White House this afternoon when the P.M. sent for me. Found him pacing his room. He turned on me:

[1] The Prime Minister thought it necessary on this occasion to advise the King to send for the Foreign Secretary in the event of his death.

'Tobruk has fallen.'[1]

He said this as if I were responsible. With that, he began again striding up and down the room, glowering at the carpet:

'What matters is that it should happen when I am here.'

He went to the window.

'I am ashamed. I cannot understand why Tobruk gave in. More than 30,000 of our men put their hands up. If they won't fight—' The P.M. stopped abruptly.

He forgot all about me, and kept crossing and recrossing the room with quick strides, lost in thought. After a little, he fell into a chair. He seemed to take a pull at himself.

'It was the President who told me; he was very kind. He only asked, "What can we do to help?" And then, although they were already allocated, the President promised me Sherman tanks. Some of them must be sent at once to Alexandria to reinforce the army.'

Only last week the Admiralty pressed that no ships should be sent through the Mediterranean, which is swarming with submarines and quite unsafe.

'I shall take the responsibility of sending them through the Mediterranean. If I give a direct order, they will carry it out.'

The P.M. got up; there was vigour in all his movements. He found comfort in action.

*June 23, 1942*

Winston's buoyant temperament is a tremendous asset. The fall of Tobruk, like the loss of the *Prince of Wales* and the *Repulse*,[2] has been a blow between the eyes. Not only Cairo and Alexandria, but

---

[1] After heavy defeats in the Gazala area (May 27–June 18), General Ritchie was intent on withdrawing his forces to the Egyptian frontier, and, in so doing, left only a weak garrison to hold the ruined defences of the Tobruk perimeter. Rommel's troops overwhelmed this force and Tobruk fell on June 20, 1942. The loss of Tobruk was the rallying point for those who had lost confidence in Churchill's leadership.

[2] The battleship *Prince of Wales* and the battle-cruiser *Repulse* were sunk off Malaya by Japanese air attack on December 10, 1941. They had no air cover. Admiral Sir Tom Phillips and more than eight hundred officers and men lost their lives.

the Suez Canal and all the oilfields of the Near East seem to be at the mercy of Rommel.[1] And yet, before I left his bedroom on Sunday, Winston had refused to take the count; he got up a little dazed, but full of fight. I sat up on the night of Tobruk and last night till he went to bed, thinking he might want me. But he isn't made like that. There is never any danger of his folding up in dirty weather. My heart goes out to him. I do like a really full-sized man. With our military prestige at zero here, he has dominated the discussions.

All day and half the night, they have gone on since the news of Tobruk came through. Winston has battled with the Americans; he has not allowed the facts, damaging as they are, to handicap him. At this game, there is no one here of his own weight. He has made use of the crisis as an argument for postponing the Second Front; without any help from anyone, he has sustained the theme that only an invasion of North Africa can relieve the crisis. Marshall and Hopkins have not accepted the postponement of the Second Front, but they have agreed to divert tanks and other supplies to the Nile Valley, which is perhaps the same thing, since it means a revision of the shipping.

Harry Hopkins tells me what is happening: the big man on the American side in this dismal time is apparently the President. He reminds me of Lloyd George. Discerning people grieve over flaws in his character; they say, for instance, that he is not truthful. But now, when day after day he has to take big decisions, and the people around him are conscious of a crisis, his brain goes on working as if it were packed in ice. The stuff surely is in him; he is built for great occasions.

And if he needs a prop, there is Marshall. He has seen the British collapse in the Middle East end in the success of the P.M.'s efforts to postpone a Second Front. A smaller man would have turned sour. When our army has taken a bad knock, when its fighting spirit is suspect, Marshall has been driven to try to reassure the P.M. that the American infantry is better than the P.M. thinks. Winston has

[1] General Rommel, Commander of the Afrika Korps.

promised before he returns to England that he will go to see this
infantry for himself, and it has been arranged that we are to go
tonight in the President's train to South Carolina. However, the
coach in which the P.M. was to have slept has collided with some
railway carriages, and a worthy substitute cannot be provided at a
moment's notice. So we are to dine at the White House while they
search for rolling stock.

*June 24, 1942*
During dinner last night, when my thoughts were a long way off,
I heard my name. It was the President admonishing me:

'You, Sir Charles, do not know the South Carolina sun in June.
Be careful of the Prime Minister tomorrow.'

His words soon went out of my head, but this morning, as I
stood in a cloud of dust raised by an endless line of tanks, clattering
and crunching past the saluting post, General Marshall came up
and handed me an open telegram.

'Secret.
'To be delivered to General Marshall immediately upon his arrival at
Camp Jackson stop. You and Sir Charles Wilson are in command stop
enough said stop Roosevelt.'

It was the President's friendly way of reminding me of my duty
to my patient, his friend. All the long morning, we stood in the
open, enveloped in dust, sweating in the sun, which beat down on
the sandy stretch, as devoid of shelter as Salisbury Plain. All afternoon, still standing, we watched a battle between two mechanized
forces until my eyes watered with the glare and my feet seemed
too big for my shoes.

I suppose, instead of recording the small change of a great
friendship and telling how the President watched tenderly over the
well-being of his guest, I ought to have told how 600 men with
parachutes were dropped from aircraft and fell to earth in the
wandering, indecisive way of flakes of snow, how four of them broke
their legs, and how the guns and mortars fired live ammunition.

But while Winston, so easily bored by most things, can spend hours, apparently with profit, inspecting troops, their evolutions are quite lost on me.

I certainly ought to record what the P.M. thought of this American army. He surely said the right things; he never says the wrong ones where America is concerned. But is he convinced that they can now stand up to the German hordes in open warfare on a grand scale? It is typical of Winston that I have never heard him answer that question; he will not listen to any criticism of America, her people or her army. Nor is it necessary. His attitude to a Second Front is his answer. He does not believe that these troops are, as yet, sufficiently hardened to be war-worthy on the battlefields of Europe.

All the same, he can see that they are wonderful material. Himself half-American, he seems to understand how they feel when faced by this new job of soldiering: they will certainly bring to it a kind of cold determination to succeed, so that they can get back home.

At last we were taken to the airfield. When I got back to the hotel in Washington about seven o'clock this evening I sat down in the lift; I was glad to turn in.

*June 25, 1942*

It was a quarter to four this morning, they tell me, when the P.M.'s light went out and his exhausted secretary slunk off to bed. I can hardly credit it.

There are some in the military hierarchy to whom war is an enthralling business. But it is not like that for everyone. We had seen in the First World War what it can mean, what in the end it must mean, to any man in the ranks who keeps on his feet for any length of time: the long-drawn-out struggle with fear. It was in that mood that I went to an Intercession Service in the Cathedral here. I was brought up on the Bible and the Book of Common Prayer, and at times, often when my thoughts are quite mundane, those splendid utterances march through my mind, and I find myself repeating: 'Therefore with Angels and Archangels, and with all the company of heaven, we laud and magnify thy glorious Name.' Is it no more than a love of words? I have drifted away from church-going because the literal interpretation by the Church of what was surely meant only as symbols threatened to interfere with my own belief that scientific materialism does not explain everything.

When it was all done, I walked with Halifax to the Embassy and neither of us spoke. It was said of Lord Quickswood[1] that he could not attend church twice in one day: the emotional strain was too great for his strength.

### June 27, 1942

Our flying-boat landed on the water at Stranraer at five o'clock this morning. It happened that the sports at Geoffrey's[2] preparatory school were to be held at Sunningdale this afternoon, and my only chance of getting there in time was to return to London by the aeroplane which had brought the P.M.'s mail. When I had arranged this, I thought I ought to acquaint him with my plans. He was not at all pleased.

'Now why, Charles,' he demanded, 'do you want to break up the party like this?'

I gave him my reason. He thought it a very poor reason. He said so:

'You have taken enough risks.'

I did not argue the point. Nor did I change my plans. But Winston's words came into my head when something went wrong and we made a forced landing in long grass two miles from Worcester. But I forgot all about them when I arrived by another plane and saw the look of relief on the small, eager face of my son, who had been building on my coming.

'Hurry, Daddy. I am in the next race,' he said, pulling me along.

---

[1] Formerly Lord Hugh Cecil. He had been Churchill's best man and was now Provost of Eton.
[2] Geoffrey Wilson, my younger son.

# CHAPTER FIVE

# Another Man Made for
# Great Occasions

*July 2, 1942*

When the P.M. boarded the train at Stranraer a week ago, he was told that the Government had lost the Maldon by-election. Their candidate had polled only 6,226 votes out of a total of nearly 20,000. Winston looked pretty glum, I hear, but all he said was: 'This is Tobruk.' He was not really surprised. Before leaving Washington, he knew that Sir John Wardlaw-Milne, Chairman of the All-Party Finance Committee, had put down a vote of censure on the Order Paper of the House of Commons. The only way to stop the rot, the P.M. said to me later, was to convince the House that no one could have done any better.

'I mean to do that,' he added, setting his jaw.

*

Winston had been out of the country only ten days, but he felt out of touch with affairs; he wanted to know what his critics were likely to say, so that he might be ready with an effective answer. Sir Stafford Cripps, the Leader of the House of Commons, was asked for a report. But when it came it was not at all what the P.M. had hoped for. There was not a single point in the whole paper that he could make in his speech.

Sir Stafford said bluntly that Maldon 'shows the profound disquiet and lack of confidence of the electors.' There was 'a general feeling of dissatisfaction that something is wrong and should be put right without delay.'[1]

The Prime Minister was inclined to dismiss these strictures as 'all theory.' 'You can't run a war as if you were in a laboratory,' he growled. Sir Stafford had spoken of lack of confidence; he, Winston, did not agree that there was any lack of confidence – except, of course, among a few cranks in the House of Commons, and they were well known to everyone. He had been a lifetime in politics, and he knew how to handle the House without anyone's help.

It was in this mood that he rose to wind up the two-day debate. Is it so surprising that he let himself go? 'Naturally, I made every point which occurred to me,' he said. But they were debating points; they were not those Sir Stafford had made. These remained unanswered. If the public wanted information on the succession of defeats, the P.M. did not give it to them. Instead, he gave them a superb demonstration of his skill in debate. One heard on all sides that 'his handling of the House was indeed masterly.'

And it must be said that those who led the attack went out of their way to make his task easy. Wardlaw-Milne argued that the Prime Minister interfered too much in the direction of the war, whereas Sir Roger Keyes,[2] in seconding, said he did not interfere enough. And when Wardlaw-Milne proposed that the Duke of Gloucester should be appointed Commander-in-Chief of the British Army, the House ceased to take him seriously. When Keyes had resumed his seat, a Member pointed out that if the motion was carried the Prime Minister would have to resign. Was that what Sir Roger thought desirable? Whereupon Sir Roger jumped to his feet.

'It would,' he exclaimed, 'be a deplorable disaster if he had to go.'

Members were frankly mystified. What were these critics of the

---

[1]  Winston Churchill, *The Hinge of Fate*, p. 354.
[2]  Sir Roger Keyes, Admiral of the Fleet, Director of Combined Operations 1940–1.

Government trying to say? They wanted to put something right, but what was it? The House had been unhappy about things for some time, but would they be any better if these people had their way? The figures that the Prime Minister produced were positively devastating. The House was now becoming restless; all interest had gone out of the debate. And when a division was taken, only twenty-five members voted for the motion, while 475 were against it.

The P.M. sat back; he was well content. The noisy minority had had their noses rubbed in the mud. Perhaps it would be a lesson to them. Walter Elliot had reminded the House that after eight years of ignominious defeat in the field only twenty-five members had gone into the opposition Lobby against Pitt. The P.M. was deeply interested. It was certainly curious that the number should be repeated like that. Macaulay had recorded that every disaster that happened without the walls of Parliament was regularly followed by triumph within them. And that, too, was happening again. The Prime Minister's mind went back to Pitt's problems, and when I saw him after the debate he compared them with his own. As for Sir Stafford's analysis of the causes of discontent which had led to the vote of censure, he did not think there could have been much in it after all, for the House was nearly solid. Anyway, he had other things to think of.

The P.M. had gone to Washington in June to persuade the President to agree to the invasion of North Africa as an alternative to landing in Normandy. He had failed – at least that was his impression – because of the loss of prestige of the British after the fall of Tobruk.

Roosevelt's advisers took a rather different view. In their eyes, the Prime Minister had been only too successful. He had got what he wanted indirectly; he was altogether too clever for them. They spoke of his influence with the President as a positive menace, and when Mr Churchill went off to meet the House of Commons, he left behind him in Washington a sense of uneasiness, and even alarm. It did not appear that there would be a Second Front in 1942, or 1943 either. Even the steadiest minds around the President seem to have been affected by the feeling of disappointment and frustration. Marshall himself, at a meeting with the President on July 15, supported Admiral King[1] in his claim that the war in the Pacific should have priority.

The President took this clash of opinion very much to heart. For the first time in the war he found himself at variance with his Chiefs of Staff. But he did not hesitate. Flouting the sentiments of his countrymen, he made it clear, once and for all, that there could be no question of transferring to the Pacific the full weight of American effort. He determined to send Hopkins, Marshall and King to London, and with them he sent written instructions. They were to press as strongly as they could the case for invading France in 1942. If they failed to get this, they were to report to him, but, he added, in that event they must find another place for American troops to fight the Germans in the autumn. He wanted an agreed plan now.

In London, Marshall found that the British had quietly made up their minds that an invasion of France that autumn must end in disaster. In vain, with Hopkin's able help, he argued his case. Nothing that they said appeared to make the slightest impression on General Brooke's settled convictions. As Hopkins put it, he kept looking into the distance.

'I feel damn' depressed,' Harry wrote.[2]

At the second meeting on July 22 it was apparent that a complete deadlock had been reached, and Marshall said he would have to report to the President that the British were not prepared to go ahead with the invasion that year. The President's reply was prompt and even categorical. If they could not get agreement about France, they must search for an alternative – perhaps the invasion of North Africa. To Marshall, as a soldier, these were orders from his Commander-in-Chief, and with a heavy heart he accepted TORCH, the plan to land in North Africa.

Marshall could see many good points in the African plan. It was

[1] Admiral King, Chief of American Naval Operations.
[2] Robert E. Sherwood, *The White House Papers of Harry L. Hopkins*, Vol. II, p. 610.

strategically sound, certainly, but to land at Algiers, Oran and Casablanca in the autumn of 1942 would take up so much shipping that it meant inevitably the postponement of the invasion of France until 1944. That was why Lewis Douglas[1] said that TORCH was the most important decision taken during the war: why it was in the President's judgment a turning-point in the whole war.

This brings me to the Prime Minister's part in these proceedings. Winston had used the fall of Tobruk to persuade the Americans to divert to the Nile Valley material set apart for the invasion of France. He thus set in train a series of events which led to TORCH, and so to the postponement of the invasion of France until 1944. Did he, by his sagacity and wisdom, save the Allies from a disaster of the first magnitude that might have led to the loss of the war, or was he responsible, by what the Americans call his pigheadedness, for dragging out the war into the sixth year? Was Winston himself sure that this postponement was in England's best interest? Anyway, as far as I know, he has never claimed credit for postponing the invasion of France, though the Secretary of the Cabinet held it to be his most solid achievement after what he did in 1940. Was his silence a kind of escape clause or insurance in case posterity held him responsible for prolonging the war?

Nor, perhaps, was that the end of the train of consequences of this signal decision. It may well be that the failure of Britain to bring the First World War to a victorious conclusion in 1916, combined with our inability to win the Second World War in 1942, imposed a drain on the resources of a small country, in men and in material, from which it has never completely recovered. It was not enough to win a war; it must be won quickly, or victory might be as disastrous as defeat.

---

[1] Lewis Douglas, U.S. Ambassador to the Court of St James's 1947–50.

# CHAPTER SIX

# A Sad Business

My diary for 1942 has the same backcloth to every scene: Winston's conviction that his life as Prime Minister could be saved only by a victory in the field. It accounts for the sharp exchanges he had at this time with General Auchinleck.[1]

I find a pencilled note with February scrawled in the margin:

> 'Found the P.M. in an explosive mood today. Auchinleck will not be ready to take the offensive in the Desert till June. "The bloody man does not seem to care about the fate of Malta. Anyway," said Winston, setting his jaw, "we can't settle this by writing letters."'

It appears that on March 8 he sent a telegram to Auchinleck telling him that he would be glad if he would come home for consultations. The General replied that he could not leave Cairo at that juncture.

*

*March 14, 1942*
The P.M. is furious with the Auk. He wants to relieve him of his command and talks of Gort[2] taking over. My informant spoke darkly of the Ides of March. 'In your jargon,' he said to me, 'I would not call the Auk a good life.'

---

[1] Sir Claude Auchinleck, Commander-in-Chief, Middle East 1941–2.
[2] Lord Gort, Governor of Malta 1942–4.

*

Alan Brooke in his diaries put this in a different light. He spoke of
the Prime Minister's persistent attempts to prod Auchinleck into a
premature offensive when the P.M. himself was not familiar with
all the aspects of the situation, and when he knew that the Chiefs
of Staff were against an offensive at that time. Brooke wrote on
March 24: 'It is very exhausting, this continual protecting of
Auchinleck.'

It was not only the political situation that was worrying the P.M.
The plight of Malta had become an obsession with him. He was
anxious to help the island by an attack in force on Rommel, but
Auchinleck persisted that he was not ready to give battle. And then
early in May he offered to send strong forces to India. This was
the last straw. It was decided to send him definite orders for an
early offensive, which he must obey, or in default be relieved of his
command. 'This was,' the P.M. writes,[1] 'a most unusual procedure
on our part towards a high military commander. There was,' he
continues, 'a considerable pause, during which we did not know
whether he would accept or resign.' At length the General inti-
mated that he would carry out the P.M.'s instructions. The P.M.
urged him to take personal command of the army, but the General
replied that he was very reluctant to 'become immersed in tactical
problems in Libya.' This unfortunate phrase stuck in the Prime
Minister's gullet. Twice he spat it out with great scorn.

The battle that began at the end of May seemed to bear out
Auchinleck's fears. Rommel attacked on May 26, and by the end
of June our army had been thrown back to Alamein. I think that
it was at this time that the P.M. made up his mind that Auchinleck
must go. My diary takes up the story at this point.

*July 28, 1942*
I was summoned this morning to No. 10 Downing Street, where
I heard that we should soon be on the move. The P.M. has decided

---

[1] Winston Churchill, *The Hinge of Fate*, p. 275.

to fly to Cairo. From Gibraltar he will fly south to Takoradi on the Gold Coast, and so across Central Africa to Cairo. It means about five days in the air, landing at places where malaria and yellow fever are rife. The P.M. wanted my advice about inoculations. I did not like the plan and gave my reasons.

As I was leaving I met John Anderson.[1] He said that certain members of the Cabinet were concerned about the Prime Minister's travels and the dangers he was running in flying over hostile territory in an unarmed bomber. He and Cripps had arranged to see the P.M. this afternoon, and, as health might come up, he would like me to be there.

At the appointed hour I joined them in the Cabinet Room. I was most concerned with the actual risk of the protective measures against yellow fever.[2] While we were discussing these problems, the door opened and the Prime Minister hurried in, beaming at us disarmingly – always a sign that he is up to mischief. He began to unfold a large map, spreading it on the table.

'Vanderkloot says it is quite unnecessary to fly so far south. He has explained to me that we can fly in one hop to Cairo. Come here and look.'

Sir John knelt on a chair to get nearer the map, while Cripps leant over his shoulder. The P.M., with a pencil, traced the route from Gibraltar across Spanish Morocco till he struck the Nile, where his pencil turned sharply to the north.

'This changes the whole picture,' the P.M. added confidently.

I ventured to ask who Vanderkloot was. It appeared that he had just crossed the Atlantic in a bomber, and it is in this machine that we are to fly to Cairo. I wondered why it was left to an American pilot to find a safe route to Cairo, but that did not seem a profitable line of speculation.

'You see, Charles, we need not bother about inoculations.'

Anderson and Cripps pored over the map like excited school-

---

[1] Sir John Anderson, Lord President of the Council.
[2] That there was substance in my fears we learnt later when more than half of those inoculated against this fever developed an obstinate form of jaundice.

boys, and the party broke up without a word of warning or remonstrance about the risks the P.M. was taking in flying over hostile territory in an unarmed bomber by daylight. The P.M. gets his own way with everyone with hardly a murmur.

*August 1, 1942*
Called at No. 10 to see if anything was wanted. The P.M. seemed abstracted.

'There's something very wrong there,' he muttered half to himself. 'I must clear things up.'

For a long time he has been worried by the reverses in the desert, and when he told me that he had asked Smuts[1] to join him in Cairo, I knew he meant to bring things to a head. As I was leaving, he put down a telegram the secretary had just brought in.

'We may go to see Stalin. He won't like what I have to say to him. I'm not looking forward to it.'

The P.M. is turning over in his head how he can break the news to Stalin. He has to tell him that there will not be a Second Front in France this year.

*August 3, 1942*
It was after midnight when we left Lyneham in the unheated bomber. Two mattresses had been dumped in the after-cabin, and I passed the night in comfort. The P.M. was less happy; he dislikes draughts – and after all it is rather a feckless way of sending him over the world when he is approaching his seventieth year. However, he soon forgot his discomforts in sound sleep, and when we got to Gibraltar this morning he was ready for anything.

*August 4, 1942*
Vanderkloot has brought it off. We landed safely near the Pyramids and drove into Cairo. The Embassy is hot and steamy, but the P.M.'s bedroom is air-conditioned, and anyway he does not feel extremes of heat and cold like other people. He is in great heart.

[1] Field-Marshal Smuts, Prime Minister of South Africa 1939–48.

No longer is he compelled to deal with great events by correspondence; he is 'the man on the spot.' Twice he has said this to me. A great feeling of elation stokes the marvellous machine, which seems quite impervious to fatigue.

When I left the P.M., I found my hostess anxious to learn the habits of her formidable guest. Lady Lampson,[1] I have just discovered, is the daughter of the Italian physician, Castellani, who had enjoyed a considerable measure of success in practice in Mayfair before he went to Rome to help Mussolini with his medical arrangements. I found this interesting. A fortnight before we left London, Lord Dawson pestered me, as President of the Royal College of Physicians, to remove Castellani's name from the list of Fellows. He said that he was the Axel Munthe type of doctor, living in some comfort by his wits, and that he was now helping the enemy.

For my part, I have no liking for this witch-hunting. Besides, as an Italian he is doing the right thing. And there can be no doubt about his ability. After all, living by one's wits is an elastic term which might be stretched by some to include rather more conventional types.

After Lady Lampson had learnt that I held no recipe for the taming of Winston, I talked for a time with Smuts. His weather-beaten face is dominated by the penetrating gaze of the cold, measuring, grey-blue eyes, which are set deep above the prominent cheek-bones.

I do not feel that I have got to the bottom of him yet, any more than I can fathom Roosevelt. If Smuts had been born in Germany, he might have been one of the great captains of war. He collects his facts like a man of science – listening, sifting and rejecting what has not been proved. No other soldier I know has quite the same approach to evidence.

I am glad he is here. The P.M. hates the thought of removing one of his commanders. Smuts is more ruthless, and if the P.M. has to make changes in the higher command, even, it may be, to get

---

[1] Wife of Sir Miles Lampson, British Ambassador in Cairo.

rid of General Auchinleck, Smuts's presence and counsel will fortify and comfort him.

*August 5, 1942*
Very early this morning the P.M. drove with Auchinleck to his head-quarters behind the Ruweisat Ridge. There, in a kind of wire cage, we breakfasted with some men burnt brown by the desert sun. There were flies everywhere. When they were disturbed they rose in a cloud with a buzzing sound. Wandering over the world with the Prime Minister, one meets new faces almost every day, until one hardly tries to put a name to them. From time to time, however, one encounters someone who refuses to be dismissed in this perfunctory fashion. Here was a face that interested me very much. There was nothing distinctive about the alert blue eyes set in a brick-red face, but there was about this man an air of authority. Those near him appeared to listen very attentively whenever he spoke. When I asked his name, they said, 'Straffer Gott,' and added that he had a way of turning up in the desert when things had gone wrong, and putting them right, so that he was much beloved by his men. After breakfast the P.M. took him off in his car to the airfield. He is clearly interested in him. It is said that Gott, after three years in the desert, is a tired man, but I fancy that the P.M. must have decided that he is not too tired to take over the Eighth Army.

At the airfield we took leave of Gott and were handed over to Tedder[1] and Arthur Coningham[2] – another personality. We flew with them to Coningham's headquarters in a tent in the desert. Here were all the heads of the Desert Air Force. A special luncheon, which Shepheard's Hotel had sent from Cairo by car, got lost, and while we waited I had time to look round. It is a new atmosphere. These men have not taken a bad knock; they are on top and know that they are on top. In an impersonal war of millions they remain individuals. These fellows were not groomed in a mess before the war. Their thoughts are not borrowed from others and their speech

[1] Arthur Tedder, Air Officer Commanding-in-Chief, R.A.F., Middle East.
[2] Air Marshal Arthur Coningham, Commanding Desert Air Force.

is forthright. They are critical of the Army, and they say what is in their minds without batting an eyelid. The P.M. is apt to be lost among his own species, but I think he caught the drift of their talk. Certainly the Army's shortcomings were set forth succinctly. It is not to them that one will look for a recommendation for mercy when the Commander-in-Chief stands in the dock.

And there is Tedder to speak for them if the P.M. is in doubt. Tedder's father, a rough diamond, fought his way from the bottom to become head of the Excise. In the son the facets have been polished, but the hard stone is left. I drove with him to the airfield. He seems quite unlike anyone in the service I have met – a quick mind and a sharp tongue. He admires Smuts, thinks he is a greater man than the Prime Minister, and says so. As we retraced our steps towards Cairo at the end of the day, the P.M. remained sunk in his own thoughts. He did not speak once, but I have a feeling that it is all settled.

*August 6, 1942*
All day the P.M. has shut himself up with Smuts and the C.I.G.S. – we have seen nothing of him, but tonight he came out to sit on the lawn under the stars, and as he talked it was possible to follow his thoughts. The Ambassador's son is here on leave. He is in the Guards and what he had to say about the morale of the troops in other units – though it leaked out in driblets – was disquieting. The P.M. said presently:

'There is something wrong somewhere. I am convinced there has been no leadership out here. What has happened is a disgrace. Ninety thousand men all over the place. Alex told me there are 2,000 officers in Cairo who wear a smart uniform called a gabardine, and that they are called the gabardine swine.' His voice rose: 'There must be no cozening. The Army must understand there are very serious penalties for not doing their duty.'

*August 7, 1942*
I have discovered that when the rest of the party go off to change for dinner, Smuts comes out on to the lawn and sits by himself for

perhaps half an hour. Tonight I joined him, and when he quoted from *The Ring and the Book* and found that I could carry on where he left off, he began to speak about many things. I offered him my books, but he said he did not read fiction. The people in the house say that he takes his Greek Testament to his bedroom. When it slipped out that I had once passed an examination of sorts in botany, he began to talk of the different species of grass in South Africa. There were thousands of them. He carried his manual on botany about with him. Presently, when I had been talking to him of the value in war of the appraising, measuring mind, he began to show signs of impatience, drumming with his fingers on his chair. What I said he accepted, but he went on to speak of the supremacy of the man of ideas.

'That is why Winston is indispensable. He has ideas. If he goes, there is no one to take his place. Men of action,' he said, 'live on the surface of things; they do not create.' He rose at last. 'We must go in. They may be looking for us.'

During dinner there was a discussion on the profit motive; perhaps it would be more accurate to say that there was a dialogue between the P.M. and Smuts. I need hardly add that it was Smuts who raised the subject; the P.M. was plainly not interested. The P.M. is very conservative and Victorian, but Smuts feels that big changes are coming.

P.M.: 'As I get older I begin to see a pattern in things.'

Smuts: 'There is a pattern in history, though it is not easy to see or follow.'

Smuts spoke of Gandhi: 'He is a man of God. You and I are mundane people. Gandhi has appealed to religious motives. You never have. That is where you have failed.'

P.M. (with a great grin): 'I have made more bishops than anyone since St Augustine.'

But Smuts did not smile. His face was very grave. The cast of his own mind enabled him to measure just what this limitation had meant to this man for whom he had so deep an affection. As I listened to Smuts my mind went back to a Christmas morning at Carthage. There was an Early Service in a barn, with the Coldstream as communicants, and when the service had begun a dove flew in and perched on a rafter; so that the men said there would soon be peace. Alex told me later that when he repeated this to the P.M. he had only mocked; 'There is nothing in such stuff', he said. But Alex said: 'If I am living for nothing and there is no second life to come – it seems to me intolerable'.

While they talked I kept asking myself what kind of a man is Smuts. Is he the Henry James of South Africa? Does he think of his fellow Boers as James came to think of the American scene as perhaps a little primitive? A South African here speaks of him as 'remote'; even to his own people he is a stranger. No one really knows him. It appears that this solitary, austere Boer with his biblical background lives in a world of his own. It is as if he had been cut off from his kind.

He lives to get things done. Anyone who steps in his path is ruthlessly pushed aside. As for his colleagues in the Cabinet, they are kept at arm's length. The whole political apparatus is just a necessary nuisance. He is taken up with the war and with world events; social affairs in South Africa mean little to him: he is not interested in the slums of Johannesburg. Like Winston, he is sure that there is nothing in the world which he could not do as well as anyone. There is nothing that cannot be thought out. Certainly he has an extraordinary mind, thinking out everything for himself. And yet in the end, human nature being what it is, I am fearful that his arrogance will trip him up.

In my conversation on the lawn, I got an impression of a hard man – it is not to him that I should look for a reprieve for Auchinleck – a man interested only in ideas, and not much nearer the mark than the P.M. when it comes to summing up a man. He is one of the few men – I can think of only two – who have Winston's ear because he respects their mental processes; the other, of course, is the 'Prof'.[1] Winston is encouraged when he hears from Smuts that he is proceeding along the right lines.

As for Auchinleck, Brooke tells me that he is a man of splendid

[1] Professor Lindemann, afterwards Lord Cherwell.

talents, a very able soldier, and a man, too, of great strength of character. He has come to grief, it would seem, because he could not pick the right subordinates. Those he appointed had so dispersed our forces in the desert that Rommel, with his more effective tanks and guns, had little difficulty in defeating the scattered fragments piecemeal. There is another reason: the Auk does not understand Winston.

As the P.M. went to his room after dinner, Jacob stopped him and told him that Gott had been shot down and killed flying to Cairo, on the same route which the P.M. had flown two days ago without an escort. He stood staring at the carpet, then very slowly he pulled himself up the stairs. It had been decided that Gott should be given the Eighth Army. I wonder what the P.M. will do now.

*August 9, 1942*
The end of the story came this morning. I had taken a book and was sitting under one of the two trees on the Embassy lawn. The soldiers were in conference, and I had the lawn all to myself, except for a sentry who passed up and down the raised path that separates the garden from the Nile. I was watching two hoopoes extracting worms from the grass with their long bills when Brooke appeared with Auchinleck; they took seats under the other tree. I could not hear what the C.I.G.S. was saying, nor could I see the expression on Auchinleck's face, but I did not need any help to follow what was happening. Auchinleck sat with his forearms resting on his thighs, his hands hanging down between his knees, his head drooping forward like a flower on a broken stalk. His long, lean limbs were relaxed; the whole attitude expressed grief: the man was completely undone. After a time they got up and went into the house. I tried to get on with my book, but I was somehow made miserable by what I had seen.

# CHAPTER SEVEN

# Breaking the News to Stalin

*Moscow, August 12, 1942*

It was five o'clock in the evening when our Liberator made a good landing at the Moscow airfield. A small crowd of officials, headed by Molotov,[1] met us, and a guard of honour goose-stepped past the P.M., while a band played the National Anthems of Britain, the United States and Russia. Then we got into cars and were driven at a great pace through Moscow to a house or dacha in a pine wood called 'State Villa No. 7.' The P.M. was preoccupied with the coming interview with Stalin; he was silent, abstracted and short-tempered.

The elderly concierge on the door mumbled something. As I was getting out of my greatcoat I heard loud shouts coming from upstairs. I went up them, two at a time, to find Winston sitting in a large bath, shivering and damning.

'The water is bloody cold and I don't know which is the hot tap.'

Their taps do not work like our taps, and the Russian lettering did not help. Sawyers had gone off to fetch something. I took a chance. There was a sudden big gush of icy water under terrific pressure. It caught the P.M. amidships. He gave a loud shriek and when he got his breath he cursed me for my incompetence. I flew to get help.

I am lodged in the nursery, a large room with a clever wallpaper and lined with cupboards full of ingenious toys.

[1] Vyacheslav Molotov, Soviet Commissar for Foreign Affairs.

The conference with Stalin, at which Molotov, Voroshilov,[1] Harriman and Archibald Clark Kerr, our Ambassador, were present, began at seven o'clock and lasted four hours.

The P.M. on his return was full of what had happened:

'The first two hours were bleak and sombre. I explained at length, with maps and arguments, why we could not do a Second Front. Stalin said he did not agree with our reasons. He argued the other way, and everyone was pretty glum. Finally, he said he did not accept our view, but that we had the right to decide. The only way to swallow a bitter mixture, as Charles will tell you, is to take it in a single gulp. At any rate, I did not attempt to sweeten it. I asked for plain speaking, and I certainly got it. But if Stalin was bitterly disappointed, he listened patiently to my explanation. He never once raised his voice, never once lost his temper. When I had told him the worst, we both sat in silence for a little. Then I spoke of the bombing of Germany, and he seemed a little more friendly. I thought that was the time to produce TORCH. Stalin was at last listening with both his ears. "May God prosper this undertaking," he said.'

'Did he really say that?' I asked.

'Oh, he brings in the Deity quite a lot. And before I had come to an end of my explanation of TORCH he astonished me by giving four reasons why this operation must help. First, it would surprise Rommel's troops in the rear; secondly, it would soon put Italy out of the war; thirdly, it would end in fighting between Germans and the French; fourthly, it would frighten Spain into staying neutral. I was astonished that he was able to master an intricate problem of this nature that was quite new to him in a few moments.

'It is typical of Stalin that the only reason he left out was the opening of the Mediterranean. He is a land animal. I put my cards on the table, and when I left we were good friends and shook hands cordially. I mean to forge a solid link with this man.'

If the P.M. was pleased, the Ambassador was delighted; he was

---

[1] Marshal Voroshilov, Commissar for Defence.

obviously greatly relieved that the first meeting had gone so well. Harriman turned to me:

'You will be glad to know, Sir Charles, your fears were ground-less.'

Clark Kerr took me aside.

'Things were pretty grim,' he said, 'until the Prime Minister described our bombing of Germany. Then Stalin, for the first time, became really interested. He said his information was that the bombing was upsetting the civilian population. He wanted to blast the German workmen out of their homes.'

'Did that break the ice?' I asked.

'Well,' the Ambassador went on, 'when Stalin began to thaw, the Prime Minister adroitly produced TORCH. He drew a croco-dile – and explained to Stalin how we intended to rip open the soft underbelly.

'That was what TORCH meant. Stalin had not taken his eyes off the interpreter; he was following every word; and then he held up his hand' – here the Ambassador imitated his action – 'to stop the Prime Minister. He wished to ask a question. At what date did Mr Churchill plan to land in North Africa? When the Prime Minister said October, the Russians grinned with pleasure – though Molotov did ask if September was a possible date.' Clark Kerr chortled: 'There was one touch typical of Stalin. When the Prime Minister stressed the importance of secrecy, Stalin's face wrinkled with amusement. He said that he hoped nothing would appear in the British Press.'

It was now after midnight, and the P.M., who had had no dinner, proceeded to eat a huge meal; in between the courses he nursed his head in his hands and said nothing. At the end he yawned wearily.

'I will only do half a dozen telegrams and then go to bed,' he said rather petulantly.

Presently he put his half-finished cigar across the wine-glass, and got up and stretched himself; the telegrams, he decided, must wait till the morning. He was plainly very weary. After all, he had been on the aerodrome at Teheran this morning at six o'clock. I took him to bed, and while he was undressing I asked him what he thought of Stalin:

'Was he quick at getting on to your points?'

'Extraordinarily quick,' the P.M. replied. 'This alone was worth the journey. My strategy was sound,' he went on. 'For an hour and a half I told him bluntly what we could *not* do. At the end Stalin said he was, of course, very disappointed, but he thanked me for my very frank statement. He had not expected very much. Then I told him what we could do. He ended enthusiastic – in a glow.'

*August 13, 1942*

After luncheon the P.M., who was looking through the window at the blue sky, said he would like to walk in the wood – which surprised me a good deal, because he hardly ever walks for the sake of exercise. As we wandered among the trees he said:

'Now I have broken the news to Stalin I have a feeling the rest should be plain sailing. I spoke very plainly to Molotov this morning. I thought he ought to know that Stalin would not be wise to be rude to us when we had come all this distance to help him.'

'What did Molotov say?' I asked.

'Oh, he promised to tell Stalin what I had said, and from the way he said it I think he will. "Stalin is wise, and he will know how you feel, even if he argues." Those were Molotov's words. Of course, I don't know how much the interpreter altered what he actually said. But if he really did say that – well, it's very interesting.'

The P.M. stopped at a great glass tank full of goldfish of different kinds. He sat down on the edge of the tank and proceeded to demonstrate to me the various kinds. Could we get any food for them? he wondered. When I went off to look for a Russian who spoke English, I discovered that the wood was surrounded by a green palisade about twice the height of a man. There were four or five green gates at intervals. Finding one without a guard, I came nearer until I could see a kind of peephole, the size of a brick; looking through this, I saw police and soldiers and barbed wire. They are plainly prepared for trouble with their own people.

When I returned to the P.M. he was with one of the Russians. This man wanted to know if Mr Churchill would like to see the air-raid shelter. He directed us to a place in the wood, some distance from the house, where an electric lift took us down to a long passage lined with coloured marbles and wooden panelling. There were perhaps ten or eleven elaborately furnished rooms, with heavy, swinging doors, offices, a completely equipped kitchen with refrigerators and servants' quarters – like a section of the Strand Palace Hotel gone underground. In all the rooms there were candles in heavy silver candelabra, in case the electricity failed. The P.M. isn't interested in that kind of thing. His mind is with Stalin in the Kremlin, and when he could he thanked the Russians and went off to his room.

He saw Stalin at eleven o'clock this evening at the Kremlin. The meeting was a flop. It was as if yesterday's meeting, with its good humour and apparent agreement, had never taken place.

'I am downhearted and dispirited,' the P.M. complained on his return. 'I have come a long way and made a great effort. Stalin lay back puffing at his pipe, with his eyes half closed, emitting streams of insults. He said the Russians were losing 10,000 men a day. He said that if the British Army had been fighting the Germans as much as the Red Army had, it would not be so frightened of them. He was most uncomplimentary to our Army. He said we had broken our word about a Second Front.'

The P.M.'s lips were pressed together.

'I can harden too. I am not sure it wouldn't be better to leave him to fight his own battles,' he muttered. 'Losing all these British ships; only three out of fourteen got through in the last convoy . . . I am sure that Stalin knows that we are right. His judgment is too sound not to know.'

At this point Sir Alexander Cadogan,[1] who isn't exactly pro-Russian, interjected:

'Should I tell Stalin in confidence that you are hesitating whether

---

[1] Sir Alexander Cadogan, Permanent Under-Secretary of State for Foreign Affairs 1938–46.

to accept his invitation to dinner tomorrow after what has happened?'

The P.M.: 'No; that is going too far, I think.'

When Cadogan had gone, the P.M. said half to himself:

'We're a long way from home – four days' flight.' He looked up at me. 'And the journey is not without danger.'

While the P.M. was undressing he kept repeating what Stalin had said to him at yesterday's meeting. He used exactly the same words he had used on his return from the Kremlin. He repeated the four reasons Stalin gave why TORCH would help, and told me again how he had invoked the blessing of the Deity on the under-taking. What Stalin said to him had lodged in his mind.

*August 14, 1942*

Cadogan always attends these conferences in grey flannels and black coat. I should take this as a subtle compliment to the Prime Minister's sartorial eccentricities if I had not learnt that the Permanent Under-Secretary would bend the knee to no man. He has all the coolness and nonchalance of the English . . . I imagine he contrives to combine all the things for which the Foreign Office is criticized by the vulgar. I do not say this is necessarily against him. In his cups he gets more sympathetic.

The Ambassador told me that Cadogan called on Molotov this afternoon, bearing a written reply to Stalin's memorandum; at the same time he told Molotov frankly that the P.M. felt 'puzzled and disheartened.' It seems that the tone of this outspoken document was not lost on Stalin. He has had time to turn over in his mind what might happen if the P.M. left Moscow in his present mood. It would be awkward if the democracies left him to his own devices. At any rate, by nine o'clock, when we dined at the Kremlin, it was obvious that Stalin had thought better of his truculent attitude and was anxious to make amends. He went out of his way to be agree-able to the P.M. I was too far away during dinner to hear what they were saying, but Clark Kerr told me later that it went all right for a time, though the P.M. had not yet forgiven Stalin for the things he had said about our soldiers. They talked about Lloyd George and Lady Astor. Stalin told how he had asked Lady Astor about politicians in England. "'Chamberlain," she said, "is the coming man." 'What about Winston?'

"'Oh, he's finished," she replied.'

Stalin had retorted: 'If your country is ever in trouble, he will come back.'

During dinner Winston said: 'When the Germans declared war on you, I consulted nobody, but made my broadcast speech.' That went straight home, Clark Kerr told me.

At another time Stalin said: 'I am a rough man, not an experienced one like you.' He begged that his roughness should not be misunderstood.

The dinner dragged on; the list of toasts appeared interminable. John Reed, acting Head of Chancery at the Embassy, said to me: 'Voroshilov challenged me to a competition in pepper-vodkas, and when I declined he refused all further conversation.'

At length Molotov got up and proposed the health of Sir Alexander Cadogan. Cadogan, who had noticed that the P.M. was not enjoying himself and was indeed beginning to betray some impatience, seized the opportunity to break up the banquet. When Molotov sat down he said quietly that with Stalin's permission he would himself propose a toast. 'I gave them: death and damnation to the Germans.' That did the trick. There was no one present to reply, and after a brief pause Stalin got up and left the table.

When Stalin had gone, Mikoyan[1] staggered out with his arm round a colleague's neck.

After dinner Stalin and the P.M. were photographed together; Stalin seemed to take the initiative in this and made it plain that it gave him pleasure. Then something went wrong. The P.M., Harriman and Molotov went over and sat at a table, where Stalin joined them, taking a chair next to the P.M., who, however, went on reading some document, and hardly spoke to Stalin. I received the impression that Stalin wanted to be friendly, but that the P.M.

[1] A. Mikoyan, People's Commissar of Foreign Trade.

would not meet him halfway. At last the P.M. got up and said 'Goodbye' and moved off. He walked very quickly, with countenance overcast. His face was set and resolute. Stalin accompanied him through the vast and empty halls which separated the dining-room from the door by which we had come into the Kremlin. I had never seen Stalin move except in a slow and measured fashion. Now to keep up with the P.M. he had almost to trot. Watching him, I thought of the importunity of the small boy who is asking for a cigarette card and will not take 'No' for an answer. Perhaps Stalin realized that he had gone too far, and that this might be the end; he saw what that would mean.

The P.M. strode into the waiting car. He asked Alex Cadogan to drive with him. Cadogan told me in his dry, factual way of the P.M.'s mood when they left the Kremlin:

'I was surprised in the car to find the violence and depth of the resentment that he had worked up. I don't know what would have happened at the Kremlin if the party had gone on much longer. Nor was I able to discover the exact cause of the P.M.'s mood. Anyhow, he was like a bull in the ring maddened by the pricks of the picadors. He declared that he really did not know what he was supposed to be doing here. He would return to London without seeing Stalin again.'

I followed in another car. On alighting at the villa, I was told the P.M. wanted me. I found him with Cadogan and Rowan,[1] sitting at a long table. They took no notice of me, but went on talking. There was a long dispute whether the proposed communiqué describing the results of the P.M.'s visit should be worded as the Russians proposed. The matter under discussion was so plainly secret that I rose to leave.

'Don't go, Charles,' the P.M. interjected, and went on talking.

He said the communiqué would be 'disastrous,' because it would be interpreted everywhere as meaning that the Russians and British had disagreed and that there was to be no Second Front. Cadogan said he could not see how it could be disastrous. It was, like all

---

[1] Leslie Rowan, Assistant private secretary to the Prime Minister.

communiqués, bosh, but he could not see why it should be interpreted as meaning no Second Front.

The P.M. replied that there was no reference to any offensive
action. Cadogan kept repeating that he could not see how it could
be disastrous. I had never seen anyone talk to the P.M. like this. At
last the P.M. said:

'Well, you have been in the Foreign Office all this time. Do as
you think. But I want it recorded that I thought it would be disastrous.'

Cadogan retorted: 'Molotov, when I see him, will ask me how
it is disastrous, and I must be able to answer.'

P.M.: 'I will authorize you to take the line you want.'

Whereupon Cadogan said he could not take a line if the P.M.
thought it would be disastrous. There was a silence. The P.M. rose
to go to bed. Cadogan got up, said 'Good night,' and left the room.
Rowan followed him. I went after the P.M. to his bedroom. He had
flopped into an armchair and sat staring at the carpet. When he
noticed me he said:

'Stalin didn't want to talk to me. I closed the proceedings down.
I had had enough. The food was filthy. I ought not to have come.'

The P.M. got up, pacing the room in nothing but his silk under-
vest, mumbling to himself. At last he pulled up before me:

'I still feel I could work with that man if I could break down the
language barrier. That is a terrible difficulty.'

He wondered whether he should make another attempt. He
might be snubbed. I said he must risk that. It wasn't a question of
whether Stalin was a brigand or not, but if we did not work in with
him it would mean at least a longer war and more casualties. But
the P.M. wasn't listening. He said he wouldn't go near Stalin again.
He had deliberately said 'Goodbye' and not 'Good night.' If there
was any fresh move, Stalin must make it. He wouldn't. He got into
bed, put on his black eye-shade and settled his head in the pillow.
I turned out the light. When I left the room I looked at my watch.
It was a quarter to four. The night was nearly over. I could not
sleep; the consequences of leaving Moscow like this with Stalin and
the P.M. at loggerheads frightened me.

*August 15, 1942*

After breakfast I ran into Reed on the drive. I said to him that I would like to see the Ambassador, but hesitated to ring him up. Reed said at once, 'He said to me only this morning you're the best diplomatist of the lot. I'm sure he'd be glad to see you. He's with Alex Cadogan now.'

As he spoke they came up the drive, the Ambassador puffing at his pipe, and passed us by. When I saw there was no chance of getting Clark Kerr away from Cadogan, I went into the house and wrote to him. I confessed my fears, prayed him to forgive my butting in, but I wondered if it would be possible to put into Stalin's ear:

(i) That the P.M. must not leave Moscow without seeing Stalin.

(ii) That the P.M. had said after the first meeting 'I'd like that man to like me' and after dinner: 'I feel I could work with that man if I could break down the barrier of language.'

(iii) That Stalin must be made to understand that the P.M.'s success or failure in Moscow with the Russians would not influence the electorate in the United Kingdom; only continued defeats could weaken Winston's position.

(iv) That the P.M.'s only interest was to defeat Hitler; that was an obsession with him.

At the same time it would help if the P.M. could be persuaded:

(i) That a quarrel with Stalin meant more British casualties.

(ii) That Stalin coming to the door to see the P.M. off was, according to Molotov, without any precedent in the history of the Soviet Union.

(iii) That they both wanted to come together, but something was keeping them apart.

(iv) That it was up to the P.M., with his vast experience, to handle the situation so that this was brought about.

When I had finished the note, I was on the point of tearing it up. It seemed impertinent. At that moment Reed passed through the room, and that settled the matter. I gave my letter to him and through the window I watched him hand it to the Ambassador. About an hour afterwards Clark Kerr came up to me:

'I'm more hopeful,' he said. 'The P.M. listened and said to me at the end, "It was my fault."'

Winston was thinking of his mood at the dinner. I, too, was hopeful as the hours passed, because there is no word yet of our leaving Moscow.

The P.M. must have made up his mind to see Stalin before he goes, or we should by now be packing up.

While we were waiting for tea they brought me a letter from the Embassy. It was from John Reed. I read:

'From all that H.E. told me on the drive back to Moscow from the dacha after his interview with the Prime Minister I was left in no doubt at all that the P.M. intended to leave this afternoon. The Ambassador was cock-a-hoop because he had dissuaded him from doing so. The P.M. told him he could hardly bring himself to shake Stalin's hand. "Did he not realize who he was speaking to? The representative of the most powerful empire the world has ever seen." The Ambassador had a very difficult task talking the P.M. round; he considered it his greatest diplomatic triumph.'

As I put Reed's letter into my pocket Cadogan came into the room. He had been ringing up the Kremlin at intervals to arrange a call on Stalin by the P.M. He was told that 'Mr Stalin is out walking.' As the hours passed he kept on telephoning the Kremlin and the reply was always the same – Stalin was still out walking. Cadogan did not dare to pass this on to the P.M. for fear it might bring on another crisis. At last – it must have been about six o'clock – when Cadogan had given up hope, the news came that Stalin would see the P.M. at seven o'clock.

The P.M. was resolved to make one final effort to break down the wall of misunderstanding which separated him from Marshal Stalin. He said he would be back at half-past eight, and ordered dinner for that hour. A good deal seemed to hang on this final

interview and when 8.30 came and there was no sign of the P.M.,
I found myself pacing up and down the passage by the front door.
Then nine o'clock, then ten o'clock, eleven, twelve, and still no
sign. Was it a good or a bad omen, this prolonged interview? What
did it mean? General Anders, the Commander-in-Chief of the
Polish Army, had been asked to come at eight o'clock. As the hours
went by, he seemed never to stop abusing the Russians. We were
rather embarrassed, wondering if the Russian servants understood
English. About midnight I decided to have something to eat. As
the night wore on, the rest of the party slept in their chairs or read;
one of the secretaries put his feet up on a chair and was soon fast
asleep. His deep breathing and Anders's voice were the only sounds
that broke the silence. At half-past three in the morning the P.M.
burst in. A glance at his face told me things had gone well. He
spoke a word to Anders and then went to his room, where I followed
him. He was full of the interview.

'During the first hour,' he said, 'I was very cordial, but there
was no response from this hard-boiled egg of a man. About eight
o'clock I prepared to take my leave. Stalin asked when we were
to meet next. I replied I was leaving at dawn. He then said: "Are
you preoccupied?" He meant engaged. I answered, "Not at all."
He invited me to come to his apartments and to have some drinks.
We walked about a hundred yards to his simple rooms, a dining-
room and work-room and a bedroom. Then on the spur of the
moment he asked me to dine with him and sent for Molotov to
join us.

'Dinner began simply with a few radishes, and grew into a
banquet – a sucking pig, two chickens, beef, mutton, every kind of
fish. There was enough to feed thirty people. Stalin spoilt a few
dishes, a potato here, an oddment there. After four hours of sitting
at the table, he suddenly began to make a hearty meal. He offered
me the head of a pig, and when I refused, he himself tackled it with
relish. With a knife he cleaned out the head, putting it into his
mouth with his knife. He then cut pieces of flesh from the cheeks
of the pig and ate them with his fingers. Stalin's daughter, a red-
headed, well-favoured girl, came in and kissed him, but was not

allowed to stay. An old woman appeared, rather frightened; otherwise we waited on ourselves.

'Stalin is as keen as I am on a landing in Norway. He said if this fell through he might have difficulty in keeping his vast armies supplied. He wants lorries. He is making his own tanks. Stalin seems sure he can hang on till the weather breaks.

'When I raised the question of the collective farms and the struggle with the *kulaks*, Stalin became very serious. I asked him if it was as bad as the war. "Oh, yes," he answered. "Worse. Much worse. It went on for years. Most of them were liquidated by the peasants, who hated them. Ten millions of them. But we had to do it to mechanize our agriculture. In the end, production from the land was doubled. What is one generation?" Stalin demanded as he paced up and down the length of the table.'

Sawyers came in and out of the bedroom: 'We shall be late, sir, at the aerodrome.'

The P.M. took no notice.

'I was taken into the family,' he continued. 'We ended friends. It was true that argument broke out later, but it was very friendly argument. I said to Molotov when I was leaving: "I will not trouble you to come to the airfield. I will say goodbye to you here.' "Oh, no," said Stalin. "He is a younger man. He will see you off!"'

And at 4.30, as dawn was breaking, Molotov arrived at the villa to accompany the Prime Minister to the airfield.

*

My diary of the four days in Moscow was taken down at the time; it sets out in some detail what happened in the seventeen hours that intervened between Winston leaving the dinner table in the Kremlin at half-past one in the morning of August 15, and his arrival at the Kremlin to say goodbye to Stalin at seven o'clock in the evening of the same day.

The P.M., incensed by Stalin's insults, resolved not to see him again. Cadogan underlined the depths of his resentment; the P.M. had told him that he meant to return to London without seeing Stalin. The Ambassador was satisfied that he intended to leave

Moscow that afternoon. The following morning, after a night spent in turning over the incalculable consequences of a quarrel between Winston and Stalin, I sent a message to Clark Kerr in the hope that he might be able to persuade the P.M. to change his mind. The Ambassador found Winston in a difficult mood and he was cock-a-hoop when he at last persuaded the P.M. to see Stalin before leaving Moscow.

There is a discrepancy between this account of the conference and that of Winston in *The Hinge of Fate*. The Prime Minister, back in Cairo after the conference, reported to Mr Attlee that the dinner had passed off in a very friendly atmosphere. He can hardly have forgotten the events of the night of the 14th. It is more probable that he saw little point in perpetuating in detail his own stormy reaction to Stalin's insults and generally provocative attitude in the course of their meeting on August 13, particularly now that the conference could be acclaimed as a complete success.

As one reads of these now-distant days, they seemed to be smoothed out, and as it were edited; the terrifically alive, pugnacious, impatient and impulsive Winston Churchill has been dressed up as a sagacious, tolerant elder statesman, pondering good-humouredly on the frailty of men and the part chance plays in their fluctuating fortunes. He himself once said that he was not designed by nature for that particular role.

This brings me to Winston's memory. I recall that he declaimed to me 'King Robert of Sicily', a poem of eighty-six lines, five days after his stroke in 1953, with only a few mistakes. He then asked me what part of the brain stores memories, and went on to tell me that he could recall in detail many incidents in his trench life at Plug Street in the First World War, whereas in the Second War one great event toppling over another seemed to wipe out the last, so that in writing his book he came to depend on what had been committed to paper. There were, however, times when everything was at stake which were stamped indelibly on his mind. I have heard him describe the scene in a deep shelter at Uxbridge on September 15, during the Battle of Britain, perhaps half a dozen times, and on each occasion in almost the same words.

Winston's first meeting with Stalin was another instance. He was keyed up to what was even in his life an unusual experience. He came back from his talks with Stalin in a state of suppressed excitement; he wanted to tell us what Stalin had said. I took it down at the time. Next day, while he was undressing, he repeated what Stalin had said to him in exactly the same words. We know now that they were Stalin's actual words, because Winston's account of these talks in *The Hinge of Fate* was taken from the interpreter's script.

# CHAPTER EIGHT

# A Soldier Uninhibited

*Cairo, August, 1942*

Cairo feels airless after Moscow, and the news from home is not exhilarating. The Dieppe raid was, it appears, a fiasco; three-fifths of the Canadians – about 3,000 men – were either killed or taken prisoner. But the P.M. will not hear of the word 'failure.' The casualties were heavy, but the results were important. We had learnt a lot.

'You ought to remember, Charles, that in the air it pays us to lose machine for machine.'

I seemed to be back in the First World War, listening to the Brigade people explaining away an unsuccessful raid.

'It is a lesson,' the C.I.G.S. grunted, 'to the people who are clamouring for the invasion of France.'

*August 19, 1942*

I heard the P.M. singing in his bath this morning, and he was in high spirits when Alex[1] arrived at the Embassy to drive him into the desert. All day we bumped and jolted, through the blinding heat, until towards evening we came to a caravan tucked away among the sand-dunes by the sea. Monty[2] appeared in battle-dress and beret, and then we bathed. A little way off a lot of our men were shouting

[1] General Alexander, who succeeded General Auchinleck as Commander-in-Chief Middle East on August 12, 1942.
[2] General Montgomery, Commander Eighth Army in North Africa, August 12, 1942.

and splashing in the waves. Then Monty took the P.M. away to explain the battle, and we saw no more of him; Alex may be in supreme command, but I get the impression that it is Monty and his Eighth Army who have taken charge of this business. Which is all to the good, for this man clearly knows his job.

*August 20, 1942*

The P.M. set out early to examine the ground near the Ridge, where the battle will be fought. On our way, we kept passing bunches of grinning, cheering soldiers, naked except for a loin-cloth, and burnt brown by months under the African sun. When we got out of our cars, the P.M. came up to me.

'Can you explain this, Charles? When I was at Omdurman forty-four years ago, it was a military offence to appear without a pith helmet, and we were clad so that our skins were shielded from the sun. Why don't these fellows here get sunstroke and heatstroke?' he demanded.

About noon we came to Freyberg's[1] canvas oven, where we were to lunch.

'Monty has worked a miracle; the atmosphere is completely changed.'

Everywhere the P.M. went he sensed quiet confidence and a good spirit. He was, indeed, well content.

'Where is Monty?' he asked cheerfully when we were about to begin luncheon.

We found him in his car eating sandwiches. He explained that he made a point of never lunching with a unit under his command.

The P.M. was full of all that he had seen. He talked on many things late into the night, while his little audience, revelling in this new experience, marvelled at the man – his boyish enthusiasm, his consuming vitality, his terrific vocabulary. As for our host, Monty had withdrawn to his caravan, according to his habit, at ten o'clock sharp.

\*

[1] Sir Bernard Freyberg, Commander of New Zealand troops in North Africa.

I find this note on Monty written later in my diary:

> The average Army officer tends to conform to a type; it is dinned into him at school that he must not be different from other boys until the approval of his little community becomes essential to his peace of mind. For my part, I can own to a liking for these inhibitions, which are a small part of good manners, even if they mean no more than a concern for the convenience of others. Ernest Bevin, for instance, talked about himself – non-stop, as they say – while Anthony Eden, a vainer man, has learnt reticence. To remain gentle and self-effacing after climbing to the top of a profession, as Wavell and Marshall have done, is to me an endearing trait.

There is, of course, none of this nonsense about Monty; he wanted it made plain at the very beginning that he is not at all like other people; he appears to be intent on creating a particular image in the public mind. Nor would you expect Winston to submit to inhibitions of any kind. After all, they imply a desire to placate, and Winston is singularly free from that urge; they call, too, for a measure of control and he has 'devoted more time to self-expression than self-discipline.'

Monty's boastfulness has been held against him as a breach of good manners, but it is, of course, largely irrelevant when sizing him up as a soldier. On the other hand, there was nothing new in his training methods. He has told us at some length how he made it his business to go among his men, how he deliberately set out to make the Eighth Army a *corps d'élite*, and every man in it cocksure of victory. This is the pride in arms of the Brigade of Guards, or, for that matter, of the Roman Legion. At least it was all to the good to have nothing to do with the impersonal leadership of the First World War. In my time in the trenches I saw the Divisional General once – at a horse show.

The P.M. spoke of it as an astonishing transformation; he said it was plain already that Monty knew the secret of preparing his men for battle. I ventured to argue that there were others – Straffer Gott and Alex himself – who had won the hearts of their men while shunning publicity. Winston gave a great snort. It is foolish, of course, to argue with him.

*

*August 21, 1942*

Brooke is sure that Monty is big enough for the job. When he talks to me about the retreat to Dunkirk, I notice that he picks out the generals who were imperturbable in adversity. A note of affectionate pride crept into his matter-of-fact speech as he explained how, when the position looked quite desperate, Monty was still cocky and full of confidence that he could carry out the orders given to him. His quick brain took in the situation almost at a glance; it was a great comfort to Brooke to have a lieutenant like that at such a crisis. And it was Brooke who brought him here; the P.M. took a lot of persuading. Knowing what the C.I.G.S. thought of Monty, I asked him how he had settled down in the Eighth Army. Brooke is usually pretty thrifty in praise, but to my surprise he then let himself go. He was astounded by what Monty had done.

'Why, he's only been here a few days, but he has got about and sized up the position. And he has placed pretty accurately, I think, those under him. Why, he even told me what Rommel will do!'

Brooke smiled.

'I believe he is right, too.'

*

I shall leave my diary here to record a conversation with General Eisenhower in the White House in the summer of 1954. Ike had been talking to the Prof and me of the importance of faith. And then he rather abruptly changed the subject: Patton[1] was an unusual general; he was not much good at fighting a battle, but he was the best pursuit general of recent years. If Monty had been as good in

[1] General George Patton, Commander (successively), U.S. 7th and 3rd Armies.

pursuit as he was in fighting a battle, then he would have been one of the great captains.

*

*August 22, 1942*
While we were in Moscow the siege of Malta was raised. Five ships out of a convoy of fourteen successfully ran the gauntlet of submarine and bomber, and made it possible for the Governor, Lord Gort, to fly to Cairo to report to the Prime Minister. The P.M.'s relief is a joyful sight. The plight of the island – short of food and ammunition – has been distracting him. We found Gort at the Embassy on our return from the desert. He is hardly recognizable – stones lighter. The fat boy, as he was called, has disappeared, and in his place is a man years older, with sunken cheeks and tired eyes. The island has been on short commons, and the Governor has been setting an example in rationing.

Gort has sustained without bitterness the cruellest disappointment that can befall a soldier, in that he was dislodged from the supreme command in the midst of a world war. But he tackles his present job, so unimportant in comparison with his responsibilities in France, with all his might. He simply hadn't enough wits for a really big post, but he has character enough for anything.

The P.M. dabbed his eyes with a handkerchief as he listened to Malta's story. This morning the King has sent his congratulations on the success of the Moscow visit. There was a message, too, from Smuts. He showed it to me.

'Your handling of a critical psychological situation was,' I read, 'masterly. You have firmly and finally bound Russia to us for this war at least.'

It is at these moments that the P.M. is inclined to take the bit into his teeth and, kicking up his heels, gallop about for the fun of the thing. I thought it would do him no harm to show him a telegram I had just received from General Smuts. It was handed in at Pretoria and deciphered here:

'Following is personal message for Sir Charles Wilson from General Smuts:

'Please continue your efforts for Prime Minister's health. I feel convinced he cannot continue at the present pace without a breakdown. Grave national responsibility rests on you for Leader's health. All good wishes.'

'I am very well,' the P.M. pouted. 'Come. Let us go and see if anything has come in. We have clapped Gandhi into gaol.'

# CHAPTER NINE

# Turning-point

In 1953 I asked Winston to pick out the two most anxious months of the war. He did not hesitate: 'September and October, yes, 1942.' And yet, if I can trust my diary, I was not unduly worried about him then. It is true that whenever I appeared at No. 10, there seemed to be some fresh burden on his mind, but he met these calls with such abounding energy that I felt his reserves had hardly been touched.

On our return from Cairo on August 24, 1942, the P.M. received from Washington what he calls in his book a 'bombshell,' though the epithet he used at the time was even more descriptive. The Chiefs of Staff of the two countries had come to a complete deadlock. The Americans wished to reduce the scope of TORCH; they wanted to confine it to attacks on Casablanca and Oran, abandoning altogether the plan for a landing at Algiers. The Prime Minister was shocked. Algiers, he felt, was the key to the whole operation. Why, he wondered, were the Americans tearing the agreed plan to pieces in this fashion at the eleventh hour? Were they afraid to commit their forces to a major operation in an inland sea because their lines of communication ran through the Straits of Gibraltar? Perhaps Lewis Douglas, years later, gave me the explanation when he said:

'Asquith,[1] I am told, in his day hardly made a major decision without seeking a parallel in the past. Winston isn't like that. But

[1] Herbert Asquith, Prime Minister 1908–16.

in the case of the Mediterranean the long history of the inland sea was always present in his mind. The control of the Mediterranean meant in his eyes the control of the Western world. We owe a good deal to Winston for keeping the historic importance of the Mediterranean in men's minds during the war.'

Did Marshall fail to understand the importance of the Mediterranean? He had always been opposed to TORCH, but the Prime Minister did not believe that he would allow a personal judgment to weigh with him once agreement had been reached. This correspondence with the President distressed the P.M. He was never so unhappy as when he was at odds with his military advisers or his American allies. Besides, he had promised Stalin TORCH, and he felt that to fob him off with a simplified version was to break his word. One day, when I called on him, he said:

'If the Americans are obstinate, the whole plan for invading North Africa may fall. Ike[1] and Mark Clark[2] are very much upset about it. They cannot understand what is happening in Washington.'

And then, on September 5, the President gave way. The pent-up feelings of the two men flashed across the Atlantic:

President Roosevelt to Prime Minister – 5 Sept., '42: 'Hurrah!'
Former Naval Person to President Roosevelt – 6 Sept., '42: 'O.K. Full blast.'

These events, though disturbing to the P.M., could be matched by the disasters of any similar period in the past two years. What made these months so crucial to him was not the number or severity of the reverses, but the steady deterioration in the political situation at home.

One day Brendan Bracken[3] sent for me.

---

[1] General Dwight D. Eisenhower, Commanding General of the U.S. forces, European theatre of operations.
[2] General Mark Clark, deputy to General Eisenhower.
[3] Brendan Bracken, Minister of Information, formerly Parliamentary private secretary to Mr Churchill.

'I want you, my dear Doctor, to keep an eye on your patient. There may be trouble ahead. The Prime Minister must win his battle in the desert or get out.'

I thought Brendan was fussing.

Wilson: 'I fancy the P.M. has too much on his hands to mope over things. You know, when the going is rough, he seems to find distraction in doing things.'

Brendan: 'Don't be too sure. There is a good deal going on under the surface. I'm afraid of that fellow Cripps. I think he means business. If he pulls out, there'll be the hell of a row.'

Wilson: 'I thought it was Trenchard who was making trouble.'

Brendan: 'Oh, he will make a bit of a stink, but he can't bring the Prime Minister down.'

There was something very wrong somewhere, and Aneurin Bevan made it his business to find out who was at fault. He was in the mood to make trouble. In the first months of the war, Winston and he had been good friends. The two men met at Cherkley, Lord Beaverbrook's house at Leatherhead, where, egged on by Max, they drank and argued through the night. But when in the spring of 1940 Bevan was left out of the Churchill Government, it was inevitable that he would soon become restive under the arbitrary reign of the Prime Minister.

The country was uneasy about the course of events, and Bevan made his paper, *Tribune*, the medium for ventilating this frustration. The climax came on May 1, when an article appeared in *Tribune* entitled: 'Why Churchill?' It was a devastating onslaught on the Prime Minister's conduct of the war.

Winston, himself, was disposed to dismiss Bevan as 'a squalid nuisance.' Attlee told me that Bevan's campaign was no more than an irritant. But it was another story when Lord Trenchard and Sir Stafford Cripps, the Leader of the House of Commons, put themselves at the head of the insurgents.

'Boom' Trenchard, as he was known to his friends, was a legendary figure to the pilots of this war – the man who created our Air Force in the First World War. He appeared to be a block of granite. He told me once that the chief reason why men fight is because they fear what others may say of them; that an empty seat at the breakfast table in the mess is very bad for the morale of pilots; that if there are five seats vacant after a raid, they should be filled at once. His mind went back to the days before the war, when he set out to recruit the pilots who were to win the Battle of Britain. He did not attempt to compete with safer and more lucrative callings; an ace did not bother his head about getting on in life. The kind of fighting you get in the air will never be very attractive to the worldly-minded.

All this came out in instalments, for Trenchard was barely articulate and took some time to see a point. He was, I suppose, a kind of modern edition of the bearded Duke of Devonshire of my youth – the Lord Hartington of Gladstone's day – who eventually arrived at the right decisions, though by nature he was incapable of explaining how he had reached them. Trenchard had been so often right in the past. Who could say with certainty that he was wrong now?

Lord Trenchard himself had no doubts. 'We must avoid the stupendous drain on manpower of an attempt to win victory by land warfare. You must get this into the Prime Minister's head. If he puts his faith in bombers, it will save millions of lives.' I explained that the P.M. did not rely on his doctor for his strategy. I do not think he heard. 'If only I could get sense into their heads!' he went on. 'I want to help, but when I get on to my feet to speak, I cannot make what I want to say as clear to them as it is to me. I get no better,' he said to me sadly. 'In fact, I get worse. They don't seem able to follow what I am trying to say.'

Trenchard had said that if we put our faith in bombers, it would save millions of lives. 'He might be right,' the P.M. said, half to me and half to himself – Winston's imagination is not always a good friend. From what he then said, I believe that he, too, had doubts about the verdict of history on the way that England had 'got mixed up in land warfare in the two World Wars.'

But it was not the occasion for musing on the past. He was being attacked. There might, he said, be repercussions in the House and in the country. Lord Trenchard's personality and record certainly lent weight to his views in the Services and in the inner circle of Government, but the Prime Minister knew that, in time of war, his criticism would not rock a Coalition Government. He was pained, but he was not perturbed.

While this correspondence was passing between them, a more formidable critic had taken the field. Sir Stafford Cripps had long been dissatisfied with the direction of the war. In September he felt so out of tune with the Prime Minister that he felt he could no longer postpone his resignation. The two men were not designed by nature to run in double harness. Cripps's subtle intelligence, trained in the law, made him impatient of short-cuts, but when he went to the Prime Minister to get from him an important decision, he came away grumbling:

'The man simply will not listen to evidence.'

Cripps's case had rested, perhaps, on half a dozen premises, and he would have liked to examine each in turn, but when he was in the act of developing the second something he said sent the P.M.'s mind off at a tangent. He had started an idea, and it went ricocheting in Winston's head until it became plain to Cripps that the Prime Minister was no longer listening to what he said. The P.M. seemed to arrive at his conclusions by what I can only call a *saltus empiricus*. It was all very trying to the precise Sir Stafford.

The austerity of Cripps's nature, combined with his mental processes, were equally unintelligible to the P.M. One night he described Cripps to Stalin. He began by dilating on his virtues, then after a pause he went on:

'The trouble is, his chest is a cage in which two squirrels are at war, his conscience and his career.'

Sir Stafford's indictment of the direction of the war fell under three heads.

In the first place, he complained that, in a war which would be won by the scientists, effective use had not been made of our pre-eminence in science. He saw that the trouble began at the top – that the Prime Minister's mind was ingenious rather than scientific. Portal long afterwards said to me:

'The P.M. never really understood the air.'

Tedder said the same thing. It was true that he would always welcome any new idea; even if it did not sound plausible, he would insist that it be given a fair trial. He played, too, a considerable part in initiating some of our more fruitful inventions – such as the Mulberry Harbours used in the invasion of France in 1944 – but the scientific habit of mind was wholly foreign to his mental processes.

Our equipment suffered in consequence. We met reverses in the desert because our tanks were inferior to those of the Germans and, in particular, because the guns in our tanks were outranged by the guns in their tanks. In this connection, I recall a conversation with a prominent Fellow of the Royal Society during the late summer of 1942. If, he said, we had been as inefficient in providing aircraft as we have been in turning out tanks, the war would have been lost already. It seemed to him incredible that the Prime Minister received scientific advice from one source only – Lord Cherwell.

In the second place, Cripps wanted more time to be devoted to the broad strategy of the war. The Chiefs of Staff were engulfed in routine.

Finally, Cripps doubted whether some of our generals had any aptitude for handling mechanized forces on a large scale. Their ideas and methods were obsolete.

In the correspondence that followed Cripps's paper, the Prime Minister challenged him to name those in whom he had no confidence. Cripps bluntly replied that the Chief of the Naval Staff, Sir Dudley Pound, was past his work. The P.M. was pained by this attack on Pound, to whom he had long been deeply attached.

The Prime Minister was still living on his balance at the bank that had accumulated in 1940. Broadly speaking, he got his way in everything. Lord Beaverbrook explained the position to me: 'The Prime Minister, Brendan and I used to meet every evening. We settled most things.' But the P.M. knew how far he could go. He knew that the resignation of the Leader of the House on such an issue as the conduct of the war must lead to a political crisis of the first magnitude. 'Anything might happen,' he said. During

September the P.M. used all his powers of persuasion to convert Cripps, and in the end Cripps, whose high sense of duty had never been in question, was persuaded to postpone his resignation until after the battle in the desert.

It was with a sense of relief that the P.M. turned to the preparations for the impending battle. But it was no more than a respite.

\*

*September 30, 1942*
Brendan Bracken came to see me today. He says that if Rommel is victorious the position of the Prime Minister will become very difficult. 'You see, Charles, important changes in the direction of the war would then be inevitable, and Winston will never submit to any curtailment of his powers. If we are beaten in this battle, it's the end of Winston. Is he sleeping all right? You see, he is going through a very bad time.' So far as I can tell, Brendan is alarming himself unnecessarily. Of course, these thoughts may be passing through the P.M.'s head, but his confident nature is able to dismiss them from his mind. Why should he waste his time picturing what might happen if Rommel won? He does not for a moment believe he can win.

\*

I can see now that I was completely taken in by the bold front the P.M. put up during those two critical months. This man, who is, after all, my patient, had been distracted by his cares. He knew what defeat would mean. Brendan did not exaggerate the turmoil in his mind when he said: 'Winston is finding the suspense almost unbearable.' Greedily he devoured the reports from the desert. It appeared that everyone in the Eighth Army was cock-a-hoop when the battle began on October 23.

The Prime Minister and his colleagues in the Cabinet were therefore both surprised and shocked when, after a week's hard slogging, there was nothing to show for 10,000 casualties. The offensive seemed little nearer its goal than at the beginning. When I had to see the P.M. about a sleeping pill, they warned me that he was in an explosive mood. I was with him only a few moments, but as I left he grunted half under his breath: 'If this goes on, anything may happen.' I found Brooke waiting for me. 'Is the P.M. all right, Charles? I thought he was going to hit me when he demanded: "Haven't we got a single general who can even win one battle?"'

Three more difficult days went by. All day and all night the devastating fire of 1,000 guns was supported by incessant bombing from the air, where we were dominant. I did not see the P.M. during that time, but it appears that he waited for news with mounting apprehension. And then Monty attacked. The P.M. breathed again. He was in a state of great excitement when he heard that Rommel was in full retreat. I find this note in my diary:

'The victory in the desert has brought great joy to the P.M. He talks of ringing the church bells all over Britain. But he won't do anything till the prisoners number at least 20,000. He will take none of the credit, though the changes he has made in the desert command have been triumphantly vindicated. He is lyrical about Monty and Alex. This victory will silence criticism, and it seems that for the moment all his troubles are at an end.'

Four days later there was more good news: the first British and American troops landed at Algiers on November 8. The invasion of North Africa had begun. The details of this vast operation had been carefully thought out. Six hundred and fifty ships passed through waters infested with submarines without loss; the actual landings at Algiers and Casablanca were made without heavy fighting; even at Oran the opposition was soon overcome. Coming on top of the victory at Alamein, the imagination, fore-sight and careful attention to detail shown in this brilliant oper-ation left the country with a feeling that there could not be much wrong after all. Perhaps the worst was over.

Looking back, we can see that the battle was a turning-point in Churchill's fortunes during the war. He himself has told us that in

September, 1942, his position was more vulnerable than at any other period in the war. After El Alamein, he was never again in danger of losing his job as long as the war lasted.

# CHAPTER TEN

# A Great Friendship

*January 13, 1943*

I left my cottage at Harefield at nine o'clock after listening to a recording of the Brains Trust in which I had taken part, and kicked myself for the things I ought to have said if I had thought of them in time. It was raining as, with the help of a torch, I picked my steps through the pools on the garden path to the gate, where an Army car was waiting to take me to the Annexe at Storey's Gate.[1] I found the P.M. in high spirits, elated to be once more on the move. The airfield near Oxford was wintry, damp and dismal, but after ten hours in the air we breakfasted in a bungalow outside Casablanca, with the sun streaming in from a blue sky and oranges, with their leaves, on our plates.

The P.M. is full of zest, though the night was not a success. In the stern of the bomber there were two mattresses, stretched side by side, one for the P.M. and one for me. The rest of the party slept in their chairs. I woke with a start to find the P.M. crawling down into the well beneath, where Portal was asleep. When he shook him vigorously by the shoulder, I thought it would be well

---

[1] The cellars underneath the Office of Works in Storey's Gate were converted into a fortress, with a concrete roof 15 feet thick and steel doors. There was a Cabinet room and a Map room and bedrooms for the Prime Minister and his Ministers. It was from his room here that Churchill made some of his famous broadcasts. Over the cellars a flat was prepared for Churchill and his family, and was known as the Annexe. They moved there when a bomb demolished part of 10, Downing Street.

to find out what was wrong. Winston said he had burnt his toes against some metal connections of the improvised heating arrangements at the foot of the mattress. 'They are red hot,' he explained. 'We shall have the petrol fumes bursting into flames. There'll be an explosion soon.'

Winston was thoroughly worked up about the business; the simplest thing seemed to be to turn off the heating. How long I slept after we had settled again I cannot say, but I awoke to discover the P.M. on his knees, trying to keep out the draught by putting a blanket against the side of the plane. He was shivering: we were flying at 7,000 feet in an unheated bomber in mid-winter. I got up, and we struggled, not with much success, to cut off the blast. An hour or two later he woke me and we returned to the attack. The P.M. is at a disadvantage in this kind of travel, since he never wears anything at night but a silk vest. On his hands and knees, he cut a quaint figure with his big, bare, white bottom.

*Anfa, Casablanca, January 16, 1943*
This afternoon I went for a walk. The same idea had occurred to the Chiefs of Staff, and I found them talking at the water's edge. Dill, who was with them, gazing at the white breakers, said they had been very lucky in the weather for the invasion of North Africa: if the sea had been as rough as it is now, the landings would not have been possible. War is a game of chance, and luck had given them the one day in fifty when we could land. We walked slowly back. Portal, who is full of odd scraps of information, which he usually keeps to himself, explained to Dill how the sap travels in a cactus plant.

When I got back I found that there had been a great hunt for the P.M., who had been missing. Anfa Camp, the name given to the hotel and the villas surrounding it in which we live, is encircled by a wire fence in which there are only two entrances, guarded by sentries, but the P.M. had somehow slipped out and had gone for a walk. The Sappers are putting a wooden covering over the steps to our front door so that the President's chair can be wheeled up the ramp into the house when he dines with us tonight.

The worst of these trips is that I am the only person of the whole party who has nothing to do; I'm here only as insurance . . . I rise at 8 am and after breakfast write the book till lunch. Then if there is any sun, I sit in it and do a little more book. After that my daily walk. Then a bath and dinner at 8.30. Bed about 11pm.

*January 19, 1943*
I asked Harry Hopkins today whether he thought these conferences are worth while. He grinned broadly:

'The President came here because he wanted to make the trip; he is tired of sending me to London and Moscow. He loves the drama of a journey like this. They are always telling him that the President must not fly; it is too dangerous. This is his answer.'

As for the P.M., when he gets away from his red boxes and leaves London, he puts his cares behind him. It's not only that he loves adventure; he feels, too, at times that he must 'let up'; even a week or two away from the unending grind helps. He wants to shed for a little the feeling that there are more things to do in the twenty-four hours than can possibly be squeezed in. Perhaps Roosevelt has that feeling too. It's the instinct to escape, to take a long breath. Besides, neither of them, in a way, has ever grown up.

However this may be, they both came to Casablanca for one purpose: to decide where to fight next, when there are no Germans left in Africa. The Chiefs of Staff have been hammering away at the alternatives for a week. Yesterday it was finally agreed to attack Sicily. Harry doesn't seem very happy about this decision; as he puts it, he is 100 per cent. with Marshall in wanting to get on with the invasion of France.

*January 22, 1943*
The President, Harry told me, cannot return to Washington without patching up this de Gaulle–Giraud[1] feud. It will not be easy. de Gaulle positively goes out of his way to be difficult. He seems as sure about everything as when I first met him in the hall

[1] General Giraud, High Commissioner, French North Africa.

at Chequers, just as he was about to leave for London: an improbable creature, like a human giraffe, sniffing down his nostrils at mortals beneath his gaze. When I questioned him about his book on the use of the tank in wars of the future, he began speaking very rapidly in French, leaving me staring up at him like an urchin gazing in awe at a Palace guardsman.

Since then he has popped in and out of the pages of my diary, and whenever he appears he has a crack at the P.M. The P.M. is a bad hater, but in these days, when he is stretched taut, certain people seem to get on his nerves: de Gaulle is one of them. He is so stuffed with principles that there is no room left for a little Christian tolerance; in his rigidity, there is no give. Besides, men of his race do not find it easy to accept any foreigner as a superior being, and Winston does not like that kind of agnosticism.

However, it is plain that the President has set his mind on making peace between the two generals; they must be friends. And time is running short. So Anthony Eden has been given the job in London of getting de Gaulle out here – a pretty stiff task, for the General is a haughty fellow and crammed full of grievances.

At first, apparently, Anthony made no progress at all. Indeed, de Gaulle's curt refusal seemed final. It was only when the P.M. despatched a sharp message, intimating that if the General could not be more helpful the Allies would have, in the future, to get on without him, that de Gaulle at last thought it prudent to come here. He came with no good grace this morning, and even now half the day has been spent in persuading him to meet Giraud; it was like entraining a difficult horse. Nor was his interview with the Prime Minister more successful. When at last they emerged from the little sitting-room in our villa, the P.M. stood in the hall watching the Frenchman stalk down the garden path with his head in the air. Winston turned to us with a whimsical smile:

'His country has given up fighting, he himself is a refugee, and if we turn him down he's finished. Well, just look at him! Look at him!' he repeated. 'He might be Stalin, with 200 divisions behind his words. I was pretty rough with him. I made it quite plain that if he could not be more helpful we were done with him.'

'How,' I asked, 'did he like that?'

'Oh,' the P.M. replied, 'he hardly seemed interested. My advances and my threats met with no response.'

Harry Hopkins had told me of the President's quip that de Gaulle claimed to be the lineal descendant of Joan of Arc. I repeated this to the P.M. He was not amused. It did not seem at all absurd to him.

'France without an Army is not France. De Gaulle is the spirit of that Army. Perhaps,' he said sadly, 'the last survivor of a warrior race.'

If this Frenchman's arrogance, his defiance of everyone and everything, do at times get on the P.M.'s nerves, there are days when he cannot withhold his admiration. He was in tears when he said:

'England's grievous offence in de Gaulle's eyes is that she has helped France. He cannot bear to think that she needed help. He will not relax his vigilance in guarding her honour for a single instant.'

I wonder what will happen tonight when de Gaulle sees the President. Roosevelt is in no mood, if Harry can be trusted, to make allowances for Gallic pride. And, as Winston said, de Gaulle is the quintessence of an inferiority complex.

*January 23, 1943*

It appears that when the President met de Gaulle things went better than any of us had anticipated. The President was attracted by 'a spiritual look' in his eyes, which the P.M. had somehow missed.

*January 24, 1943*

The President and the P.M. were with de Gaulle before the Press Conference, when, to everyone's astonishment, Hopkins walked in with Giraud. I am sure Harry had planned this bringing together in public of the two French generals. Roosevelt, though he was taken aback, seized the opportunity. Before they could recover from their surprise, he had arranged that this historic moment – for such both the President and the P.M. deemed it – should be recorded for posterity by the camera. There were plenty of volunteers to take the picture, for a flock of photographers were waiting for the Conference, and the President decided that the lawn behind his bungalow should be the site of this interesting ceremony. The picture which the photographer obtained may be stuff for the historian. He will see the long, stiff-necked de Gaulle gingerly proffering his hand, though his face is without a flicker of a smile. Behind the outstretched arms he will detect the seated President, his head thrown back in hilarious enjoyment of the moment, while Winston sits demurely on the edge of his chair, his face wearing the expression of a child who has the sixpence in his hand, and is anxiously waiting for the opposite side to call 'Up, Jenkins.'

The Conference has lasted ten days. The soldiers and sailors are returning by air to England, while the P.M. goes by road to Marrakesh for twenty-four hours; after which the President will go home and we shall go to Cairo.

We set off in a fleet of cars, taking a picnic lunch with us. All the way to Marrakesh, 150 miles across the desert, there was an American soldier stationed every hundred yards, and when we paused by the roadside for luncheon fighter planes hovered protectingly over us. We were about to take the road again when Randolph went back to find the President's car to read him an extract from Machiavelli, which he thought appropriate.

While yet a long way from Marrakesh, we saw on the horizon the foothills, with the snow-capped Atlas Mountains behind them. And so we came to a house on the fringe of the town that had been set apart for us.

It was the hour when the sun was setting. To see the colours changing over the snow-capped mountains, Winston climbed on to the roof. It was so lovely that he insisted the President must see it. Two of his servants, by holding hands, made a chair with their arms, and in this fashion he was carried up the winding stairs to the roof-top, his paralysed legs dangling like the limbs of a ventriloquist's dummy, limp and flaccid. We stood gazing at the purple hills, where the light was changing every minute.

'It's the most lovely spot in the whole world,' the P.M. murmured.

When the President had been carried back to his room, I walked with Winston in the garden among the orange trees.

'I love these Americans,' the P.M. said. 'They have behaved so generously.'

At night there was a family dinner party, when the President and the P.M. made little, affectionate speeches to each other, and Winston sang. There were choruses, which grew in gusto as the night went on. The President proposed the health of one who would very much like to have been here – the King.

In the morning the P.M., who intended to see the President off at the airfield, kept putting off, as usual, the moment when he must get out of bed, until he made himself late. Then we heard his bedroom slippers flopping on the stone floor, and he appeared at the door in his most flamboyant dressing-gown, covered with red dragons. He got into the President's car in this gay garment and drove with him to the airfield.

The P.M. tells me that the War Cabinet are being very obstinate about Turkey. 'They don't want me to go to see Inönü,' he said. As far as I can make out, Anthony has made a stand for once. He is cautious, and feels that nothing will come of it. Besides, he must dislike the negotiations being taken out of his hands. But in the end the P.M. has had his way, of course, and expects that an answer from Inönü will be awaiting him in Cairo. He seems to be convinced he will be able to bring Turkey into the war, and is in great heart about it all.

About noon the P.M. got out his paints, which I have not seen before,[1] and, climbing the tower, gazed for a long time in silence at the Atlas Mountains. He seemed reluctant to break the illusion of a holiday, which for a few hours has given him a chance to get his breath.

---

[1] This was the only picture the Prime Minister painted during the war.

# CHAPTER ELEVEN

# Faith Abounding

*January 30, 1943*

Ever since the collapse of France and the appearance of the Germans in the Caucasus, Turkey has been kept on tenterhooks; her army has been permanently mobilized to resist invasion. The Turks have been so circumspect in their dealings with Germany that it was a milestone when the wise and prudent President of Turkey[1] agreed to meet the P.M. on Turkish soil. It means that our stock has risen as the German military position has deteriorated.

As we climbed into the aeroplane at Cairo, bound for somewhere in Turkey, we had a feeling that this particular trip was a little off the beaten track. Landing at Adana, where a number of cars met us, we drove through narrow, flat, muddy roads to a train in a siding. There was no platform, but we heaved the P.M. up into his compartment, and the train proceeded to meander along, at about eight miles an hour, under the shadow of the Taurus Mountains, until out of the snow-capped hills there crawled, 'like an enamel caterpillar,' the President's train: I have borrowed this image from the P.M.; he likes it and has repeated it several times.

Our train pulled up with a great clanking of carriages in a siding. The President of Turkey descended from a compartment and climbed into our saloon, which had been prepared for luncheon. The President, his Prime Minister and his Foreign Minister are all deaf, and the Marshal who commands the Turkish Army, dour and

[1] Ismet Inönü.

aloof, may have been deaf too: he took so little part in the exchanges. On our side the P.M., the C.I.G.S. and Alex shouted cheerfully. Jumbo Wilson[1] paired off with the Turkish Marshal, and no one feared that either would be guilty of any light indiscretions.

The President, in spite of his deafness, has an air of great alertness and was all smiles; he speaks English and made a good impression on the P.M. I was on the point of mobilizing my halting French for the benefit of the President's secretary when he informed me in fluent English that he listened every week to the Brains Trust.

There were more conferences in the afternoon, but the train was stuffy, and I jumped down and went for a walk along the sleepers. Before dinner I found the P.M. in his bedroom at the back of the train. He was pleased with the talks.

'This is about the best day's work I have ever done,' he said to me. 'The President put both hands on mine. I now understand how he seduces people. I'm sure I have completely won him over. But I don't want the Turks to come in until they are ready. I don't want them massacred. Let them be armed, and then, if it is in their interest, they will come in. I only pressed that this rearmament business should be thoroughly organized.'

To an onlooker there does not seem to be any danger of precipitate action on the part of the Turks.[2] They will not do anything rash. They are much too scared of the Russians and of what may happen when peace comes.

The American Ambassador, Steinhardt, however, was as optimistic as Winston: 'Let them take their own time. Don't hurry them. You'll see events will bring them in.' The British Ambassador, Sir Hughe Knatchbull-Hugessen, seemed to agree with his colleague's point of view. He had, I think, borrowed it from him. Both of them appeared apprehensive that the P.M. would go too quickly. It seems that the Turkish Prime Minister told the P.M. that Russia would be very powerful after the war, and that Turkey must

[1] General Sir Henry Maitland Wilson, Commander-in-Chief, Middle East.
[2] The manuscript notebook K.4/1/1, which is very close to the published account of this trip, carries Moran's less equivocal heading, 'P.M. taken in by the Turks'.

be prudent. The P.M. retorted that there would be an international organization to see that Russia was kept in her place. The Turk complained that he was looking for something more 'real.'

'I don't know what he means by "real,"' the P.M. grumbled when he got back to his compartment. 'I should have thought an organization of this nature is real enough for anyone.' The Turk made it plain that he feared a Russian occupation of the Dardanelles and not German bombing. But neither Winston nor the Ambassadors would listen.

At night there was a great feast and much liquor was drunk in toasts. The P.M., becoming quite hilarious, did all the talking. He was entirely taken up with the task of converting some of his stories into his own brand of French. It isn't French, and it isn't English, but something in between. When he quotes poetry, he gabbles it like a self-conscious schoolboy, but now he was too busy with his speech to bother about us. Before we arrived, the Turks may have wondered how things would go, and no doubt there was a sense of relief at the turn of events. Anyway, when they found the P.M. in tearing spirits they, too, laughed immoderately. At times there was so much uproar that I could not hear what Ismet Inönü's A.D.C., who was sitting on my right, was saying. However, after his tongue had been loosened by many drinks, I had less difficulty in following his talk. He said that the 'high-ups' in Turkey give Germany four months before she collapses.

### January 31, 1943

We slept in the train, and today the Turks came to lunch. Then the train returned as it came, at the same cautious pace, and the same cars took us to the same aerodrome, where the Turks had assembled in force to see us off. We bade friendly farewells and climbed into the big bomber. The engines roared, we began to move, and at that moment the pilot carelessly allowed the right wheel to leave the runway, whereupon the big tyre at once sank a foot into the mud. The engines raced, but nothing happened. We were bogged. The Turks looked sympathetic. I was afraid that the P.M. might be upset by the delay, but when I looked round he was nowhere to be seen. I found him surrounded by Turks, who were all talking at once. Winston had taken charge in his best Sidney Street[1] manner, and kept pointing to the wheel and gesticulating to the Turks. If only he could make them understand his plan . . . Lorries with chains appeared, but all were of no avail. The Turks crept away. Spades were produced and men dug round the sunken wheel. The P.M. removed his hat and mopped his head. At last it was decided that we must change aeroplanes. The afternoon had slipped away; it would be dark before we landed at Cairo.

Brooke was fretting because the P.M. kept changing his mind. First he wanted to stay another night in Turkey. The negotiations with Inönü were of vital importance; they must on no account be scamped. Then, when he had talked to the C.I.G.S., he decided that no time must be lost in getting back to Cairo, where a pile of work had accumulated. The engines began warming up, and suddenly the P.M. decided that he would not go to Cairo after all. He would spend a night in Cyprus.

After a flight of less than an hour, we landed and drove to Government House, a comfortable mansion that had been built at the expense of the islanders in expiation of their crime in burning the old residency to the ground. Across the middle of the main reception-room is a wooden partition, which, on pressing a button, rises slowly like a curtain and finally disappears into the ceiling. This new toy greatly intrigued Winston. Three times the performance had to be repeated, up and down. Tomorrow our bomber will take us back to Cairo.

*February 3, 1943*
To Tripoli by air. The military situation here is full of problems. The C.I.G.S., sitting opposite me is, however, serenely indifferent

---

[1] The siege of Sidney Street took place in 1911. Foreign anarchists murdered a policeman in the course of burglary and then barricaded themselves in a house in Sidney Street, East London. Churchill was Home Secretary at the time, and when the police asked for his permission to bring in armed soldiers he clambered out of his bath and went to the scene of the fighting to take charge of operations himself.

to everything but Lansborough Thomson's *The Migration of Birds*, in which he has been immersed since we left the airfield at Cairo. The P.M., removing his cigar from his mouth, began advising Randolph to give up smoking. It made him cough for an hour every morning, leaving his voice husky, and as a politician his voice was part of his stock-in-trade; he was prejudicing his career for these wretched cigarettes. The plane was noisy and they were still bawling at each other as I fell asleep in my chair.

When our bomber landed at Castel Benito, a lot of figures in khaki, fringing the airfield, rushed forward to greet the P.M. as he emerged in his Air Commodore's uniform. The P.M. advanced towards Monty and clasped his hand in both of his own. The Eighth Army had fought their way here hardly a fortnight ago, and now, in a grassy space, bounded by eucalyptus trees, the P.M. was in his element when he addressed the troops. No one can do this sort of thing so well.

A few miles outside the town of Tripoli, a little off the main road, we came to three caravans, outspanned like those of gipsies on a heath. One is for the P.M., a second for Alex and the third is mine. Commanders-in-Chief no longer live in comfort, as they did in châteaux in France in the First World War. It is not that they fear attacks from the air, but rather that they dread democracy. They want to persuade the soldiery that their leaders are not lounging in luxury while they grovel in discomfort.

Haig[1] would have been shocked by this modern, thought-out approach to democracy, of which Monty is a master and the others eager disciples. Alex's caravan is a one-room affair with a bed, a small table, a chair and a washstand.

\*

This morning, immediately after breakfast, we left army head-quarters and went by car to the Piazza Italia where the 51st Highland Division was drawn up waiting for Winston to inspect

---

[1] Field-Marshal Earl Haig, C.-in-C., British Expeditionary Force, 1915–19.

the troops. When Roosevelt flew to Cairo he came through Freetown which had been a British colony for donkeys' years and I gather he was rather shocked by what he saw: no attempt to build or plan a place that would be a credit to us and a place of comfort to the inhabitants. But the Italians do things differently. They are great builders. There was something spacious and impressive about their Tripoli . . . the Bank of Rome and other buildings give one an impression they were built in the Roman way for all time.

*

A week after our return to London from Algiers, the P.M. started a cold in the head. He kept to his room, but during the evening of February 16 his temperature shot up, and, after examining his chest, I had to tell him that he had a patch at the base of the left lung. 'What do you mean by a patch?' he demanded impatiently. 'Have I got pneumonia?'

Next day an X-ray showed a small shadow, and bulletins became inevitable; I therefore called in consultation Dr Geoffrey Marshall of Guy's Hospital. It was not until the 24th that the temperature fell, but we were at no time concerned about his condition. When a man approaching his seventieth year gets pneumonia it is, broadly speaking, the heart and not the lungs that decides the issue. Winston's heart, which nine months later was to cause us anxiety at Carthage, did not worry us then.

The patient himself took a more serious view of his illness. Apart from his appendix, he had never been seriously ill, and his attention was caught now by the high fever; his imagination did the rest. He tells us that it was 'a very disagreeable experience,' and that he 'sometimes felt very ill.' To Harry Hopkins he wrote that he 'had had a bad time and might easily have been worse.' To the President he spoke of the fever as 'heavy and long.' While his mind was busy conjuring up possible complications of his illness, Marshall, a genial but off hand physician, told him that he called pneumonia 'the old man's friend.'

'Pray explain,' said Winston.

'Oh, because it takes them off so quickly,' Marshall answered unabashed. He was soon established high in the P.M.'s favour.

It is one of Winston's foibles to pretend that he never allowed any of his illnesses to interfere with his work, though he admits on this occasion that the flow of his minutes dried up for a week. President Roosevelt, who was also on a sick-bed, sent a cable claiming that he had been dubbed a thoroughly model patient. He exhorted Winston to live down the reputation he had won in the American Press of being 'the world's worst patient.' He is, of course, nothing of the kind. I keep my chiding for him who turns his face to the wall, whereas Winston has no intention whatever of dying if sheer will-power will keep him going. Besides, no intelligent man, properly handled, can ever be a bad patient. On the contrary, when Winston is sick he does what he is told, provided, of course, that he is given a good reason.

In fact, he positively beseeches his physician to try fresh remedies. He does not believe in leaving things to Nature. 'Can't you do anything else?' he will ask reproachfully.

If there is a blot on the certificate I have given him, it is that, alas, he takes instinctively to a quack, gulping down his patter and his nostrums indiscriminately. During the twenty-five years he was in my care, I had to call in a number of doctors for various parts of his body, and it is, I think, substantially correct to affirm that he took to them in inverse ratio to their scientific attainments.

# PART TWO

# The President Digs In

# CHAPTER TWELVE

# Their Minds Made Up

When the P.M. got about after his illness at the end of February, I tried to keep an eye on him – a pretty thankless task – though there are no entries in my diary until late in April, when he told me that he was going to Washington.

Before Winston crossed the Atlantic he appeared to go through a period of indecision: one day he would decide to go by sea and the next he was sure that he could not spare the time and must go by air. If he travelled by sea he had a feeling of being out of touch with things; something might happen and he would hear of it too late to do anything. Furthermore, he had always had a horror of time wasted; during the war this became an obsession with him and in mid-Atlantic he would say, 'If we had flown as I wanted we should be in London now and could do business.' On the other hand, he disliked flying. I think this may date back to the time when he was piloting a small plane and crashed. His passenger was dreadfully mauled, breaking both legs. Winston, however, was so made that he would not give way to fears of that kind; because he disliked the air, he was more likely to fly. On this occasion he credits me with the decision to go by sea, affirming that I did not want him after his pneumonia to fly in a bomber at perhaps ten thousand feet.[1] It may be so, but I had little say in matters of this kind. It was the P.M. himself who weighed the pros and cons; I was never allowed to touch the scales.

[1] Winston Churchill, *The Hinge of Fate*, p. 700.

His purpose was to persuade the President that the only fitting sequel to the victory in North Africa was to drive Italy out of the war and to bring Turkey in as our ally. He did not believe that an easy task lay in front of him, and throughout the voyage he remained engrossed in the preparation of his case. It was the business of a large party of experts to provide chapter and verse for his arguments, and here they were at his beck and call at any hour of the day or night.

The P.M. was interested in the *Queen Mary* as a troopship. She repeatedly carried a whole division, about 15,000 men, eastbound from New York to the Clyde. At first the Americans were reluctant to put too many eggs in one basket. Then one day General Marshall said bluntly to the Prime Minister: 'If you had to give the order, would you take a risk and send a division on this ship, knowing that if it were torpedoed there would only be boats for a fraction of that number?' That is the kind of awkward, sleep-disturbing decision which the men at the top were always taking. The P.M. did not hesitate; he would accept the risk.

The third day out Sir William Beveridge,[1] who happened to be a passenger, came to luncheon. In my diary the occasion was dismissed with the laconic statement: 'The atmosphere was correct without being unduly cordial.' It generally happened like that when the P.M. summoned to his table an acquaintance in whom he had little interest. Then, as if exhausted by his act of civility, he would make no further attempt at conversation, sitting all hunched up and scowling at his plate, with his thoughts a long way off. Besides, his guest on this occasion was not particularly congenial. Sir William, no doubt, was conscious that he, too, had done a good job of work for the country. The trouble was that this did not occur to the P.M.; at any rate, if it did he kept it to himself, and at about half-past two the bleak little function just petered out.

When I went back to my cabin after Beveridge had taken his leave I felt hot, and taking my temperature, found it was 103°. It

[1] Sir William Beveridge, Economist and author of the Beveridge Report on the Social Services.

was soon plain that a microbe, the *Colon Bacillus*, which had bothered me before, had come back, and I spent the next forty-eight hours in a somnolent condition. Winston was always uncomfortable and put out when anybody about him was sick; he would have liked to do something, but did not know what to do. He hated doing nothing. The ship's doctor told me how upset the P.M. had been when he heard I had taken to my bed. 'Damn it,' he growled. 'Have you seen him? Well, what is the matter? I trust it's not serious?' I must have been half asleep as he marched in. But I remember him, rather vaguely, standing in the middle of the cabin, as if I were infectious, and demanding: 'Are you taking care of yourself? Is there anything I can do? Anything I can get?' There was a short silence, and then he turned to the doctor: 'I shall want to know all about the temperature. Pray keep me posted.' And with that he turned on his heel and marched out.

However, if Winston's bedside manner was poor, his heart was kind, and when the *Queen Mary* docked at New York on May 11 I found he had been busy. Though no one was to be allowed to land before morning, it had been arranged that I should be taken at once on a stretcher to the Presbyterian Hospital, where Harriman had arranged accommodation in the Harkness Pavilion. Looking round the spacious room assigned to me, I began to be concerned about the economic consequences of my illness. When my surgeon appeared I was reassured to find that I was in the hands of a man who knew his job and did not depend on his personality for practice. When he went the pathologist came; he pricked my finger and said presently, 'What have they been doing to you?' I learnt that the white cells in my blood which normally number 8,000 per cubic millimetre had fallen to 2,000. These cells are there to wage war with invading microbes, and it appeared that the mechanism on which my immunity depended had been put out of action by a surfeit of sulpha tablets.

When I caught up with the P.M. in Washington a few days later I had to explain it all to him. He seems fascinated by nature's processes. 'Some day, when I have time, I shall write a thriller,' he said. 'The villain, a doctor, will destroy his victims by breaking down their immunity.'

The P.M. was looking for work after his week-end at Shangri-La, the President's mountain refuge in the Catoctin Hills in Maryland; Harry Hopkins had come back full of stories about Winston's 'marvellous memory.' The President, too, was in good fettle, and Harry told me how he began quoting poetry: two lines from some verses about Barbara Frietchie, a semi-legendary character of the Civil War. 'Then when he was stuck and could not go on Winston came to the rescue and gabbled the whole poem. While we were still asking ourselves how he could do this when he hadn't read the darned thing for thirty years, his eye caught a sign pointing to Gettysburg. That really started him off.' No doubt encouraged by their interest in his feat, the P.M. went on to give a masterly review of the battle, ending with a lengthy disquisition on the characters of Stonewall Jackson and Robert E. Lee, two of his heroes.

Hopkins was a good deal less flattering about the P.M.'s contribution to the discussions, which had begun on May 12 in the oval study of the White House. Indeed, he looked pretty glum as he assured me that I had not missed anything. Winston, he said with a sour grin, recalled the last time they had met in that room, a year ago, when they learnt that Tobruk had fallen. It was not a very happy beginning. The Americans had not forgotten the occasion. They had gone to the White House to clinch the plan for the invasion of France, when news had been brought to them of the disaster. Then in some manner – they were even now not quite clear how – they found themselves agreeing to the diversion of ships and troops to North Africa that were meant for the invasion of France. They could not help admiring the P.M.'s gift of dialectic, but they had made up their minds that it was not going to happen again. And here, damn it all, was the old story once more, shamelessly trotted out and brought up to date.

Harry was in one of his sardonic moods; imitating Winston, he said: 'The great prize when Sicily falls is to get Italy out of the war. Bulgaria's defeatism in 1918 brought about the collapse of Germany; might not Italy's surrender now have similar consequences? It will surely cause a chill of loneliness to settle on the German people and might very well be the beginning of the end.'

The words were the P.M.'s, but somehow they sounded less convincing when put by Harry like this. I asked him what the President made of all this. 'Not much,' he answered. 'This fighting in Italy does not make sense to him. He wants the twenty divisions, which will be set free when Sicily has been won, to be used in building up the force that is to invade France in 1944.'

I enquired of Hopkins what was the effect of the President's attitude on the P.M. 'I thought he was a little subdued – for Winston, that is,' and Harry grinned broadly. For my part I was sorry for the P.M. He had been so sure in London that when they got together after dinner in the White House he would be able to bring the President over to his view. Since those disasters of a year ago, which the Prime Minister had so rashly recalled, a good deal had happened that was not known to him. The Americans had done some very hard thinking, and Marshall was at the President's elbow to keep in his mind the high urgency of a second front. The results, according to Hopkins, were very satisfactory. The President could now, Harry felt, be safely left alone with the Prime Minister. The P.M. is, I think, puzzled; he had not expected the President to lay down the law like this, but I don't believe he is really depressed. He still feels it can all be put right. There had been so much to settle during this visit, but if he could get Marshall to himself, perhaps in Algiers, he is certain it would all be plain sailing. Marshall would agree with him about the invasion of Italy. I own I am rather worried about the P.M.'s optimism. It seems to be interfering with the cold functioning of his judgment.

*

*May 18, 1943*
I am still bothered by a smouldering fever and my notes are thin.

Washington is hot and humid, but it does not seem to affect Winston. Today he spoke to Congress for fifty minutes and though he said nothing new it went down well. At least Harry Hopkins was sure that it had made a very good impression. 'They're saying,' he grinned broadly, 'that the only time they're told anything is when Winston addresses Congress.' The P.M. was a good deal worked up beforehand, saying: 'It was a great responsibility; a much more diffi-cult speech than the first time I talked to Congress after Pearl Harbour.' I asked him why. He replied that he feared what he had to say would be 'inadequate,' and that he 'regretted taking it on.'

I was in the diplomatic gallery with Mackenzie King and the Duke and Duchess of Windsor. As the Duke descended to his seat in the front row, he got as much clapping as Winston, or more, by which we were surprised. He has lost his boyish good looks, and does not somehow fit into middle age. Winston was loyal to his King to the very last, but, I think, he learnt a long time ago that he had been wrong about the abdication. It is not Winston's habit to live long with his mistakes. He is a very loyal servant of King George and is no longer – it must be said – interested in the Duke; when they tell him that the Duke has asked for an appointment, the P.M. sighs and arranges the day and hour.

*May 25, 1943*
Found the P.M. pacing his room. There was no welcoming smile. When I asked him how he had been he did not answer. He had other things to think about besides his health. He stopped and said abruptly, 'Have you noticed that the President is a very tired man? His mind seems closed; he seems to have lost his wonderful elas-ticity.' I could not follow all that was in the P.M.'s mind, and when he saw that I was not going to help him he seemed to forget about me.

For a long time he went up and down his room, scowling at the floor. I could see that he did not want to talk, that he had work to do. I felt I was in the way, and left him. Perhaps he thought that he had been rather abrupt. At any rate, later he sent for me on some pretext. He seemed less worried and then the mood came back.

'The President,' he said, 'is not willing to put pressure on Marshall. He is not in favour of landing in Italy. It is most discour-aging. I only crossed the Atlantic for this purpose. I cannot let the matter rest where it is.'

There were forty-eight men lunching today at the White House. I sat next to General Stilwell, a sour, dried-up little man whom they call Vinegar Joe. He complained bitterly that Winston wasn't interested in the Pacific, implying that, if he were, the President would pay more attention to their needs in those parts. He is pretty critical of the British.

As the Conference unfolded (to use Winston's word) it was plain enough that the Americans had made up their minds. The P.M. was concerned because no definite recommendations had been made by the Combined Chiefs of Staff to follow up the conquest of Sicily by the invasion of Italy. Why, these Combined Chiefs of Staff would apparently be content with the capture of Sardinia; that was to be the proud objective for the rest of 1943 for all the mighty forces gathered in the Mediterranean. The P.M. deplored the prospect. The invasion of France had been fixed for May 1944. Was it conceivable that a million and a half of our best troops should be kept idle for nearly a year?

I hear tonight that he made a final appeal to the President to let General Marshall come with us to Algiers, and perhaps to his surprise, and certainly to his great satisfaction, Roosevelt has agreed.

*May 26, 1943*
This morning we took off from the Potomac River in a flying-boat. I wish we were bound for London. It is not easy to do my job with these bouts of high fever.

*May 27, 1943*
I was awake when there was a small 'pop' accompanied by a little flash of light like a small bulb fusing. I wondered what it was, and then I must have gone to sleep. This morning I learnt that in a storm the flying-boat had been hit by lightning.

*May 28, 1943*
I am back in London, when I ought to be in Algiers with the Prime Minister, and in pretty poor heart about it all. When we landed at Gibraltar yesterday my fever still hung about. I might be a nuisance, travelling round Tunis like this; it would be better, I thought, if I

cut out North Africa altogether and flew direct to England. When I broached this to Winston he vigorously insisted that I must get fit. 'I am very well,' he said, 'and if anything went wrong you could fly out in a few hours.' So I spent the afternoon in a quiet corner of the Convent[1] wondering if it would have been better to have gone to Algiers without bothering the P.M. about my ailments.

The light had nearly gone when they brought me to the small aircraft in which I was to travel to England. Its floor, as far as I could see by torchlight, was almost entirely taken up by a stretcher bearing a young soldier with a brain tumour, who was being sent home. The night in the air seemed to stretch out interminably. Would that loud, stertorous breathing never stop? I could not help listening to it as it rose noisily to a climax; then there was a pause that made me wonder if he had died, and then it began all over again. There was plenty of time to ruminate. I ruminated.

For three years the Prime Minister has been doing everyone else's job as well as his own, wallowing in detail; and there is no end to it in sight. It is easy to get into the way of thinking of him as different from other people, someone unique, a law to himself. But I know better. There will be trouble one day. I wonder in what shape it will come.

If in the end he is defeated I feel sure it will not be by a break-down in body or mind, but rather by a gradual waning of his powers, brought on by his own improvidence, by his contempt for common sense and by the way he has been doing the work of three men. There is no hour of the night when I can be certain that he is in his bed and asleep. Of course, this cannot go on for ever.

However, it takes a lot of hard work to leave its mark on a robust constitution. I would go further. I doubt whether men at the top often go to bits through overwork by itself. There are generally other and less obvious factors dragging them down.

*

[1] The Residence of the Governor of Gibraltar is called the Convent, though the nuns left it two centuries ago.

In the P.M.'s case it took me some time to find out what they were. They are recorded in some notes that I found in my diary; they bear no date but they must have been written a long time after this. I print them here because they may help the reader to understand how the Prime Minister's strength was gradually undermined: '. . . Is there something else sapping his strength? Is Winston's impressionable nature itself a source of weakness in war? The idea is, of course, far from novel. That a man's imagination may run riot in battle is indeed as old as the literature of war. "More life," wrote Thomas Hardy, "may trickle out of a man through thought than through a gaping wound." But does Winston Churchill suffer from that handicap? And if so, how does he show it? I learnt in the First World War what to look for; the danger signals I used to call them. They told me when a man was in distress. Often this waverer was most fearful when there was no danger; it was his own thoughts that festered in the mind and in the end brought defeat. Because there was no danger, his apprehension, fear in its infancy, was labelled imaginative fear, but it had its roots in reason, it fed on the memory of things.'

Once more it was my business to pick up these signals. In mid-Atlantic, as I have told, Winston touched me on the knee, 'Do you realize we are fifteen hundred miles from anywhere?' That is the kind of confession that I find, not very often of course, in my diary when we were on the high seas or in the air, and it was these signs of apprehension in Winston that first caught my ear.

When I found out for myself that Winston was by nature very apprehensive I was slow to credit my own evidence. Very gradually, however, it came to me that he was completely without the self-protective mechanism which is the only gift, as far as I can tell, common to men who last in war: a way of looking at things which alone makes it possible to carry on. In the First World War we spoke of men 'sticking it,' and I wrote then of the 'sticker' that he 'is just one who has contrived to cut off those messages from the outer world that reach the brain at times like these and threaten its balance. His business is to become insensitive, to give up thinking. The wise man lives only for the hour.'

Winston Churchill was less fortunate. And I had him in my head when I scribbled in pencil in the margin of my diary:

'If it should happen that a man of action, exercising supreme power, is also an artist, then God help him. He will have to change his nature to survive.'

Winston could not change his nature. As First Minister of the Crown in time of war he was bound to receive in the course of his lonely mission wounds deeper and more lasting than any weapon can inflict; it was vital to him that he should be able to shed the kind of thought that might distract or distress his mind; forget, if he could, for a short space at any rate, the anguish of the hour. He could not do it.

I find this note in my diary of December 11, 1941:

'Paid a routine visit to the Annexe. I ran into Mrs Hill leaving his room. "He has just heard some very bad news." I said I would not bother him. "I think he would like to see you," she said. I found him with his head in his hands. After a time he looked up; he seemed dazed.

'"You know what has happened?"

'I had not heard of the sinking of the *Prince of Wales* and the *Repulse*.'[1]

As I put down the diary, the whole sad business came back to me. He had sent those ships to Singapore without air cover, and against the advice of the First Sea Lord. And Smuts was not the only one who had sensed disaster. After his stroke in 1953, when it appeared that he might die, Winston told me that he had had a very bad dream. I asked him what he had dreamed. But he could not bring himself to talk about it. He did not speak for a long time, and then he turned to me: 'Do you know anything about dreams?

[1] Captain Roskill writes to me: 'It is beyond doubt that Churchill initiated the idea of the two ships going East, and that the First Lord and the First Sea Lord, Mr Alexander and Admiral Pound, strongly opposed it at many meetings of the Defence Committee and Chiefs of Staff Committee ... Smuts telegraphed a prophetic warning of the disaster which was likely to ensue from the despatch of those two ships ... In the end Alexander and Pound gave way.' Cf. *The War at Sea*, by Captain S. W. Roskill, R.N., Vol. I, pp. 553–9.

Can doctors tell what they mean?' When I answered, 'Only up to a point,' there was another long pause. 'You know when the *Prince of Wales* and the *Repulse* were sunk?' He could not go on; he seemed to be so upset that I was frightened he might have another stroke.

# CHAPTER THIRTEEN

# The Conversion of Marshall

In my diary there is a break in the narrative after I had parted from Winston at Gibraltar. I could not tell the story of his visit to Tunis and Algiers, because I was not there. The gap is bridged by two brief entries.

*May 31, 1943*
The news from Algiers is reassuring; my misgivings are set at rest. The P.M., they tell me, is in great shape. I keep wondering if he has persuaded Marshall that his plan is sound. I cannot make out why nobody mentions this; after all, that was the purpose of Winston's visit.

*June, 1943*
Winston is back in London. This morning he said to me: 'I am more happy about the conduct of the war than I have been for some time. Things are coming out as I want them.' 'What about Marshall?' I asked. 'Has he come over to your view?' 'He doesn't, for the moment, want to make up his mind what we ought to do when Sicily is taken. But he is ready to accept my plan. He is not opposed to the invasion of Italy now.'

The P.M. seemed to have no doubts at all on this score; he was quite sure that he would get his way. I did ask him why he thought Marshall had changed his mind. For a moment he appeared taken aback. 'The merits of the case,' he said half to himself, 'are surely beyond any question.'

*

Two months later at Quebec I discovered that my doubts had substance. There Marshall gave me his own version of the conversations with Winston.

'I did not think that the moment had come for a decision. It would be better, I said to the Prime Minister, to decide what to do when the attack on Sicily was well under way. I wanted to know whether Germany meant to put up a stiff resistance in southern Italy or whether she would decide to retire to the Po as Winston suggested. I wanted more facts. I wanted to ask Winston a dozen questions, but he gave me no chance. He kept telling me what was going to happen. All wishing and guessing. When I did get a question in, the Prime Minister brushed it aside. I tried to set forth some of the factors which ought to govern our decision. I tried to argue that we must exercise great discretion in choosing what to do after the conquest of Sicily. I said to the Prime Minister that I would be content if Sardinia were taken before the invasion of France. He replied that the difference between taking southern Italy and Sardinia was the difference between a glorious campaign and a mere convenience.'

Marshall's long upper lip stretched in amusement as he told this. It appeared that this monologue went on for a week, all day and often well into the night, when he wanted to go to his bed. Winston seems to have gone on and on, talking at the American, who for his part, as far as I could tell, listened and said but little. 'I have never,' Marshall went on, 'heard anyone talk like this before.'

I told the General how my mother, when she was very old, and everyone would talk at once, used to say that 'it made her legs ache.' 'Exactly; I felt like that,' and he smiled. 'I'd never met anyone like Winston,' he continued. 'He is a very wonderful man, but he won't look at things like a man who has been all his life a soldier. I must have facts.'

Looking back, where had Winston gone wrong? When he went to North Africa he was bent on converting Marshall to his plan for the invasion of Italy, and yet he did not attempt to follow what was passing through Marshall's head. Why, for instance, did Marshall remain, up till almost the last moment, silent and cryptic? He was, after all, a straightforward soldier; his affection for Winston was undoubted, and he must have longed to discuss with him differences in strategy, to make him see the American point of view. But as Harry Hopkins explained to me: 'We have come to avoid controversy with Winston; we find he is too much for us.' Clemmie once made the same point: 'I don't argue with Winston, he shouts me down. So when I have anything important to say I write a note to him.' That was how Marshall felt. 'Oh, no, Winston heard all right, but he kept telling me what was going to happen.' That is the trouble. Winston is so taken up with his own ideas that he is not interested in what other people think. It is as if he had lived for years in a foreign country without picking up the language. He must lose a chunk of life in this way, and must often be lonely, cut off from people.

I suppose that is why the pages of his great testament so often silt up with military detail, while he apparently cannot remember – more probably has never noticed – those little personal idiosyncrasies which might have brought to life the soldiers around him.

One morning, in the autumn of 1950, I found Winston sitting up in bed in his room at Chartwell, dictating. 'Don't go far away,' he said to his secretary as she got up to withdraw. I asked him how far he had got in the book. 'You missed Algiers, Charles. I have just finished the ten days I spent there visiting the troops. When you have taken my pulse you shall read it.'

I was agape to find out how far the historian would be given the facts. I was sure Winston must have learnt at Quebec that Marshall had not changed his mind about the Italian campaign and would correct in his book the error he made at the time. Would he chuckle at the enormity of his mistake? It is, after all, from our mistakes that we learn, though it has never been a form of instruction that Winston found particularly congenial. This was, of course, rather obtuse on my part. Men who do things in the world are not in the habit of laughing at their mistakes.

Winston's own account begins:

'I have no more pleasant memories of the war than the ten days in Algiers and Tunis . . . The sense of victory was in the air. The whole of North Africa was cleared of the enemy. A quarter of a million prisoners were cooped in our cages. Everyone was very proud and delighted. There is no doubt that people like winning very much.'

And then he goes on to tell us in some detail what he said, what Cunningham said, what Alex said, what Monty said; the divisions available to Alex, on the one hand, and the distribution of the Italian Army, on the other – twelve pages in all and not as many lines about Marshall.

As I read this chapter sitting by his bed, I marvelled that Winston did not sense the atmosphere even if he did not get much help from Marshall. And then, on the impulse of the moment, I got up and put my hand on Winston's shoulder. 'You old dear. I'd not like you half as much if you had antennae.' He stared at me. 'What do you mean by antennae?' he asked. And when I did not answer he went on: 'You do say some strange things. Some of you doctors get queer ideas about what is in people's heads. You think too much about these things. It isn't healthy. I don't know where all this psychological nonsense is going to take you.'

Perhaps he felt that he had been a little hard on me. He put his hand on my arm with a benevolent gesture. 'You have not let me down yet. I haven't found you out once. How many years is it? You know, Charles, I have come to feel very safe with you at my elbow.' Winston was not often in a mood like this, when you could say anything to him. He held out his hand for the typescript.

'You've finished it?'

'I've read it twice.'

'I thought you'd like it.'

'I keep trying to fathom how your mind works.'

Winston looked blankly at me. I fancy when I said that he had no antennae that he felt there must be something wrong with his account. He went on reading and I was left to my own thoughts. Could it be that he had come to believe what he wanted to believe?

# CHAPTER FOURTEEN

# The End of an Argument

Strange stories of a young brigadier in the jungle called Wingate had recently been filtering through to the P.M. He began to wonder if this leader of the Chindits in Burma was another Lawrence of Arabia; to him that was a quickening thought.

For Lawrence made a great dent in Winston's imagination, and the impression had remained. Winston writes that he felt himself in the presence of an extraordinary being, someone outside the jurisdiction of the world, someone strangely untamed and untrammelled by convention.[1] . . . The exploits of this paladin in those sun-scorched, blasted lands, which seemed to forbid human existence, was an epic. And this epic had been marvellously told in *The Seven Pillars of Wisdom*, which Winston once told me in his judgment ranked with the greatest books ever written in the English language, with *The Pilgrim's Progress*, *Robinson Crusoe* and *Gulliver's Travels*.

There was enough in this to excite anyone's imagination. And yet we must dig deeper to unearth the roots of his affinity with Lawrence. He tells us that Lawrence had never been, in time of peace, 'in complete harmony with the normal.' Winston knew what that meant. He knew more than most what happens to a man who is different from other people; the penalty exacted from those who do not conform. In the years before the war he had come to realize that he had no real friends in any of the three parties; he could not

---

[1] Winston Churchill, *Great Contemporaries*, pp. 164–5.

remember a time when he was sure of his own reception in the country. He felt his isolation.

On July 24, 1943, ten days before we left the Clyde for Quebec, he wrote a directive to the Chiefs of Staff, in which he spoke of Wingate as 'a man of genius and audacity.' No mere question of seniority must be allowed to obstruct his advancement. The P.M. considered that Brigadier Wingate should command the Army in Burma, and gave instructions that he should come home. 'I want to have a look at him,' he said, 'before I leave for Quebec.'

Wingate arrived at the Annexe an hour before our train left London for the Clyde. When the P.M. heard that he was in the building he said he would like to talk to him about war in the jungle; he was greatly interested in the view that the Japanese could be beaten by landing men behind their lines. But there was no time then. It occurred to the P.M. on the spur of the moment to take Wingate with him on the ship. Wingate protested: 'I have no clothes. I have nothing but my tropical kit.' The P.M. brushed this aside: 'Oh, don't bother about that. I'll lend you some. I've plenty.' Wingate: 'But, sir, I've not seen my wife for a long time.' P.M.: 'Of course, you must bring her too.' So the Wingates were carried off, as you pick up a couple of books at the station bookstall to beguile the tedium of the journey.

Winston, in *Closing the Ring*, has given his first impressions of his guest. 'We had not talked for half an hour before I felt myself in the presence of a man of the highest quality.' I did not realize at the time that the P.M. had taken Wingate quite so seriously, and I only noted in my diary that he seemed to be rather unbalanced, and talked like a man full of undigested ideas.

\*

*R.M.S.* Queen Mary, *August 8, 1943*
Wingate is only a gifted eccentric. He is not another Lawrence. When this became plain to the P.M. he lost interest in him, and presently forgot all about his presence on the ship, leaving him to his own resources. The second day out Wingate came to my cabin

because he wanted my help to get rid of some microbes he had picked up in the jungle. After that I saw a good deal of him. One day I had taken my seat for luncheon when he came across the saloon and asked me to join him at his table. When we had decided what to eat, Wingate put down the menu, and without any kind of introduction said he thought it was a pity that boys at our public schools were taught by men who had done nothing in the world, and indeed had usually no experience of its ways. They went straight from school to the University, and after three or four years there they returned as masters, where they remained for the rest of their working life. Wingate wanted men who had done things to be seconded to teach; the boys would feel then that their teachers were talking to them from experience and not out of books. I asked him what was his school, and he answered Charterhouse. He went on: 'There were two masters there who had a permanent influence on my life.' He did not seem to see any discrepancy between this remark and his original thesis.

Wingate soon started another theme: 'All the things in the world that matter have been achieved,' he asserted, 'by the spoken and not by the written word.' I gave him Mahomet; however, the argument soon wilted through its own inherent weakness.

It would be easy to dismiss the mental processes of those who give way to impulsive outbursts of this kind, but I must be fair and admit that this was not the whole story. Some years later when I was talking to the Staff College at Camberley about leadership, I remember speaking in a critical vein of Wingate. When I had done, a soldier who had served under him in Burma got up and refuted what I had said. Speaking very earnestly, he defended his leader. 'We all swore by him. Of course he was a fanatic, but he believed so absolutely that there was nothing he couldn't do, that he succeeded in persuading other people he was infallible. Mind you, sir, that's not why his men would follow him anywhere. He was efficient, and they knew it. If he took them through the jungle behind the Japanese lines he would always bring them back safely.' Wingate had two bars to his D.S.O. And as your eye wandered to his face you might have noticed a scar across his throat – where he

LORD BEAVERBROOK

FIELD-MARSHAL SMUTS

FIELD-MARSHAL
MONTGOMERY

FIELD-MARSHAL ALEXANDER

MARSHAL STALIN

GENERAL DE GAULLE

TEHERAN

PRESIDENT ROOSEVELT

YALTA

*Seated*, Mr Churchill, President Roosevelt and Marshal Stalin. *Behind*, Field-Marshal Sir Harold Alexander, Field-Marshal Sir Henry Maitland Wilson, Field-Marshal Sir Alan Brooke, Admiral of the Fleet Sir Alan Cunningham, General Sir Hastings Ismay, Fleet Admiral E. J. King, Air Chief Marshal Sir Charles Portal, Admiral Leahy, General Marshall and Russian Delegates

POTSDAM

PRESIDENT TRUMAN

once tried to take his own life. He seemed to me hardly sane – in medical jargon a borderline case.

My own view of Wingate was no more than a surface impression, but one of his seniors in the Army in Burma damned the man beyond salvation: 'I did not think that he was quite sane. He was quite unscrupulous and lied for his own purposes.' General Slim told me some years later that Wingate had served under him: 'He came to me and asked for another division to turn into his irregulars. When I refused, he said that he had higher loyalties than the Commander-in-Chief. "What are they?" I asked. "To the President of the United States and the Prime Minister," he answered. "What do you mean by that?" I persisted. "I have been told to report direct to them if any General interferes with my plans. I have always got on with you, but I should have to report to them." When he said this I wrote down my orders and told him to go away and read them. The next day he was to come back at ten o'clock. I told him no one had yet disobeyed my command. If they did I should know what to do.' Slim smiled grimly, 'The next day he turned up with a sickly smile, saluted and carried out my orders. Attempted blackmail,' Slim grunted. He summed up: 'Wingate had strategical but not tactical ability. His first campaign in the jungle was a flop, his troops came out after heavy losses, disorganized. He had achieved little or nothing and used up a lot of resources in the material sense, but the psychological rewards were considerable.'

What does this all add up to? That Wingate was a size larger than I thought and several sizes smaller than the P.M.'s first impulsive appraisement.

The P.M. is not at all conventional, and his open mind has been a valuable asset in the war; no idea was too improbable, too absurd to be given a trial. But when he came to select men he was somehow less successful – the incipient genius rescued from obscurity was apt to prove a disappointment.

The P.M. has been kept in good humour by his preparations for the meeting with the President that have filled every minute of his working day on board. He has gone over in his mind, a good many times, Franklin Roosevelt's words at the White House in May. Even

then there had been a sense of urgency that was new to the P.M.,
a touch of impatience, as the President set out his views on the
invasion of France. Nothing must interfere with that. For all his
obstinacy, Winston generally knows when the time has come to
give way. Now two months have gone and a plan for the invasion
of Normandy is taking shape. The P.M. cannot help being
impressed by the numbers that will be engaged, the tonnage
involved. More than once he has spoken to me of the plan as
'majestic.' Maybe his fears of a landing on strongly held beaches
are exaggerated. Anyway, he feels the need of talks with the
President. After all, there are some things, as he puts it, which can
only be decided at the highest level.

*August 11, 1943*
I wish sometimes that one member of this singular family would
behave like an ordinary human being. Clemmie is the culprit this
time; she is being difficult – over nothing. The P.M. was in tremendous form last night. In a few hours he would be leaving Quebec
for Hyde Park to spend some days as the President's guest; then,
as he grunted with great satisfaction, things would really get
moving. I was therefore surprised to find him this morning in poor
spirits. It appears that Clemmie was to have gone with him; but
she changed her plans at the last moment; she was not sleeping
well, she said. The truth is she does not like the President; once
she confided to me that she does not like any great man except
Winston. Winston tried to argue with her; it was not very polite
to the President, he said. But Clemmie can be as difficult and obstinate as the great man himself. Besides he has 'talked at' her so often
she has become resistant and doesn't mind being 'shouted down'.

*Quebec, August 18, 1943*
The Canadian Prime Minister was our host at a Citadel dinner.
There was apparently a proposal that Canada should take part in the
Conference, but this came to nothing. As it is, Mackenzie King seems
rather like a man who has lent his house for a party. The guests take
hardly any notice of him, but just before leaving they remember he

is their host and say pleasant things. I wonder if he is as enamoured of his role at this Conference as the P.M. imagines.[1]

*August 20, 1943*

Harry Hopkins was in a curious mood this morning. He told me that at yesterday's session Winston 'came clean' about a Second Front, that he 'threw in his hand.' Hopkins said this in rather an aggressive way, as if I were in the P.M.'s camp.

'Winston is no longer against Marshall's plan for landing on the coast of France. At least, so he says.'

Harry grinned.

'But he might change his mind again, as he did last year. I don't believe he is really converted.[2]

'Why,' Hopkins went on, 'before he said he agreed we had the most solemn warning of what might happen. The old, old story of enormous casualties and the terrific strength of the German fortifications.'

Why is this man so bitter? Harry is sure that Winston's obstinacy, his drawn-out struggle to postpone a second front in France, has, in fact, prolonged the war; that if he had been reasonable earlier we might now be in sight of peace. Is Hopkins right? That must remain the riddle of the war.

It is indeed a momentous change of front on the part of the Prime Minister; the end of an argument that has gone on since the

---

[1] 'There is no doubt,' the Prime Minister said in a telegram to the War Cabinet, dated August 25, 1943, 'that Mackenzie King and the Canadian Government are delighted and feel themselves thoroughly "on the map."' King, who had been my patient, wrote to me on June 9, 1950: 'I am afraid my notes of the two Quebec Conferences are even more meagre than your own. I was, as you recall, not so much a participant in any of the discussions as a sort of general host, whose task at the Citadel was similar to that of the General Manager of the Château Frontenac.'

[2] Prime Minister to Field-Marshal Smuts, September 11, 1943: 'There can be no question whatever of breaking arrangements we have made with United States for "Overlord" [the code name for the invasion of Northern France] . . . I hope you will realize that British loyalty to Overlord is keystone of arch of Anglo-American co-operation.' This message was in response to a suggestion by Smuts that 'preparations for Channel plan should be slowed down.'

Americans came into the war. I want time to think it over and to get my bearings.

When Hopkins questioned whether the P.M. meant what he said, I wonder if he is speaking for anybody but himself. I must not, of course, make the mistake of taking him for a typical American, any more than I would argue that Max Beaverbrook is a fair sample of our countrymen. But there are Americans in high places who, though they like and admire Winston, do feel that he has been rather disingenuous about the Second Front. Before their country came into the war there was no strategy to speak of. It was just a struggle for survival. Winston Churchill became a symbol of the English will to fight to a finish; his authority was not questioned. But after Pearl Harbour America began to think of a landing in France, and the timing of this expedition became a bone of contention between us. The Americans are not in doubt that Marshall was right in resisting the postponement of the landing in France. It appears that the President and Hopkins are no longer prepared to acknowledge Winston as an infallible guide in military matters.

For that matter, it is not only the President and Marshall who are uneasy about the P.M.'s judgment. Brooke is worried by his inability to finish one subject before taking up another, by the darting processes of his mind and by the general instability of his judgment. But are his critics measuring the Prime Minister by the right yard-stick? His claim to a place in history does not rest on his strategy. His gifts are of a rarer kind.

What his critics are apt to forget is that you cannot measure inspiration. That is why it is not easy to bring home to the military hierarchy the list of assets which easily tilt the balance in his favour: the strength of will that has bent all manner of men to his purpose; the extraordinary tenacity – the Americans call it obstinacy – with which he clings for months, and if need be for years, to his own plans; the terrific force of personality that can brush aside all doubts and hesitations, and sweep away inertia, refusing to listen when weaker men begin to whine about difficulties; above all else, the superb confidence he exuded in 1940. When the Prime Minister set out to inspire the country with his will to win he made up his mind that it must begin in his own bedroom. I have been with him there at all hours, I have seen him take a lot of punishment, and not once did he look like a loser. Not once did he give me the feeling that he was in any way worried or anxious as to the outcome of the fight. Gradually I have come to think of him as invincible.

*August 21, 1943*

Some of us are going up the St Lawrence on a twenty-four hours' trip. Marshall is on board, and he began asking my views about morale. Marshall is quite ruthless when it comes to scrapping an incompetent commander. I said to him if we have a general who makes a bog of things we promote him. Marshall answered we don't think of the general, we think of the division he commands. Marshall confided in me that his heart fibrillates from time to time (a rapid, irregular rhythm of the heart). I hope he will keep on his feet; he is, too, a real friend of England and a wise man who seems to me the one indispensable man in training the American armies. I talked to him for a long time and was comforted by his wisdom.

As the light failed, a blanket of white fog enveloped the little ship, and the hooting of our siren came echoing back from the hills flanking the great river. When Marshall went to his bed my thoughts took a sombre turn, the questioning mood of the First World War came back.

Yesterday, while the P.M. was arguing that it pays us to exchange plane for plane with the Germans, they handed me a letter from home. Two young pilots in the Air Force, who, if they had lived, would have done something in the world, had been shot down. War is a hellish business when you are not right in it. I cannot get used to being a distant spectator.

These trips expose character. As an odd number who cannot promote or dispromote anybody I'm in a peculiar position among this crowd of service people. War is their great opportunity and most of them feel this. The real Sahib is very friendly and pleasant to me; indeed if you made a list of the folk who go out of their way to be pleasant to me, well knowing that it can profit them nothing, you would probably get the pick of these people. By this list

Marshall comes out first with the Mountbatten fellow a bad last. He seems a horrid, pushy go-getter. On the whole the party comes out of this list with flying colours.

*

This is from my diary of the First World War:[1]

'If the medical officer with a Battalion escaped the responsibility for military decisions which gamble in human life, nevertheless he, too, has his own distresses. It is not the wounds he binds which matter, it is when something has been destroyed in the make-up of a man that the bloody business of war comes home to him. With a background of casualties in his mind, he is prone to think that the men are being treated as pawns in the game; he may question if all this loss of life is necessary. He begins to ask himself, Who is responsible?'

That black mood came back with the loss of the two pilots. It is generally agreed that our leaders in this war are better than the 'heavy blockhead type' (it is Winston's epithet) of the First World War. But is there not the same terrifying disparity between the size and scope of the great problems of war and the capacity of those who have to deal with them? Are Marshall's brains, for instance, first-rate? I think they are, but they are not, perhaps, of the creative kind. How can one tell a soldier's quality when he has not been in action?

Marshall told me that the problem of this war was the disciplining of the citizen soldier. Anyway, that has been his task. And it has not been easy. For the American youth is self-confident; he is quite certain that he knows a better way of doing things than those who are ordering him about. Marshall had had to begin at the beginning: to plan a three months' basic training, the sole purpose of which was to get the recruit to see that he must do what he was told. And, of course, in that fashion Marshall has done a magnificent job for his country; he has shown to the full that remarkable gift for organization which is everywhere behind

[1] Lord Moran, *The Anatomy of Courage*, p. 44.

American production. But I would not call it a work of genius. Can we ask as much of a soldier? Is it reasonable to look for the creative spirit in one of our generals? In science the sterile worker soon loses caste, and even in my own calling, that is half a science and half an art, we have no patience with empty vessels. It may be that we are rather harsh, a little arbitrary perhaps, in our assessment of capacity. If a doctor adds something to knowledge – describes, perhaps, a new disease, or discovers penicillin – we count him as having a creative mind. Short of that he is bundled unceremoniously into the second category. He may be a great clinician, who notices things in a patient that others miss, but if he is not productive he remains a secondary figure. But are the soldier and the scientist truly comparable?

They are surely very different. And the crucial point of difference is this: that the soldier must go on doing his job however grim the conditions. He must not quit. If he falters he is at once thrown aside. Whereas there is no certainty that the creative spirits who add to knowledge would prove as staunch. Would they keep cool heads amid the blind fury of modern war?

Winston at any rate had no doubt of the answer. In *The World Crisis* he was driven to an indictment of the General Staff. Their ideas were elementary, their scientific vision narrow, their minds rigid. They were slow to master a new mechanical idea. In short, he writes of men 'whose nerves were much stronger than their imaginations,' whom nothing could upset. Still, they were all we had; it was necessary to make the best of them. And Winston gives his reasons. 'No doubt more highly-strung men could not stand the wear and tear of high command in modern warfare.' They were necessarily eliminated in favour of those who, in his words, could preserve their sang-froid amidst disastrous surprises, 'to an extent almost indistinguishable from insensitivity.'

In war we must often be content with a modicum of brains, because other things are even more important and, on the whole, it is a better bargain than it seems. When things go wrong and there are heavy casualties, I ask sometimes: 'Would these men have got to the top in any other profession?' And it always seems to me a good enough answer that I do not know where to go to match them in strength of character.

In time to come some historian, another Trevelyan, may wonder how human nature stood up to the ordeal of the last of the Great Wars. Turning to his shelves he may find in the diaries of those days enough to piece together four unusual characters, Marshall and Eisenhower, Wavell and Brooke. Had they had their way they would have spent quiet lives in the country stillness, near some tree-reflecting stream, but that was not to be their lot. They loathed war. 'Every month,' Brooke told me, 'is a year off my life.' Yet he gave all he had to his work: a simple, gentle, selfless soul – a warning to us all not to give up hope about mankind. Taking a long view, it does not seem to matter whether soldiers win battles. What is important is that the world should go on producing men built on that pattern.

*August 22, 1943*

The P.M. is of course happy about the promotion of Mountbatten to the South East Asia Command. It is, of course, his own appointment. The Chiefs of Staff certainly display no enthusiasm; they think he is a wild fellow and from time to time murmur about Dicky's habit of bringing out ill-digested plans at their meetings. Portal in particular has little use for him, though he concedes that 'he is thorough like any other German'.

*August 23, 1943*

When the P.M. made a tour of Quebec this morning, attired in what the local papers call 'an unbleached linen suit,' the crowds gave him a noisy greeting, and he returned in very good spirits. A diet of that kind is much to his liking. By the afternoon the people had gone back to work and I had the ramparts to myself. They are still armed with the old sixteen-pounders which once guarded the St Lawrence, and my head was full of the people who first came here. I got up at last and began to mount one of the narrow cobbled streets which climb abruptly from the ramparts to the old French town. There was no one about save for a single black figure, a priest, halfway up the street, like a fly crawling up a window-pane.

When I came to the hotel the hall was full of soldiers hurrying about their business. As I was going to my room I ran into Pug Ismay[1]. As he stopped to speak to me I felt his eye roaming around the hall, seeking some more profitable anchorage. Pug graduated in a hard school at Simla under Lady Hillingdon, where he must have been an apt pup. You would not call him a very serious soldier; a gifted if rather inexperienced politician perhaps, but a born courtier without any doubt. His nickname came to him because when he smiles his face bears a remarkable resemblance to a pug dog. And this smile he works pretty hard when the P.M. is in his lighter mode; sometimes his amusement seems a little out of proportion to the wit. He is a kind of filter between the Prime Minister and his Chiefs of Staff, only letting through what is helpful and unprovocative. In the short passage between the two parties he seems to forget everything that could ruffle and anger his masters. The P.M. is of course far too knowledgeable in military matters to take Pug seriously. If Brooke says something, the P.M. listens to it attentively because it is the C.I.G.S. speaking, but Pug has to depend on seizing the right moment, and on the way he says his piece. Nevertheless, though he thinks like a politician – he never does anything without a purpose – he has a remarkable knowledge of human nature, and his influence is increasing, as the drip of water in time makes its mark on stone.

*August 25, 1943*

The P.M. likes comfort, and Colonel Clarke, our host, who owns vast forests which nourish his paper mills, is able to provide it. Even here, in a clearing in a primeval forest on the banks of the Montmorency River, our two-storeyed house, built of rudely-hewn logs, has electric light and a bathroom, while the food and drink are up to Winston's requirements. To remind us that there were wolves and moose and bear in the forest until the lumber-men

---

[1] General Sir Hastings Ismay, Chief of Staff to the Minister of Defence (Winston Churchill).

came, there is a huge black bearskin rug in front of the fire – a fire in August sounds strange, but we are sixteen hundred feet above the sea.

*August 26, 1943*

We made an early start climbing over rough roads to Snow Lake, the highest point in the Laurentian Mountains, four thousand feet above the sea. This morning each one of our little party sallied forth in a canoe, with a French Canadian paddling, and fished with a wet fly. The trout in this lake are big, and if a man is a fisherman he is often rewarded by big catches; Brooke and Portal, when they came here not long ago, took 151 trout, averaging one pound, in a single day. When it was learnt that I was the only one to draw a blank the P.M. became much concerned. 'Nothing,' he repeated. 'Clemmie,[1] Charles has got nothing.' 'Where is my fishing rod?' he demanded, and when it was brought he proceeded to initiate me into the art of casting a fly. When he had done, he sent for the chief guide, and, after a spirited little speech, I was committed to his care. I was paddled to a little bay, reputed to be prolific in fish, but still nothing happened. My guide, in desperation, set off for another part of the lake. Only the lapping of the water broke the silence; I sat watching the changing lights on the wooded hills which guard the lake, while my thoughts kept wandering back to Fenimore Cooper's Red Indians. I suppose I had been trailing my line in the water for, all at once, I felt a tug, and to my joy I landed a trout – a three and a half pounder. I was relieved that honour was satisfied. As for the P.M., he became almost hilarious at my achievement. Already he is full of theories and laying down the law about the fisherman's art. This mountain air should bring new life to him. Even the Marine Orderly is stirred, and became so excited in a struggle with a big fish that he fell into the lake. While we were rescuing him, a loon flew over the water, making an unfamiliar cry. When night fell, Winston came out on the wooden pier, gazing up at the Aurora Borealis. This quiet life is doing him good, but he feels he is playing truant.

[1] Mrs Churchill.

*September 1, 1943*

Last night, before we left Wolfe's Cove, on the outskirts of Quebec, at seven o'clock, I made this note: 'The P.M. stood for some time at the window of his car giving the victory sign to odd workmen in the fields, who could see nothing but a train rushing through the countryside.'

*Washington, September 2, 1943*

I went this morning with Clemmie to see the Lincoln Memorial. There he sits, an immense figure of a man, grasping the sides of the chair with his bony, gnarled hands. You feel that the sculptor understood the elemental grandeur and the spiritual force of the man. That is what we have missed in two world wars. The earnest goodness of the leaders. With Winston war is an end in itself rather than a means to an end. It fascinates him, he loves it . . . he neither believes in nor is interested in what comes after the war . . . Smuts's words on Winston's lack of any religion come into my mind.

# CHAPTER FIFTEEN

# How Churchill Learnt his Craft

*September 6, 1943*

On the train to Boston I found I was running a temperature again. One might think, from his irritability, that the P.M. had the bug. For some reason, which I have not yet fathomed, he is taking the speech he is to make at Harvard very seriously. The President, too, is interested. He was at Harvard in 1904, and he wants the ceremony at his old University to be up to English standards in pomp and colour. I think he has been sticking pins into Conant, the President of Harvard. At any rate, there has been a to-do about the P.M.'s robe. Conant wants him to wear his Oxford D.C.L. It is a scarlet affair, and certainly more impressive than the austere American gown, but it is too late to get a robe from England; however, they have unearthed one at Princeton and have borrowed it for the occasion.

When the P.M. came on to the stage of the Sanders Theatre at Harvard, it was plain that he had tried to make his own contribution to an academic event. He was attired in a black coat and a bow tie. But Winston would not be Winston if he was strictly conventional. Beneath the gorgeous scarlet robe appeared a pair of rather inadequate grey flannel trousers. Holding his quaint black velvet hat in his extended arm, he beamed on his audience as they welcomed him.

He began by reminding them in a few sentences of the bombed cities of Britain, recalling the last time he had worn academic robes. It was at Bristol, which had been heavily bombed during the night;

indeed, 'many of the University authorities had pulled on their robes over uniforms begrimed and drenched.'

'Here now today, I am once again,' the P.M. paused, and there was a twinkle in his eye, 'in academic groves – groves is, I believe, the right word – where knowledge is garnered, where learning is stimulated, where virtues are inculcated and thought encouraged.'

It was a very mild quip, but his audience were in an indulgent mood as they thought of the bombing of Britain. Then, very gently, he told them of the price of greatness:

'One cannot rise to be in many ways the leading community in the civilized world without being involved in its problems, without being convulsed by its agonies and inspired by its causes.'

The subtle flattery of this passage was well designed to pave the way for what was to come. He could now lay bare the full scope of the workings of his mind:

'The most potent factor in human society at the end of the nineteenth century, Bismarck said, was the fact that the British and American people spoke the same language – this gift of a common tongue is a priceless inheritance and it may well some day become the foundation of a common citizenship.'

There, the cat was out of the bag, but how gently, how patiently, how prudently, were the audience prepared for its appearance!

With the end in sight, the main motif of his speech was allowed to peep out once more:

'I am here to tell you that nothing will work soundly or for long without the united effort of the British and American people. If we are together, nothing is impossible. If we are divided, all will fail. I therefore preach continually the doctrine of the fraternal association of our peoples, not for any purpose of gaining invidious material advantages for either of them, not for territorial aggrandisement or the vain pomp of earthly domination, but for the sake of service to mankind and for the honour that comes to those who faithfully serve great causes.'

That was as near as he dared go to proposing a closer union after the war. Winston told me on our way back to Washington that a little time ago he could not have gone so far. I do not doubt that he tried 'common citizenship' on the President before he launched it at Boston.

The speech ended on a typical Churchill note:

'And here let me say how proud we ought to be, young and old, to live in this tremendous, thrilling, formative epoch in the human story.'

'Now, God be thanked Who has matched us with His hour,' sang Rupert Brooke at the Dardanelles, and this old tough, so near to seventy years of age, throws up his hat that he is alive to play a part.

\*

Neville Cardus wrote of the bowling of Wilfred Rhodes:

'Flight was his secret, flight and the curving line, now higher, now lower, tempting, inimical; every ball like every other ball, yet somehow unlike; each over in collusion with the others, part of a plot. Every ball a decoy, a spy sent out to get the lie of the land; some balls simple, some complex, some easy, some difficult; and one of them – ah, which? – the master ball.'

It would serve as a description of this speech of Winston Churchill. Each sentence is a spy sent out to get the lie of the land, and one of them is the master sentence.

\*

*September 7, 1943*

When the P.M. has a speech on the stocks, it takes possession of him, and he usually banishes from his mind everything that is not connected with his script. But when he spoke at Harvard, I found that his thoughts kept wandering to the coming landing at Salerno.[1] That is where his heart is. As the appointed day draws near, the

---

[1] On September 9, 1943, the U.S. 5th Army and the British Xth Corps landed at Salerno with the object of outflanking the Axis armies in Southern Italy, following the 8th Army's invasion of the toe of the peninsula.

P.M. can think of nothing else. On this landing he has been building all his hopes. There are no doubts of any kind in his mind; anyway he admits none. It *must* succeed, and then Naples will fall into our hands. Last night, when the stream of his conversation was in spate, he talked of meeting Alex in Rome before long – the capture of Rome has fired his imagination; more than once he has spoken about Napoleon's Italian campaign.

*Washington, September 9, 1943*
For some time stories have been going about that Dudley Pound drops off to sleep in important committees, even at meeting with the Cabinet, but people add, with a knowing air, that he always wakes up when the Navy is mentioned. They would have me believe that he gets bored with anything that does not affect the Navy, and cannot be bothered to keep awake. But it does not seem much of a compliment to this sailor if they can detect no difference between his mental process now, when he is a very sick man, and the time when he was fit and well.

I first noticed this at the Guildhall one morning during a Freedom ceremony when I happened to be seated on the platform next to Pound, and I noticed that he had fallen asleep; his head had sunk until it almost touched my shoulder.

As for the P.M., he does not notice this kind of thing until it hits him. And here at Washington it has hit him pretty hard. Today a message came from the White House. The Prime Minister would like to see me.

'I'm worried about Pound,' he began. 'I thought things weren't right when he got out of coming to Snow Lake. You know he is a keen fisherman. Last night after dinner he came to see us. The President asked him some very ordinary questions, and I was very surprised when he answered wide of the mark. I said to him: "But, Admiral, you don't really mean that?" He sat up straight and said he would let me have a full report in the morning. After that he rose, saying that he felt tired and would go to bed. After he had gone the President said that he had noticed at some of the meetings that Pound was torpid, and had decided that he was finished.

'This morning,' the P.M. went on, 'Pound asked to see me. In view of what had happened last night I felt he was going to say something very important to me. It did not seem right to receive him in bed. I got up and sat at a table in my dressing-gown. When he appeared I asked him to sit down. He said at once: "Prime Minister, I have to tell you that I am no longer able to carry out my duties and must ask to be relieved of them. I have had a slight stroke, my right foot does not work properly and my hand is affected so that I cannot write my name properly. My general activities are affected." I told him that in saying this he had behaved like a man and a gentleman, and that arrangements would be made forthwith to relieve him of his duties. I asked him to return with us in *Renown*. Can nothing be done, Charles? Will he get better?'

*September 12, 1943*
When our troops landed on the Salerno beaches it did not prove to be at all a walk-over. On the contrary, the news that filtered into Hyde Park, where we had followed the President, was disquieting: the Germans had launched a strong counter-attack and the situation was very uncertain. 'These things always seem to happen,' grumbled the P.M., 'when I am with the President.' Poor Winston, he had been so anxious to convince Roosevelt that the invasion of Italy would yield a bountiful harvest at no great cost. When we left Hyde Park tonight, on the long train journey to Halifax, the situation was still very obscure.

*September 13, 1943*
This morning things are no better. The P.M. is as irritable as if he had a big speech hanging over him. I have never seen him more on edge during a battle. Three 'bloodys' bespattered his conversation, and twice, while I was with him, he lost his temper with his servant, shouting at him in a painful way. He got up and walked down the train. He was sure that Alexander was doing the right thing, but he could not help wondering what he was doing and whether he was on the spot. He did hope Alex would keep him

posted. 'Has any news come in?' he kept demanding. In truth, the reports that are reaching him only leave him more anxious. There is a dreadful hint, though it is carefully covered up, that we might be driven into the sea. It appears, as far as I can tell, that the P.M. is largely responsible for this particular operation; if anyone is to blame, he is the man; and, from the way things seem to be going, I suppose he is beginning to think that there might be a good deal to explain. None of the generals in command, he tells me, has fought a battle before. Could he do anything to help, he wondered. He cannot stay still for long; twice in the last hour he has gone off wandering down the train as if he were looking for someone. At last he felt he must pour out all his fears to Alex, he was sure he would not resent it.

'Prime Minister to General Alexander. 14 Sept. 43

'I hope you are watching above all the Battle of "Avalanche" which dominates everything. None of the commanders engaged has fought a large scale battle before. The Battle of Suvla Bay was lost because Ian Hamilton was advised by his CGS to remain at a remote central point where he would know everything. Had he been on the spot he could have saved the show. At this distance and with time lags I cannot pretend to judge, but I feel it is my duty to set before you this experience of mine from the past.

'2. Nothing should be denied which will nourish the Battle of Naples.

'3. Ask for anything you want, and I will make allocation of necessary supplies, with highest priority irrespective of every other consideration.'

*September 16, 1943*
On board *Renown* the P.M. has become a little less abstracted. It is with a real sense of relief that he counts the days before the ship will drop anchor. He told me that he was anxious to get back to London to pick up the threads again. All the same, he has not

found it easy, while the telegrams kept coming in, to settle down to his speech for the House of Commons. His habits in a ship don't help. Instead of coming on deck for a little exercise, he remains immured in his cabin. Today, when he had been brooding over his plate, he looked up, and, addressing no one in particular, said: 'My feeling is we are going to win.' He admits now that it has been touch and go, that for three days the issue hung in the balance. Anyway, he is pretty sure that we are out of the wood now. When he rose from the table to go to his cabin, I think we were all a little surprised – though we are accustomed to his moods – at this sudden revulsion of feeling: his spirits have come back, his dark fears are exorcised.

*September 21, 1943*
Back in London, the anxious days, when it seemed we might be driven back into the sea, are forgotten. The P.M. is in high spirits; he knows he has the country solidly behind him. Even the small group of members of the House of Commons, who had set themselves up as his mentors, held their peace on this occasion.

*September 22, 1943*
When the P.M. woke, and rang his bell for the newspapers, he was shocked to read of the sudden death of the Chancellor of the Exchequer, Sir Kingsley Wood, with whom he had been on very friendly terms. Sir John Anderson, the Lord President of the Council, who is now to become Chancellor, is a very different man. There has indeed been nothing quite like him in the Civil Service. His astonishing efficiency depends on an unusual combination of qualities. In the first place, he has an appetite for facts, which he has indulged freely for many years, so that it is almost impossible to catch him out in anything. This grip of detail is reinforced by what Maynard Keynes termed 'the gift of instinctive judgment.' Anderson only speaks as from the Bench. To this catalogue of virtues I must add his immense experience of administration and his shining moral courage, what Winston calls 'Sir John's firm spirit.' The Prime Minister has great need of such a man. Absorbed

himself in the conduct of operations, he has been happy to leave the Home Front to Anderson; he knew nothing would go wrong. A special committee – the most important of all the Cabinet Committees, the P.M. used to call it – was set up to supervise all matters on this front, with Anderson as Chairman.

Sir John was thought by some to be censorious, but he felt he had the right to be critical. The world, after all, had accepted him as a great man, and he saw no reason to demur. It is said that he was pompous as an Edinburgh student, and in the days of his fulfilment they called him Jehovah. I remember once saying to him: 'Winston is hopeless with strangers.' He agreed, but added, in his pontifical manner: 'Winston must not only get to know a man, he must also find him congenial,' and Sir John permitted himself a slight smirk. He would indeed have been pained if he had known that his own solid gifts were not those to set the P.M.'s mind on fire. Winston trusted him, he respected his judgment, but he did not always find him congenial.

*October 24, 1943*

The P.M. told me that he saw Pound the day before he died.[1]

'His face was set,' and here the P.M. imitated Pound's expressionless countenance: 'He could not speak. But he took my hand, and when I said things that might be agreeable to him, he gripped it hard. His mind was all right; he knew what I was saying. He died on Trafalgar Day,' the P.M. mused. 'Death is the greatest gift God has made to us.'

*October 26, 1943*

The P.M. is already beginning to have his own doubts and hesitations, a good deal of his optimism after Salerno has oozed away. But on one point his mind is made up. He is resolved not to let Alex down. When I called at No. 10 this morning I found the P.M. glowering over a telegram from Eden. His face was glum, his jaw set, misgivings filled his mind.

[1] October 21, 1943.

'Stalin seems obsessed by this bloody Second Front,' he muttered angrily. 'I can be obstinate too.'

He jumped out of bed and began pacing up and down.

'Damn the fellow,' he said under his breath. And then he rang for a secretary. When he began dictating a telegram to the Foreign Secretary I got up to leave the room.

'No, Charles, don't go. This,' grumbled the P.M., 'is what comes of a lawyer's agreement to attack on a fixed date without regard to the ever-changing fortunes of war.'

Alex's fears had upset the P.M. His mind was now made up. He turned to the secretary, who held her pencil ready.

'I will not allow the great and fruitful campaign in Italy to be cast away and end in a frightful disaster, for the sake of crossing the Channel in May. The battle must be nourished and fought out until it is won. Molotov must be warned,' the P.M. continued striding to the door and back, 'that the assurances I gave to Stalin about OVER-LORD in May are subject to the exigencies of the battle in Italy. Eisenhower and Alex must have what they need to win the battle, no matter what effect is produced on subsequent operations. Stalin ought to be told bluntly that OVERLORD might have to be postponed.'

The P.M. seemed preoccupied and short-tempered today.

*October 29, 1943*
Went to the House of Commons yesterday to hear the P.M. speak on what he calls 'the physical aspect of the new House.'

'If,' he said, 'the House is big enough to contain all its members, nine-tenths of its debates will be conducted in the depressing atmosphere of an almost empty, or half-empty, Chamber. The essence of good House of Commons speaking is the conversational style, the facility for quick, informal interruptions and interchanges. Harangues from a rostrum would be a bad substitute for the conversational style in which so much of our business is done. But the conversational style requires a fairly small space, and there should be, on great occasions, a sense of the importance of much that is said, and a sense that great matters are being decided, there and then, by the House.'

This morning when he talked to me of his beloved workshop, the old House of Commons, his voice broke:

'There I learnt my craft, and there it is now, a heap of rubble.[1] I am glad that it is in my power, when it is rebuilt, to keep it as it was.'

His mind travelled back over the long and painful apprenticeship that he had served. For some time he went lovingly over the past, and, as he tried to tell me the tale, the tears ran down his cheeks. For my part, though I had heard it all before, when he asked me a question, I could not speak to him.

Winston seemed concerned chiefly with his early struggle to win the confidence of the House. He spoke as it were of a vocation, and, in fact, few men have stuck so religiously to one craft – the handling of words. In peace it made his political fortune, in war it has won all men's hearts. Without that feeling for words he might have made little enough of life. For in judgment, in skill in administration, in knowledge of human nature, he does not at all excel.

Winston found that out for himself quite early. 'You see, Charles, it all began at Harrow.' Sitting at the bottom of the school, under something of a cloud, he discovered that he could do what other boys could not do – he could write. And when, as a subaltern in India, he began to read Gibbon, already he knew what he wanted to do in life. He confessed that from the beginning 'personal distinction' was his goal, and he knew, too, that it could only be achieved by cultivating this inborn aptitude; if he had always done what he liked in life, that did not mean that he was afraid of hard work. Above all, he had set his heart on one thing: he wanted to be an orator. He read everything he could get hold of about Chatham; he studied his father's speeches; he practised his own before the looking-glass. Even then he dreamed of the day when he would dominate the House of Commons, when they would have to listen to him.

He told me this very simply, stopping when his voice threatened

[1] During the night of May 10, 1941, a German bomb severely damaged the Parliament buildings at Westminster.

to get out of control, while I marvelled at his will and purpose. The wonder to me was that he had not lost heart. For, in truth, he did not seem to be designed by nature for his part. Small, tongue-tied, with an impediment in his speech, when he rose in the House, he was always fearful that he might blurt out something that would get him into trouble, and that he would wake in the morning to find that he had blighted his prospects. When he told me this he hesitated and then went on: 'I did not get completely rid of that until the war.'

'Without the most careful preparation,' he continued, 'I could not speak at all in those days. And even then I always kept strictly to my notes.' Moreover, in spite of all the pains he took, he was always in danger of breaking down in the course of a speech. Once he had found himself on his feet, with his mind a complete blank, while the awful silence was broken only by friendly, encouraging noises; he stood his ground until at last he could bear it no longer; back in his seat, he could only bury his head in his hands.

After his breakdown in the House of Commons he dreaded getting up to speak more than ever. Sometimes he would persuade himself that what he was about to say had already been said, or that the time to say it was past. Any excuse served to keep him in his seat. But he obstinately refused to give in. He would not admit defeat.

Perhaps at this point it occurred to him that he had already told me too much. Anyway, when he had solemnly warned me against my practice of speaking without notes, he began to ask me about medicines, and I knew that the conversation was at an end.

*November 7, 1943*
The P.M. seemed in a better mood today. He had heard from the President that no more landing-craft would be withdrawn until December 15. Looking at me over his spectacles, he said, 'We need not take that date too seriously.' He needs a fillip, for October was a bad month, and now there is a good deal of grumbling over the inoculations.

# CHAPTER SIXTEEN

# On the Way to Teheran

*H.M.S.* Renown, *November 16, 1943*

The P.M. is in the doldrums. He came on board with a heavy cold, and inoculations against typhoid have left him with some fever. I had been looking forward to the sea voyage to get him into good fettle for the strenuous days that lie ahead. I pictured him ticking over for a time, cut off from things. But Winston is upsetting all my plans. For four hours yesterday he and Randolph sat in his cabin hunched over their cards, and then after a break for dinner, Winston said to Randolph: 'What about another cut of the cards?' It was after five o'clock in the morning when they went to bed.

Gil Winant[1] breaks pleasantly our ordered lives. Other men have to win the confidence of those they meet; Winant is allowed to skip that stage. Before he utters a syllable people want to see more of him. He has the rapt gaze of a monk; the big dark eyes, buried in his head, look beyond you – I do not wonder that Epstein wants to do a bust of him. I have heard some say of Winant that he is just an impressive façade, that there is nothing behind that prophetic presence. They say that a man's face is sometimes his fortune. Yet to me he seems a discerning man. When I said to him that Winston had no informed likes, meaning that he likes people in a superficial way without really knowing what there is in them – a kind of surface impression as it were – he nodded eagerly, saying that he had not heard it put that way. How typical of Gil when I

[1] J. G. (Gil) Winant, U.S. Ambassador to the Court of St James's, 1941–3.

try to bring him to life that I cannot call to mind anything that he said, but have to fall back instead on something I said.

Winant holds men, but that is as far as they get. He has wrestled with the world and has hidden, like Brooke, behind a curtain of his own making. It appeared to lift a little when the two men came together. There was Winant talking eagerly about *Fallodon Papers* and Brooke – a new Brooke to me – hardly able to wait his turn as he thought of some lines from *The Prelude*. When Winant had done, how his words cascaded!

Winant worries about the P.M.; he thinks that he is wearing out and that there is no one to take his place. Winant is concerned to build a better world after the war, and he has Winston in mind as the architect. 'Tell me, Charles, do you think he is interested?' Winant came closer to me in his excitement. I had to own that Winston has come to look askance at change.

The P.M., of course, is not blind to Winant's quality. There was talk tonight of the possibility of putting France on her feet again, and of the great difficulty of doing this because so many Frenchmen were quarrelling among themselves. Winant would not accept this; those who were helping in France and working for us stood, in his sight, for a sounder France. The P.M. intervened: 'The ambassador always stands out for the larger view, and he is, of course, right.' The P.M. is attracted by Winant's optimism, but it is not to him that he turns for advice. He prefers the tart cleverness of Harry Hopkins, for the same reason that he is drawn to Max Beaverbrook. Some readers may say that if the silent Winant could enliven our proceedings we must be a pretty solid party. There may be truth in this. If the reader joined us on our travels and waited patiently for something good, he might wait for a long time. Desmond MacCarthy once wrote of Asquith that in the social give and take he exercised a strict intellectual economy. The heads of the services who come with Winston carry a heavy burden. They must be glad to throw it off for a time and tick over. Besides, what they have most in their minds is least suitable for public discussion, on their discretion many lives depend. And they come of a clan that only unbuttons in intimate talk with old and true friends. Whatever the explanation out of school we shall pass for a pretty humdrum lot.

When there was a break in the conversation, Winant rose to go on deck – the temperature of Winston's saloon is kept at 73 degrees Fahrenheit. 'These great men,' he said, as he took a long breath of the cool night air, 'are very thrifty in the expenditure of their time.' It did not seem a particularly appropriate observation at that moment, when we had been at the dinner table for more than two hours. 'Roosevelt,' he went on, 'has many interviews, timed to last from ten to fifteen minutes; when he does not want to be asked questions, he just goes on talking till his secretary appears, saying he is very sorry, but Senator So-and-So has been waiting a long time. Whereupon the President's visitor takes his leave. This is the point, Charles. He goes away not at all dissatisfied, though he may not have succeeded in asking the President a single question. Tell me, is Winston clever, like the President, in getting rid of people?'

I sensed that Winant wanted to know more about Winston, but I dodged the question. For Winston is not at all clever at that sort of thing. We do not think of him as in any way subtle; if he talks, it is because he likes talking and is, at best, but an indifferent listener; and, if he dreads being left alone with a stranger, it may be because he can find nothing to say which will bridge the silences. His dislike of strangers, never very well disguised, often flusters the unfortunate intruder, who arrives full of what he is going to say, the arguments tidily and carefully arranged. And then somehow there is no time, or so it seems, to say it in an orderly manner as he had planned; sometimes he even wonders if Winston is attending to what he is telling him. It is all very awkward and unexpected. After a little the Prime Minister holds out a limp hand with a rather unconvincing smile, and it is with a feeling of disappointment but also a sense of relief that the caller finds himself on the stairs.

If Winston is not interested in the strangers he meets, he does not, to be sure, know much about those with whom he works. I said to him the other night that Leslie Rowan might one day be head of the Civil Service. He stared at me in bewilderment. 'Now why did you say that?' seemed on his tongue. It would never occur to Winston to wonder about Leslie's future. I suppose that is because he is not interested in people and cannot follow their thoughts – he speaks with scorn of anyone who pretends he can. I am on the black list. It happened like this. War has always fascinated him; he knows in surprising detail about the campaigns of the great captains; he has visited nearly all the battlefields and he can pick out, in a particular battle, the decisive move that turned the day. But he has never given a thought to what was happening in the soldier's mind, he has not tried to share his fears. If a soldier does not do his duty, the P.M. says that he ought to be shot. It is as simple as that. When he dipped into the manuscript of my little book, *The Anatomy of Courage*, he said that the picture of what goes on in a soldier's head, as I had painted it, would discourage the young soldier; it might affect recruiting. I had tried to unravel the behaviour of men in war, to discover what was happening in their minds. In those years in the trenches in the First World War we had lived on our will-power. It was our capital, and when it was spent we were finished. We had learnt painfully how it could be eked out for a little longer, and I was disappointed that Winston did not think it would help if I put this on paper.

*Malta, November 17, 1943*

There is nothing new in the P.M.'s impatience with 'all this psychological nonsense.' In fact, I gave it so little thought that I was not prepared for a letter from Dorothy which I found awaiting me at Malta telling me that Macmillans had refused to publish the book. They took the same line as Winston. I replied:

'My dear Dorothy,

'I have just got your letter. It is, of course, a blow. I cannot reconcile it with Desmond's[1] opinion. Though it is a little disturbing that Winston seems to agree with Macmillan. It would not be fair to hold him to his promise to write a preface to the book when he feels like this. I shall just forget about it. Now I feel more deter-

---

[1] Desmond MacCarthy, literary and dramatic critic.

mined than ever to get it published. The next publisher to try is, I think, Constable. I have not yet decided how to approach them. The delay is the main bother. Don't worry about me. These things stir in me some primal fighting instinct, and I will not let them beat me. I am going straight on with my three articles for the *Sunday Times* when I have finished this letter.

'My dear Child, I sometimes long for a more peaceful way of life without all these setbacks, but I see clearly I was so made that these things will pursue me to the end. What I do most regret is that you with your very different temperament should have to share in these blows. I see that you and the boys and this book have become what I value in life, and that the rest is nothing. This book has become part of me, my apologia. It was a declaration that the little administrative, competitive life in which I have been caught up was not really me, but it was more, much more than this, for in a way it was inspired by the constant feeling (which never leaves me) of the loss in war of all these boys. I have scribbled this hastily that you may not sorrow about the effect of this news on me. The time is gone when anything can really get me down as long as John is all right.'

I decided to ask Winant's advice. Winant was a pilot in the first war; he has read *The Anatomy of Courage* in typescript twice, and understands what I am trying to say. The following conversation took place:

Moran: 'Macmillans have refused my book.'

Winant: 'Good God! Well, you'll have no difficulty in finding an American publisher.'

Moran: 'I wonder.'

Winant: 'You are bound to be down about it for the moment.'

Moran: 'I am not sure you understand. When I began to write about courage I soon found I was writing about fear. My book is all about how courage is spent; it is the story of man's failure to control his animal instincts. You see, Gil, I don't know enough Americans to hazard a generalization, but I have got it into my head that as a race you are not really interested in failure.'

Winant (nodding vigorously): 'That might be true.'

Moran: 'Whereas we English rather like a man who hasn't come off, anyway if he is staunch and uncomplaining in adversity. You see, it's a man's character that counts with us, not his achievements. Ask anyone who matters to put our soldiers in some order of merit and at once he begins talking about Wavell. But it was Wavell who said to me, "I have had a bad war."'

Winant: 'Yes, I agree. It's not failure you like, but the fact that some men grow in adversity. I think it is because you people are so interested in character and put it before anything else that you find failure not unattractive.'

Moran: 'There were times before the war when I have come home sick at heart with the ugly ways of the little competitive world and have said to myself: Is success after all pathological?'

Winant (smiling): 'Well, I guess my countrymen would not have much sympathy with that line of thought.'

Moran: 'Winston seems to me a hundred per cent American in his feelings about failure.'

Unless a man has done something in life, something really worth doing, he does not interest Winston. The fact that he has not come off and is a bit of a failure merely depresses him. It is what a man does, not what he is, that counts. I suppose the trouble is that Winston has no nose for character; he is not very good at spotting a wrong 'un. You will find him rigidly adhering to his own almost finicky standards of rectitude and at the same time quite oblivious that some of his friends have fallen short of his own standards. It is, Winant argued, what you would expect in a man of action.

*Malta, November 18, 1943*

It seems that, for security reasons, the authorities do not wish the P.M.'s presence on the Island to be known, so he was driven last night by a devious route to the Governor's Palace. Lord Gort has placed his own bedroom at the disposal of his guest; this room on the second floor overlooks a street which is a favourite promenade of the Maltese. The P.M. was resting when I paid him a visit. From the street below came a great hubbub of voices. His brow darkened. He threw his legs out of bed, and striding across the room thrust his familiar head through the open window, bawling:

'Go away, will you? Please go away and do not make so much noise.'

The P.M. is still mouldy; a cold in the head has dragged on; he will not take any precautions, but expects me, when summoned, to appear with a magic cure. Meanwhile he has relieved his feelings by drawing up an indictment of our operations in the East Mediterranean since the army landed in Italy.

I went for a walk with Martin this afternoon and he told me how the P.M. saw the Japanese Ambassador before Japan came into the war and had an important conversation with him. Now the Foreign Office prides itself on keeping exact records of conversations so he was asked about this particular interview. 'I remember what I said,' he answered, 'but I can't remember what the Ambassador said.' Put differently he was more interested in what he said than in what he heard. He is also losing opportunities of learning by his desire to instruct or at any rate to lay down some proposition. This is the secret of his inability to pick the right people. He isn't interested in them.

*Cairo, November 23, 1943*

I was asked yesterday to see Madame Chiang Kai-shek, who is living in a well-guarded villa near Mena House. I waited in a room on the ground floor, while they brought her doctor, a middle-aged Chinese, who seemed intelligent and apprehensive. I am not sure that his expectation of life was as good as that of his patient. At any rate, what I said to Madame might have a decisive influence on his future. 'You know the history of Madame?' I explained that I knew nothing about Madame. He gave it to me shortly and coherently. Madame had been to many doctors in America for diverse maladies. She got nettle-rash at times of mental stress; it first appeared after the death of a relative. It was this which was troubling her now. She was sensitive to many things, such as shell-fish. Every conceivable investigation seemed to have been done in America; some of them had led to active measures. Indeed, every form of treatment seemed at one time or another to have been confidently advised.

I suggested that Madame, who had been told that I had come, might wonder what plot we were concocting. Would it not be well to see her? Her doctor nervously agreed. I followed him upstairs to a room where I found Madame in bed. She is no longer young, but there is about her an air of distinction; there is still left a certain cadaverous charm. She speaks English, so that I soon discovered that she was very intelligent. She was always tired, as the nettle-rash interfered with her sleep. She wanted to get well quickly, so she was willing to try anything new which might be suggested. At that point the door opened and a man stood with his hand on the doorknob. Madame spoke to him in Chinese, and he advanced towards me. He was a formidable-looking ruffian, with a square jaw, carelessly shaven, dressed in a black robe like a monk. Madame explained that it was Chiang Kai-shek; he shook hands and withdrew. When I had finished my examination she fixed me with a searching look.

'Well, what is wrong?' she demanded.

'Nothing,' I answered.

'Nothing?' she repeated.

A slight smile played round her lips. She looked at me with more interest than she had so far shown.

'I shall soon get well, you think?'

'Madame, you will only get better when the strain of your life is relaxed.'

She scrutinized me intently.

'I have seen many doctors in the States; they have all told me stories saying that if I did something I should soon get well. You are about the first honest doctor I have seen.'

She rang a bell and said something to a Chinese servant, who reappeared in a few moments with a parcel, which Madame handed to me with a pleasant smile and suitable expressions of her gratitude. It contained an ivory tablet, exquisitely carved. I saw that the audience had come to an end.

*November 24, 1943*

Madame brought Chiang Kai-shek to dine with the P.M. She acted as interpreter; without her, things would have dragged. The P.M. is always attracted to a soldier who has done something in the field, but he is sceptical of China as a great power and grudges all the time that Roosevelt has given to her affairs. To the President, China means four hundred million people who are going to count in the world of tomorrow, but Winston thinks only of the colour of their skin; it is when he talks of India or China that you remember he is a Victorian.

*November 25, 1943*

Ran into Harry Hopkins, and found him full of sneers and jibes. He had just come from a meeting of the Combined Chiefs of Staff, who were framing a plan of campaign to put before Stalin at Teheran. According to Harry, Winston hardly stopped talking, and most of it was about 'his bloody Italian war.' Harry went on in his dry, aggressive way:

'Winston said he was a hundred per cent for OVERLORD. But it was very important to capture Rome, and then we ought to take Rhodes.'

Harry made it clear that if the P.M. takes this line at Teheran and tries again to postpone OVERLORD the Americans will support the Russians.

All Hopkins's views on strategy come, of course, from Marshall, but in changing hands they seem to go sour, as a microbe gains in virulence when it passes from one host to another. However, making allowance for the fact that Harry is a born partisan, I have noticed lately a certain hardening of purpose in the American camp. They left Quebec in great heart, assured that everything was settled for good. And here is the British Prime Minister at his old game again. There is an ominous sharpness in their speech when they say that they are not going to allow things to be messed about in this way indefinitely. 'Some of us,' Hopkins snarled, 'are beginning to wonder whether the invasion will ever come off.'

Harry thinks that the P.M. is trying to get out of his commitments. When I argued with him he got up impatiently: 'Sure, you're not going to tell me that Winston has cold feet.' That, in fact, is the explanation of all this havering. The P.M. has always dreaded an unsuccessful attempt to land in France; it might, he feels, turn the issue of the war. He left Quebec committed, but far from happy. And the long, anxious days that followed, while the fate of the landing at Salerno hung in the balance, only confirmed his forebodings. On the way here it became plain that he is brooding on the extraordinary difficulties of this 'prodigious undertaking.' He has grown more and more certain that an invasion of France as planned must fail.

It is in that mood that the P.M. has come to Cairo. Only a spark was needed to cause him to blow up. It has not been long in coming. The twenty-five per cent increase in landing craft, which was promised at Quebec to strengthen OVERLORD, is to be used instead in the Indian Ocean. Winston was flabbergasted. Throwing aside all tact and common prudence, he argued vehemently that OVERLORD must be postponed or reinforced. The British Prime Minister, according to Hopkins's words to me, was 'explosive and obstreperous'; and the President, torn between Winston's shrill protest and the forceful arguments of his advisers, sought peace in compromise. If the forces assigned for the invasion of France are not sufficient, he is in favour of more operations in the Mediterranean in order to weaken the Germans until the time comes when OVERLORD can safely be undertaken. The P.M. thinks this is a very wise provision. The President, he tells me, is the most skilful strategist of them all. 'Better than Marshall?' I queried. 'Yes, better than Marshall.'

The effect of the President's intervention on Marshall had been rather different. He can never be sure what will happen when Winston and the President get together. With the President wobbling, he and Admiral King fear that the Prime Minister may, after all, get his own way. Harry became quite fierce as he told me this story.

'Sure, we are preparing for a battle at Teheran. You will find us lining up with the Russians,' he threatened.

What I find so shocking is that to the Americans the P.M. is the villain of the piece; they are far more sceptical of him than they are of Stalin. Anyway, whoever is to blame, it is clear that we are going to Teheran without a common plan.

# CHAPTER SEVENTEEN

# How Stalin Found an Ally

*Teheran, November 28, 1943*

The P.M. loves to be on the move once more; the thrust and parry of these conferences are much to his liking; he feels he is getting on with the war. But as he flew over the dark, jagged crags which guard the approach to Teheran, his mind was full of misgivings. When we were losing height he looked up at me and said:

'I could not justify to the House of Commons the last two months in the Mediterranean. Ever since Salerno there have been divided counsels, and the campaign in Italy has been put in jeopardy by sending landing craft home. The Germans have been allowed to get their breath after Mussolini's collapse.'

Suddenly he said with great vehemence:

'Because the Americans want to invade France in six months' time, that is no reason why we should throw away these shining, gleaming opportunities in the Mediterranean.'

The P.M. cannot get Anthony's warning out of his head. He said that when the Foreign Ministers met at Moscow last month Stalin appeared so anxious for a Second Front that our people began to wonder if all was well with the Red Army. Stalin, Eden reported, could talk of nothing else.

Roosevelt cannot understand why both men take this question of a second front so much to heart. Harry tells me the President is convinced that even if he cannot convert Stalin into a good democrat, he will be able to come to a working agreement with him. After all, he had spent his life managing men, and Stalin at bottom could not be so very different from other people. Anyway, he has come to Teheran determined, if I can trust Hopkins, to come to terms with Stalin, and he is not going to allow anything to interfere with that purpose. The mathematics of this is two to one, and before the first day was spent Brooke said to me: 'This Conference is over when it has only just begun. Stalin has got the President in his pocket.'

Hopkins tells me that when Davies[1] saw Stalin in Moscow in May he found him full of distrust. If the President wanted to see him alone, without the British Prime Minister, it could only be part of a deep-laid scheme designed to thwart his plans. It appears that Davies has not been able to dispel Stalin's suspicions. It happens that the American Legation, where the President was to stay, is some distance from the British and Russian Embassies, which are cheek by jowl, so that he would have to pass through the streets every day to the meetings. After Molotov, Harry says, had spoken about the possibility of a plot to take the President's life, Stalin invited Roosevelt to move into a villa in the Russian Embassy compound for greater security; the President at once acknowledged the Marshal's kindly thought and moved this afternoon. He will be well looked after, for his servants are all members of the NKVD, the Soviet secret police.

The P.M., too, was touched by Stalin's solicitude, and, when someone professed to be sceptical of his motives, he spoke in anger of our unhelpful attitude. All the same, no one in our party, except Winston, believes in Stalin's concern for the President's safety. Plainly it is convenient to him to have the President under his eye, where he cannot spend his time plotting with the British Prime Minister.

When the President was safely ensconced in his new quarters, Stalin lost no time in calling on him. When I heard this, I expressed my misgivings to Harry. If Winston was not invited, would it not encourage Stalin to think that the Democracies were divided in their aims? At this, to my consternation, he blew up. 'What possible objection,' he demanded hotly, 'could there be to the President

---

[1] Joseph E. Davies, Roosevelt's special envoy to Moscow, 1943; former Ambassador to U.S.S.R.

meeting Stalin by himself for a heart-to-heart talk?' Things had gone well and Harry was full of it. There was absolutely nothing to hide. And then, as if he wanted to convince me that there was no guile behind this secret conclave, he poured out the whole story. The President, Hopkins said, made it clear that he was anxious to relieve the pressure on the Russian front by invading France. Stalin expressed his gratification, and when the President went on to say that he hoped Malaya, Burma and other British colonies would soon be 'educated in the arts of self-government' the talk became quite intimate. The President felt encouraged by Stalin's grasp of the democratic issue at stake, but he warned him not to discuss India with the Prime Minister. Stalin's slits of eyes do not miss much; he must have taken it all in.

As I listened to Harry, I felt that the President's attitude will encourage Stalin to take a stiff line in the conference. But Harry is not worried. Things are going fine, he said.

When I saw the P.M. after the first Plenary Session, which began at four o'clock, he seemed so dispirited that I departed from my prudent habit and asked him outright whether anything had gone wrong. He answered shortly: 'A bloody lot has gone wrong.' He did not wish to talk about it, and I soon left him.

The session began, according to Brooke, with a lot of blah-flum. As he quoted these exaggerated sentiments, buttering up the Russians, his face hardened until it became stern and uncompromising; in this mood his features recall those of the Iron Duke. I asked him what part Stalin had played in this exchange of compliments. I was told that he had sat silent and watchful. He is always thrifty of gush. Before long the session developed into a wrangle between the Prime Minister and Stalin. Stalin said that the campaign in Italy had been useful in opening up the Mediterranean to Allied shipping, but he could see no point in the British fighting their way up Italy, foot by foot. The capture of Rome did not matter to them. General Suvorov,[1] in his day, had barked his shins against the Alps.

---

[1] The Russian Field-Marshal who led the Russian armies in Italy (1799–1800) during the French Revolutionary Wars.

The P.M. said at once that they were all agreed that the invasion of France must come first, but we were short of landing craft and there might be delays. If there were it was 'to Russia's advantage that we should not remain idle.' He wanted to get Turkey into the war. Stalin interposed quietly that Turkey had no intention of coming in. He said this as if he knew. But the P.M. said he could not believe Turkey would be so mad as to stay out.

It was the 'mixture as before,' in Harry's mockery of doctors' jargon, and I cannot help noticing that every time he has to swallow the medicine he pulls a longer face. It appears that the Americans welcomed Stalin's suggestion that we ought to abandon the campaign in Italy. As far as I can make out, the President supported Stalin. At any rate, it is plain that Stalin was pleased.

He certainly gave as good as he got. When Germany was defeated, Stalin promised that Russia would join in the war against Japan. Hopkins told me that he made this important announcement in a casual way, and without raising his voice, so that it was only audible to the interpreter, Pavlov, sitting by his side. Then he went on doodling as if nothing had happened. 'I thought we were going to be late for dinner,' Harry continued, 'when the President suggested an adjournment.'

*November 29, 1943*

When I saw the P.M. this morning he was plainly put out. It seems that he had sent a note to the President suggesting they should lunch together, but the President's answer was a polite 'No.' 'It is not like him,' the P.M. murmured. He does not, Harry explained, want an impression to get abroad that he and Winston are putting their heads together in order to plan Stalin's discomfiture.

This, however, did not prevent the President seeing Stalin alone after lunch. Harry made little of the occasion. He told me with his broadest grin how the President asked Stalin 'whether he would like to discuss the future peace of the world.' There was nothing, Stalin answered, to prevent them from discussing anything they pleased. Roosevelt then poured out to Stalin his own idea of a new League of Nations. Stalin listened patiently, but when the conversation turned to the future of Germany he became animated.

About a quarter to four this *séance* broke up and Stalin and Roosevelt went together to the large conference room of the Russian Embassy. There the P.M., who twice repeated that he was acting for the King, presented to Stalin the Sword of Stalingrad. Stalin seemed to be moved by this simple act of friendship; he bent and kissed the sword. Roosevelt said that there were tears in his eyes as he took the sword. For the first time in my dealings with the U.S.S.R. the Russians have shown themselves human beings. This afternoon this hard-boiled Asiatic thawed and seemed to feel the emotions of ordinary people. For a moment it seemed that we were meeting as friends.

Stalin has discarded his workday clothes – the grey-brown cloth tunic buttoned to the chin and the trousers of the same material, tucked into knee-boots, which became him well in Moscow last year – and has blossomed out into a mustard-coloured uniform that looks as if it has not been worn before, and gives one the impression that it has been specially designed for the occasion. It looks, too, as if the tailor has put a shelf on each shoulder, and on it has dumped a lot of gold lace with white stars. And there is a broad red stripe down the trousers, which are immaculately creased. All this is crowned by a dreadful hat, smothered with gold braid. His old rig fitted his blunt contempt for appearances; it seemed to scoff at all the uniforms around him, with their five or six rows of meaningless decorations. Has Stalin to make up and play a role like other people? I wish I could follow how his mind works. Why, for instance, did he get into uniform?

When the ceremony was over the members of the Conference took their seats around the table and the second Plenary Session began – and from what Harry told me it began on the wrong foot: 'Who,' Stalin demanded, 'will command OVERLORD?' Roosevelt appeared to be taken aback; he had to tell Stalin this was still not settled. Whereupon Stalin said abruptly he would not believe we meant business until we had decided on the man to command the operation.

Then the P.M. said his piece, and this took some time. They all wanted to help Russia, he said, and they were of one mind about OVERLORD, but . . . With this preface he proceeded to traverse systematically the northern coast of the Mediterranean. Stalin never betrays impatience; he doodled and smoked cigarettes, which looked as if he had rolled them himself and stuffed them loose in his pocket.

(Harry notices these things; he tells a story like Max. Sometimes I fancy that like him he improves upon the original text.)

When Winston had done, Stalin came to the point at once.

'If we are here in order to discuss military matters, then Russia is only interested in OVERLORD.'

He demanded that a date be fixed and that we should keep to it. The President not only forgives Stalin his impatience, he shares his feelings. When the P.M. began once more to stress the strategic importance of Turkey and Rhodes no one was surprised when the President intervened.

'We are all agreed,' he said, 'that OVERLORD is the dominating operation, and that any operation which might delay OVERLORD cannot be considered by us.'

'Sure, there was no God-damn alternative left,' Hopkins snapped. This was final. I asked Harry how Winston had taken it. He grinned broadly. 'Stalin looked at Winston as much as to say: "Well, what about that?"'

Stalin, who does not bother about the graces of intercourse, was bent on rubbing it in. When Roosevelt had finished he turned on Mr Churchill and said he would like to ask him a simple question:

'Do the English believe in OVERLORD, or do they not?'

About eight o'clock Sawyers put his head into my room.

'Can you come at once, sir, to syringe the Prime Minister's throat? He is due to dine with Marshal Stalin in an hour's time.'

I followed him to the P.M.'s room in the Legation. Winston was pacing the room, mumbling to himself: 'Nothing more can be done here,' he muttered. But once before in exactly similar circumstances the fall of Tobruk came to his rescue. In a man of Winston's temperament, defeat is never final. If Turkey can be induced to enter the war it will be reasonable to propose delay in the date for OVERLORD. From what the P.M. said to me it seems that he is turning over the next step in his mind, and that he is now looking forward impatiently to his meeting with the Turkish President at Cairo.

'You are late, Sir,' Sawyers interposed.

'Bloody,' the P.M. ejaculated as he stumped out.

I went back to Holman's[1] house, where I was staying, and found that they were waiting for me to begin dinner. The three Chiefs of Staff were the guests. They are always the same, quiet and equable, but tonight they seemed put out. It has been a bad day for our people.

I can make nothing of Portal. He is a plain man. His head is unduly small and shaped like a sugar-loaf, with a bald circle at the summit; his great beaked nose is always in some book or paper. He has a quiet, serene way with him, and that is as far as you get. His aspect checks curiosity; it seems to say, 'All trespassers will be prosecuted.' He smokes a pipe most of the day and often, after dinner on our travels, a cigar. But he has not established a tolerance of nicotine. Once, in Canada, in the train, I was sitting opposite to him, when he turned quite green. He put down his cigar, rose and left the compartment. I could see him in the corridor standing by an open window. Presently he came back, picked up his book and relit his cigar. He is not a man to be defeated easily. Trenchard once told me that Portal is equally outstanding as a pilot and as a Staff Officer – and that is not common.

Portal: 'What would happen if we went off to Cairo, saying that no useful purpose is served by our being here, and that we had work to do in Cairo?' After a pause he added: 'I think it would be all right.'

First Sea Lord[2]: 'What a waste of time this is.'

Portal: 'It is the first time at a Conference I have felt I was completely wasting my time.'

---

[1] Adrian Holman, First Secretary British Embassy.
[2] Admiral Sir Andrew Cunningham.

The C.I.G.S. turned away and came across to me:

'I shall come to you to send me to a lunatic asylum. I cannot stand much more of this. Seven hours' conference today, and we are not an inch further.'

We sat down to dinner, and presently Holman, perhaps to get a better atmosphere, said:

'How will Germany break, at the top or the bottom? Let us vote on it.'

Portal: 'At the top.'

Cunningham: 'No, at the bottom.'

In turn they gave their views. Portal said at the end:

'The Doctor shall be the judge.'

There was no escape.

'Take Ludendorff,' I began. 'Was his action in saying Germany could not go on fighting the cause or the effect of her collapse? Did he take action because he knew that the home front had collapsed, or did he himself crumble under the strain? That is the question which has not been answered. I rule that the crack may appear at the top, but all the time it may be really the bottom that has collapsed.'

Chorus: 'Very clever, but what hedging!'

About midnight I went to the Legation to the P.M.'s room to see if he needed anything. I found Clark Kerr and Anthony Eden with him, glasses of whisky in their hands. The P.M. was talking in a tired, slow voice, with his eyes closed.

'There might be a more bloody war. I shall not be there. I shall be asleep. I want to sleep for billions of years. But you will be there.' He stopped. 'Charles hasn't a drink— When I consider the vast issues,' he went on, 'I realize how inadequate we are.'

'You mean a war with Russia?'

I do not think he heard. Then he appeared to make a great effort to cast off the black depression that had settled on him.

'Stalin said we ought to take Turkey by the scruff of the neck. I said: "I think we ought to say to them: You are missing the chance of a lifetime if you do not accept Russia's invitation to be one of the victorious powers at the peace conference. If you don't, Russia has several things to settle with you. And we shall take no further interest in Turkey. If Russia has views about the Straits, that will not affect us.'" The P.M. was silent for some time. 'But Russia has not worked out a role for Turkey if she does declare war. That is obvious.' Winston re-lit his cigar; then he went on: 'The President said to me: "You may go at the Election, but I shan't." I said, "Anthony will have to wait."

Anthony: 'I'm not discontented.'

P.M. (smiling affectionately): 'No, I know. I told Stalin we wanted nothing. We desired no new territory. Stalin didn't agree with me. He rather pressed the point. You see, it would make it easier for Russia if we took something. When I asked what Russia wanted, Stalin said: "When the time comes we will speak."'

Anthony: 'It will be a poor job at the Peace Conference.'

P.M.: 'I would give them the Italian Fleet.'

Clark Kerr: 'That would be a stupendous issue. Cunningham is against.'

Anthony: 'Admirals are a Trade Union.'

P.M.: 'We must be supreme in the air, not merely in numbers, but we must lead in everything. The figures will be Air 6, Navy 3, Army 1. After the war we must have the Swiss military system. If we are strong in the air, other countries, remembering this war, will hesitate to attack us. Moscow will be as near to us as Berlin is now. I don't believe in battleships after the war.'

The P.M., who had been pacing the room, slumped into a chair.

'Stalin was ready to talk about the frontiers of Poland, but I said I had no mandate from the Cabinet nor the President's agreement. So it was left. If present ideas go, there will be a stronger Poland than before the war.'

I asked the P.M. if the President had taken an active part in the conversation. He hesitated; then he answered:

'Harry Hopkins said the President was inept. He was asked a lot of questions and gave the wrong answers.'

When the P.M. said that Roosevelt went a green colour during the first course I wondered if he was well. The strain at the top must be prodigious. Stalin himself, though he comes of tough peasant stock, is thinner and greyer than when I first saw him two years ago.

When the others had gone I took the P.M.'s pulse. It was 100. I told him that it was due to all the stuff he drank and that he ought not to go on at this rate.

'It will soon fall,' he retorted cheerfully.

When we went to his room his mood changed. He could not rid himself of that glimpse of impending catastrophe. Blurred and ill-defined as it was, it stuck in his mind. He pulled up abruptly, so that he stood looking down at me, his eyes popping.

'I believe man might destroy man and wipe out civilization. Europe would be desolate and I may be held responsible.'

He turned away with a gesture of impatience:

'Why do I plague my mind with these things? I never used to worry about anything.'

His face became very grave.

'Stupendous issues are unfolding before our eyes, and we are only specks of dust, that have settled in the night on the map of the world. Do you think,' he demanded abruptly, 'my strength will last out the war? I fancy sometimes that I am nearly spent.'

He said no more as he got into bed. I hung about for a few minutes and then asked him whether he wanted his light put out. He did not answer. He was already asleep.

I lay awake for a long time, frightened by his presentiment of evil. I own that I fear the days that lie ahead. Until he came here, the P.M. could not bring himself to believe that, face to face with Stalin, the democracies would take different courses. Now he sees he cannot rely on the President's support. What matters more, he realizes that the Russians see this too. It would be useless to try to take a firm line with Stalin. He will be able to do as he pleases. Will he become a menace to the free world, another Hitler? The P.M. is appalled by his own impotence.

*November 30, 1943*

I expected to find Winston in poor fettle this morning, but he seems to have dismissed the night's happenings as if they were only a bad dream. His fears, I fancy, are too vague and intangible to be translated into action. I may be wrong. If he has thought out any plan for meeting the threat he would keep it to himself.

After we had breakfasted, Clark Kerr gave me his version of what happened at Stalin's dinner party last night. At first, while they discussed the treatment of Germany, Stalin was grim and serious. Winston was optimistic, magnanimous and tender-hearted; he did not fear that Germany would rise again as a menace to Europe. Stalin's precarious life has left him a realist, his lessons have not been learnt from books. And what he has seen of human nature has taught him not to expect too much of it. He did not believe the German people would turn over a new leaf; obedience was in their bones.

When they had disposed of Germany, Stalin threw off care; he was, the Ambassador said, in superb form, pulling the P.M.'s leg all the evening. I asked the Ambassador:

'Was Stalin's ragging a cat-like instinct to play with a mouse, or was he just in great spirits now that he had gained his end?'

He did not answer. The P.M. had not, he said, tumbled to Stalin's game. The Ambassador was full of Stalin's talk.

Stalin: 'Fifty thousand Germans must be killed. Their General Staff must go.'

P.M. (rising and pacing the room): 'I will not be a party to any butchery in cold blood. What happens in hot blood is another matter.'

Stalin: 'Fifty thousand must be shot.'

The P.M. got very red in the face.

P.M.: 'I would rather be taken out now and shot than so disgrace my country.'

The President, said the Ambassador, then joined in the fun.

Roosevelt: 'I have a compromise to propose. Not fifty thousand, but only forty-nine thousand should be shot.'

The Prime Minister got up and left the room. Stalin followed him, telling him he was only joking. They came back together, Stalin with a broad grin on his face.

Stalin: 'You are pro-German. The devil is a communist, and my friend God a conservative.'

P.M.: 'I'd like to go to your front' – Stalin received this with pleasure – 'I'm in my seventieth year.'

Stalin: 'You need not boast about that. I'm only four years younger.'

The P.M. admitted today that he was 'pretty nearly all-in.' I daresay Stalin is in no better shape. Now they could relax, and even let themselves go.

'The conversation ended in a convivial embrace. The P.M. and Stalin stood with their hands on each other's shoulders, looking into each other's eyes. The last thing I saw of them was Stalin with his arm round the P.M. I wish,' the Ambassador went on, 'we had a record of what was said, that people might know what piffle great men sometimes talk.'

I was about to question whether it was fair to sit in judgment on this man, with all his cares, when a marine broke in on the Ambassador's story. He came to tell us that Stalin had arrived. Afterwards the Ambassador told me what had happened. The President asked the P.M. to tell Stalin the verdict of the staff meeting. The P.M. proceeded to read these decisions, which he had opposed to the very last, as if they were his own chosen strategy. There was not a trace of bitterness in his voice. It is at such moments that you get a whiff of greatness from this strange creature. I asked Winston about Stalin. 'Oh, he was reasonably affable.' His eyes twinkled. 'He can be quite friendly when he gets what he wants.' The smile vanished. 'When we were alone Stalin told me that the Red Army was warweary.' 'Is that why he wants the invasion in May?' I asked. The P.M. nodded. The President, if Hopkins is right, does not seem to have a care in the world.

'Tell me, Harry, is the President quite certain about Moscow?'

'Why, sure,' answered Hopkins. 'The President knows now that Stalin is "get-atable" and that we are going to get along fine in the future.'

Harry kept repeating the word 'get-atable'.

During luncheon, which followed this interview, the P.M. made a gesture to Stalin which, in all the circumstances, was a patent of nobility. He spoke of Russia's need for warm-water ports; he said they ought to meet the need, and, speaking for his Government, he hoped to see Russian ships on all the seas. There you have the measure of the man in defeat.

All day Stalin has been as amiable as he can be, and it was in this mood that he came to the dinner party at the Legation, to celebrate Winston's sixty-ninth birthday. The atmosphere was genial; things seemed to go smoothly from the outset. It is true that there was one discordant note. The President made a speech proposing the health of Brooke. Just as he was ending his speech, Stalin rose and said he would finish the toast. Looking across the table at the C.I.G.S., Stalin said:

'General Brooke has not been very friendly to the Red Army and has been critical of us. Let him come to Moscow, and I'll show him that Russians aren't bad chaps. It will pay him to be friends.'

While Stalin was saying this the C.I.G.S. sat very quiet and grim. Like Cunningham, he does not pretend to like Stalin; he is indeed repelled by the man's bloody record. His reply was a little involved, but when translated by Pavlov it seemed to please Stalin. At any rate, when he sat down Stalin said: 'I like that man. He rings true.'

And when we left the table and the C.I.G.S. bearded Stalin in his downright way, Pavlov said:

'The Marshal says that the best friendships are those founded on misunderstandings.'

Whereupon they shook hands as if the incident was at an end.

After dinner, when the President and most of the guests had left, Stalin lingered. Those still present were standing and talking in little groups. Randolph went over to Stalin, who was almost boisterous. Winston, coming across, said:

'England is becoming a shade pinker.'

When this was translated to Stalin he immediately said:

'That is a sign of good health. I want,' said Stalin, 'to call Mr Churchill my friend.'

P.M.: 'Call me Winston. I call you Joe behind your back.'

'No,' said Stalin, 'I want to call you my friend. I'd like to be allowed to call you my good friend.'

P.M.: 'I drink to the Proletarian masses.'

Stalin: 'I drink to the Conservative Party.'

Two of Stalin's observations have stuck. 'Without America we should already have lost the war,' and 'In Russia it is dangerous to be a coward.'

When they were all gone I followed the P.M. to his room in case he was the worse for wear. Though five minutes previously, talking to Stalin, he had been all smiles, a storm was coming up. He was pacing up and down the bedroom with quick strides. He turned to me: 'Read that.' It was a telegram from Attlee.[1]

P.M.: 'The Government may go out over Mosley.[2] Bevin is kicking.'

There followed a great diatribe over Labour's folly and stupidity. Much about Habeas Corpus.

'Where is Eden?' he said with great impatience. 'I want Eden.'

I had seen him talking in the banqueting room, so Kinnear[3] was sent to tell him that the P.M. wanted to see him. He delayed coming upstairs for a few minutes.

'Where is Mr Eden?' the P.M. shouted. 'Tell him I want to see him at once on most urgent business, and less talking there,' he said sharply to a little group at the end of the stairs. I am beginning to be worried about the P.M. He has been profligate of his resources on this trip. I don't know where this will end.

## December 1, 1943

Up to now whenever the P.M. has opened up on politics, I've dried up partly because I feel he has already so much on his plate I ought not to add to it unless some useful purpose is served, and partly because my instinct warns me that if I'm to see this job through, the fewer arguments we have the better. But at last the guard I've kept on my tongue slipped. I felt his arbitrary moods would do him

---

[1] Clement Attlee, Deputy Prime Minister.
[2] Sir Oswald Mosley was arrested after the suspension of Habeas Corpus at the beginning of the war. He was released on the orders of Herbert Morrison, the Home Secretary, in November 1943, following medical reports which showed a serious deterioration of his health. There was considerable opposition to this in the Commons, but Morrison, backed by Churchill, stood by his decision on grounds of humanity.
[3] A sergeant on Churchill's staff.

harm, that in certain matters he was dangerously out of touch with the people. I hate to see him undermining the hold he has on the country.

I said I usually stuck to my last and confined any views I brought to him to medical matters but would he listen to me for a few moments while I put a point of view to him. I said I thought a mistake had been made. It was a logical step to release all political prisoners who had not had a trial. After all it was the rights of the individual against those of the state that we were fighting for. But to release Mosley alone was a different matter . . . I said he had not the right to resign whenever he wished as in peace time. He denied this hotly. 'I shall resign when I like' . . . I said he could not govern England without Labour. It would impair unity and inter-fere with production. At this he shouted he could get on quite well without them. He would not get rid of them but they could go if they wanted. If the public held such views he'd no use for them. He had never paid much attention to public opinion. If he had in the last twelve years he would not now be in a position to help as he was. Public opinion was stupid, but he would say nothing against the people who were sound and would come to no such conclu-sions! I was a fascist . . . I explained I had never met anyone to whom I was less attracted than Mosley. 'That's it, you want to imprison someone you don't like'. If he, the P.M., were at home this wouldn't have happened. He would make one of the best speeches of his parliamentary career on this theme. Several times I made to withdraw but he called me back to shout some new contradiction. I left him with a strong sense of the corrosion of absolute power. He doesn't want to hear views contrary to his own. I felt very sad. I want to get back to my own job, but I must not hand in. I must see this job through.

I looked at my watch. It was twelve-thirty. I went to my room.

### December 2, 1943

As the Skymaster took us through the clouds towards Cairo, Clark Kerr remained absorbed in David Cecil's *Hardy the Novelist*. The P.M. seemed too weary even to read. He sat with his head in his hands; his cigar had gone out; he was not asleep; he appeared to be lost in thought.

*Cairo, December, 1943*

When we got here on our return from Teheran I knew that we were in for trouble. Winston seems to be sickening for some malady. His exhaustion is very disturbing. But he keeps insisting that he must go to Italy without delay to see Alex. I can't make out why he is so stubborn. This morning I decided that I must not beat about the bush any longer. I told him that it was madness to set off on a journey when he was under the weather like this. At that he lost his temper. 'You don't understand. You know nothing about these things. I am not going to see Alex for fun. He may be our last hope. We've got to do something with these bloody Russians.'[1]

---

[1] This meant nothing to me at the time. I put it down to his 'cussedness,' but I wonder now whether it was the first indication that Winston had arrived at the conclusion that if he wanted to help the countries of Eastern Europe he must get there before the Red Army. He looked to Alex to help.

# CHAPTER EIGHTEEN

# Touch and Go

*Casey Villa, Cairo, December 5, 1943*

There has been a final attempt to bring Turkey into the war. Yesterday Collins, the P.M.'s pilot, went to Adana to ferry President Inönü to Cairo for a conference. It is only a month since Eden met Numan Menemençioglu, the Turkish Foreign Minister, at Cairo, and nothing came of their talk. Further, the Americans are not going to help. Their Chiefs of Staff believe – and they have converted the President – that the re-armament of Turkey will mean postponing the date of the invasion of France; indeed, they make no secret of their aim to hinder any move to persuade Turkey to enter the war.

The P.M., however, is full of hope. He has persuaded himself that he can bring Turkey into the war and keeps turning over in his mind the consequences, just as if it had already happened. He does not stop to ask what the Turks themselves are thinking.

Tonight Casey[1] gave a dinner to President Inönü and his Foreign Minister before they return to Ankara. I sat opposite the Turkish President. If a man's thoughts are ever truly reflected by the expression of his features, here was a soul in torment. His face wore a distracted look; then someone would address him and he would force an agreeable smile, only to relapse once more into his own sombre thoughts. He knew he was being pressed to bring his

---

[1] R. G. Casey, Minister of State resident in the Middle East, and a member of the War Cabinet.

country into the war, and he was alive to the possible consequences if she stayed out. He was even more conscious of the certain consequences if she came in. His intelligent face mirrored his pitiful predicament.

Speaking in French, he said that when he commanded an army, before he took to politics, every soldier in Turkey was his son, but he had had to make decisions which cost thousands of their lives. He was not frightened of possible bombardment. Once it was decided that war was the best thing for his country, he would not hesitate. And his record before the war should satisfy us that this is no idle boast. Inönü went on to tell us – if only the P.M. would listen – in plain terms what would influence him when he had to decide between war and peace.

'It is for these Ambassadors, with their knowledge of Turkey, to tell us whether we can argue with truth that it will be to her advantage to enter the war.'

Inönü had made it clear at Adana that it is Russia and not Germany that the Turks fear. They fear that if the Russians come to their assistance they will remain; once the Kremlin has her troops in command of the Straits, only force will displace them.

Eden turned to me. 'What do you make of this?'

And when I replied, 'The President, I think, means what he says,' he said shortly, 'If they don't come in I have no interest in them, and I shall not lift a finger if the Straits are threatened by Russia.'

*

The P.M. believes that it is difficult to exaggerate the benefits to the Allies if Turkey comes into the war: he knows that this alone can delay a second front in France. He feels that it is now or never. He is very tired, but he will not accept defeat. He is resolved to make one last effort to persuade the Turks. He will see President Inönü alone; surely they cannot let such an opportunity pass. They came at his bidding and listened in silence as, forgetful of time, he proceeded to admonish them on Turkey's future, speaking in eloquent terms of her glorious hour of destiny.

The P.M. appears almost as distracted as Inönü himself. He has become very irritable and impatient; at times he seems almost played out. I went to his bedroom tonight and found him sitting with his head in his hands.

'I have never felt like this before,' he said. 'Can't you give me something so that I won't feel so exhausted?'

Nevertheless, he still talks of going to Italy when he leaves here. At this time of the year the climate there is vile, and Alex's tent is no proper resting-place for a man who is tired out. I feel so certain that he will get harm if we go to Italy when he is like this that I've written to Smuts in the strongest terms. He is the only man who has any influence with the P.M.; indeed, he is the only ally I have in pressing counsels of common sense on the P.M. Smuts sees so clearly that Winston is irreplaceable that he may make an effort to persuade him to be sensible. But I doubt whether even Smuts can alter his plans.

Whatever the strain, it is still broken by convivial nights, when for a few hours the P.M. seems to recover his old good spirits as if there has been a new gush of vitality pumped into his veins. Last night at the Embassy we sat at the dinner table from 8 p.m. till 11.50 p.m. Mountbatten's[1] eyes closed and opened spasmodically. I looked down the long table at the faces of the soldiers and sailors. They seemed only half awake. I was sorry for Winston: surely someone ought to show some interest in the drawn-out monologue. On the spur of the moment I blurted out: 'Do you remember Landor's lovely lines?' Winston glared at me. He hates being interrupted. 'What are they?' he snorted. I wanted to get under the table. 'What are they?' Winston shouted with growing impatience. I could think of no way of escape.

'"There are no fields of amaranth on this side of the grave; there are no voices, O Rhodopé, that are not soon mute, however tuneful; there is no name, with whatever emphasis of passionate love repeated, of which the echo is not faint at last."'[2]

I scampered over the lovely vowel sounds.

---

[1] Supreme Allied Commander, South East Asia.
[2] Walter Savage Landor, *Imaginary Conversations*, Vol. I, p. 17.

Winston (*with great contempt*): 'I call that pure defeatist stuff.'
I would not give in. I tried Milton:
'"While the still morn went out with sandals grey."'[1]
'He was on the wrong side in the Civil War,' Winston growled.
I gave it up.

After leaving the table we spent another hour and a half in the drawing-room. The servants talked in whispers. No one kept quite awake. At last, in a lull in the conversation, the P.M. was heard to make the same remark he had made three hours before. We were where we began.

\*

*December 10, 1943*
Better news this morning. Italy, thank God, is off, at any rate for the present. Tonight we go by air to Tunis and then on by car to Carthage, to stay with General Eisenhower. I have never before been so blunt with the P.M., rating him for his folly, but I take no credit for the change in plans. He knows without my help that he is at the end of his tether. Teheran seems to have got him down. It is plain that he is riding for a fall.

*Eisenhower's Villa, December 11, 1943*
Our luck is out. Soon after daybreak we came down near Tunis. A cold wind blew across the deserted aerodrome, there was no one about, no car, nothing. The P.M. got wearily out of the hot aircraft, looked around blankly and then, in spite of our protests, he sat down on a box, took off his hat and gloomily surveyed the sandy ground. The wind blew a wisp of hair this way and that, his face shone with perspiration. I pressed him to get back into the Skymaster; he only scowled. I went off to find out what had gone wrong, and learned that the airfield where we were expected was fifteen miles from this spot. There was nothing for it but to re-embark. As the P.M. walked very slowly to the aircraft there was a grey look on his face that I did not like, and when he came at last

---

[1] *Lycidas.*

to this house he collapsed wearily into the first chair. All day he has done nothing; he does not seem to have the energy even to read the usual telegrams. I feel much disturbed.

I went to bed early and woke to find the P.M. in his dressing-gown standing at the foot of my bed.

'I've got a pain in my throat, here.'

He put his finger just above his collar bone. I rubbed my eyes and got up.

'It's pretty bad. Do you think it's anything? What can it be due to?' he demanded in one breath.

I reassured him, and indeed I am not unduly perturbed. For a man with his strong constitution he never seems to be long without some minor ailment. Probably in the morning I shall hear no more of this pain.

*December 12, 1943*

I went, on waking, to the P.M.'s room. The pain had gone, he complained of nothing, but his skin was hot, and on taking his temperature I found it was 101. I could find no signs on examining his chest. We have had alarms like this before that have come to nothing, and in his position you cannot prepare for an illness without letting it be known everywhere. On the other hand, if he is going to be ill we have nothing here in this God-forsaken spot – no nurses, no milk, not even a chemist. He is, too, in poor shape to face an infection. In Cairo he had a severe bout of diarrhoea following a troublesome cold in the head. And he is, after all, in his seventieth year. It is up to me to make a decision; there is no one here whose opinion in a matter of this kind is worth having. I telegraphed to Cairo to send two nurses and a pathologist. Immediately Martin wanted to know how much we ought to tell Mrs Churchill and the Cabinet.

'Tell the Cabinet the truth,' I said.

With that he left me. Of course, if this all turns out to be nothing, and the temperature in the morning is normal, the P.M.'s faith in my good sense will be shaken, particularly when he finds the Cabinet in a flap and the Press busy. Tonight his temperature is still up. There is no bell in his room, so I left Inspector Thomson sitting outside his door when I turned in about one o'clock. He knocked at my door an hour later and said the P.M. wanted me. I found him restless and concerned about himself. He felt poorly and his pulse was shabby. Once I put the light out, thinking he was asleep, but he said:

'Don't go away, Charles. Is my pulse all right?'

*December 13, 1943*

At eleven o'clock this morning the P.M.'s temperature was only 99. He felt better; indeed, he was quite perky. He always goes entirely by the thermometer, and now he had made up his mind it was all over. At that moment Sawyers came into the room and blurted out that Dr. Pulvertaft and the nurses had arrived.

'Now, Charles,' the P.M. expostulated, 'what have you been up to? I'm not ill, and anyway what's wrong with me?'

I had no ready-made diagnosis to offer him. All I could say was:

'I'll tell you that later in the day when I know the answer.'

Pulvertaft, the pathologist, did a blood count. It was normal; there was no leucocytosis. But the P.M. did not blow up as I expected, he became interested in the enumeration of the white cells in the blood. He listened to the tale of how these cells are mobilized in an infection to fight the invading organisms, of the battle that takes place between them and the microbes, how the cells which die in the conflict are called pus cells.

'If I pricked your finger,' he said to the pathologist, 'how many white cells should I find when I examined the drop of blood under the microscope?'

'Oh, between six and ten thousand per cubic millimetre.'

'And how many have I?'

'Nine thousand nine hundred,' Pulvertaft replied, entering into the spirit of the occasion.

'Well, then,' the P.M. said, 'I'm quite normal.'

The P.M. made no objection to the arrival of a man from Tunis with a portable X-ray apparatus. But, when there was a little delay in getting the instrument to work, he grew fretful and a little petulant.

'Oh, now, damn it, come along, get this business done,' he said to the operator. 'When will you get the result?' he demanded.

'Now, sir, in half an hour.'

'Good,' he grunted.

Sawyers came in presently. The operator, he said, had developed the plates and wanted to show them to me.

'Oh, bring them in,' interrupted the P.M., 'I want to know all about this.'

I took the films from the operator and held them to the light. There was a considerable opaque area at the base of the left lung. I showed them to him.

'Well, what does that signify?' the P.M. asked.

'You've got a small patch of congestion.'

'Do you mean I've got pneumonia again?' he demanded impatiently.

At least I know where I am now. It is something to know the diagnosis within twenty-four hours of the first rise in the temperature. It means we can begin giving him M. & B.[1] straight away.

*December 14, 1943*

The temperature, pulse and respiration are all rising, the blood count is up, and there are now signs of pneumonia at the base of the left lung. Martin has sent a cable to Attlee that a signed bulletin will be telegraphed to him.

'Meanwhile, in Lord Moran's opinion, it is undesirable to delay any longer some intimation of the position to the public; he suggests something to the following effect: "The Prime Minister, who is on his way back to London from the Middle East, has contracted pneumonia and is confined to bed. A further bulletin will be issued tomorrow."'

[1] An antibiotic sulphonamide made by May & Baker.

Harold Macmillan[1] is inclined to fuss. As the only Cabinet Minister here, he claims that all decisions ought to be submitted to him. But this is a medical matter; and any decisions that have to be made are going to be made by me and no one else. Bedford[2] has just arrived from Cairo. The diagnosis has already been made and he has not suggested any change in the treatment, but his presence will keep the people at home quiet.

At six o'clock this evening the nurse came to me – would I come at once to the Prime Minister?

'I don't feel well,' he said to me. 'My heart is doing something funny – it feels to be bumping all over the place.'

He was very breathless and anxious-looking. I felt his pulse: it was racing and very irregular. The bases of his lungs were congested and the edge of his liver could be felt below the ribs. I had taken the precaution this morning to send to Tunis for digitalis, and now I gave it to him. As I sat by his bedside listening to his quick breathing, I knew that we were at last right up against things. It was four hours before the heart resumed its normal rhythm, and I was relieved to count a regular pulse of 120. A man feels pretty rotten, I imagine, when he fibrillates during pneumonia, but the P.M. was very good about it. I told him it was a temporary change of the rhythm of the heart which occurred in pneumonia; that it might become regular again at any moment. Once he asked me:

'Can't you do anything to stop this?'

But when I told him that digitalis was a specific for this condition, like quinine for malaria, and that when he was under its influence the fibrillation would probably stop, he seemed comforted. Later, when it suddenly vanished, he remembered my words that this would happen. In medical matters he always remembers exactly what I say. If it is borne out by events all is well; my stock rises. If it isn't, well, I fancy I should soon cease to be his doctor. I am often

[1] Mr Harold Macmillan, the Minister resident at Allied Headquarters, North-West Africa.
[2] Dr D. E. Bedford, Consultant for Heart Diseases, Middlesex Hospital.

astonished by the way he will reproduce verbatim something I have said months earlier.

It was half-past ten, and now that he was comfortable and drowsy, I decided to get something to eat while the going was good – it was nine and a half hours since we lunched.

## December 15, 1943

No signs of improvement yet. There are plenty of people about, but they do not add to my troubles by asking useless questions. No one greets me with, 'How is the P.M. this morning?' or 'I hope you are pleased with things.' They have learnt in these war years – probably most of them acquired the habit long ago in their self-disciplined lives – not to be curious about things which they don't know, and to bridle their tongues when they do know. At home things are different. Some of the Cabinet have been getting agitated – they seem to be in a complete dither. They have persuaded themselves that the Prime Minister is not going to come through this attack, and have been sending telegrams to Martin, urging me to agree that they should send out from England any specialists I care to name. They want to feel, bless their hearts, that they are doing something.

I went out alone, wandering among the rubble, which is all that is left of Carthage. Was all that could be done being done? I could not see that anyone, even a Prime Minister, could be properly treated by a committee. I hardened my heart and went my way. I told Martin to thank them and to say that it was not necessary to send out any doctors. I could see he did not think that I was wise. And of course if I arrive back in England without my patient they will remember this against me. I shall be another Morell Mackenzie.[1] Even now, after sixty years, the way he mishandled the illness of the Crown Prince Frederick makes a best-seller in which his infirmities, moral and intellectual, are all carefully set forth. And

[1] Sir Morell Mackenzie (1837–92), specialist in throat diseases. In 1887 he was summoned to attend Crown Prince Frederick William of Germany. The Crown Prince, who became Emperor Frederick William III in the same year, died of cancer in 1888. Mackenzie had ruled out this diagnosis when he was called in.

if there was all this fuss because a foreign Prince did not get well, what will they say if Winston slips through our hands before his job is finished? Well, if I'm going to be shot at if things go wrong, I am going to use my own judgment to prevent them going wrong.

It was left to me to compose a bulletin, which I gave to Martin when Bedford and Pulvertaft had signed it.

'The Prime Minister has been in bed for some days with a cold. A patch of pneumonia has now developed in the left lung. His general condition is as satisfactory as can be expected.'

Mrs Churchill arrived by air today. The P.M. received the news of her arrival with considerable emotion, but when I told her later how pleased he had been, she smiled whimsically.

'Oh, yes,' she said, 'he's very glad I've come, but in five minutes he'll forget I'm here.'

*December 16, 1943*

I think we have turned the corner. The temperature is still 101, but the signs in the chest are clearing up. Though this is the fifth day, Martin told me this morning that the public still do not know the P.M. is ill. Mr Attlee will tell the House at the end of Questions, and the news will be broadcast at one o'clock, just when we are no longer anxious about him.

We gave Martin another bulletin, which will appear in tomorrow's papers:

'The Prime Minister has had a good night. There is some improvement in his general condition.'

Scadding[1] arrives tonight. To placate the Cabinet, I had asked the people at Cairo to send him.

---

[1] Professor John Scadding, Physician for chest diseases at the Brompton Hospital.

*December 17, 1943*

The temperature is settling, and I have stopped the M. & B. We were able to give a more cheerful bulletin:

> 'There has been no spread of the pneumonia, and the improvement in the Prime Minister's general condition has been maintained.'

The P.M. fibrillated for an hour and a half this afternoon, but it did not distress him as it did the first time.

*December 18, 1943*

After six days' fever the temperature is normal, but when I suggested to the P.M. that there was no longer any necessity for a daily blood-count he demurred; he had been fascinated by the battle between the white cells and the pneumococci, and has insisted every day that he be told not only the total number of white cells but the percentage of the various kinds. And now he is determined to follow the demobilization of the forces which came to his rescue when he was so hard pressed.

So far the heart has not been mentioned in the bulletins, but it seems safe now to make a reference to the gravity of the illness. The public ought to know that it will be a little time before he can get between the shafts again:

> 'There has been some irregularity of the pulse, but the temperature is subsiding and the pneumonia resolving.'

*December 19, 1943*

'The Prime Minister's temperature is normal, and the signs of pneumonia are disappearing.'

*December 20, 1943*

'The temperature remains normal and the Prime Minister is making satisfactory progress.'

Now that the P.M. is beginning to be convalescent he is very difficult – on two occasions he got quite out of hand. He is tiring himself with his ebullitions. It is time he took a pull at himself. He has been savaging Bedford and Scadding, who know their job and have been helpful. Perhaps they made rather a song about the necessity for taking things very slowly. They kept saying that he had fibrillated and that this was his second attack of pneumonia in one year, and that he was nearly seventy. They want to lay down that he should not attempt to leave his bed for another fortnight. I said that if they specified an exact time he would immediately demand their reasons. It was better, I argued, to gain time and to fight a rearguard action from day to day. While it mattered I have gone my own way, and have made my own decisions, so I was particularly anxious to meet them in anything which was of less consequence. At last, against my better judgment, I agreed that they should put their point to the P.M. But when Bedford, speaking impressively, advised him to rest for a fortnight, Winston suddenly became red in the face with rage.

'Why,' he growled, 'a fortnight?'

They replied vaguely that he might get a relapse.

'Have you,' he said angrily, 'in the course of your long experience ever seen a patient get a second attack of pneumonia through getting about too early?'

Rather cowed by his violence, they admitted that they had not.

'If, Prime Minister,' they went on, 'you get up too early, you may fibrillate again.'

Once more he demanded if this warning was based on their personal experience and once again they owned that it was not. I was upset by Winston's rough handling of my colleagues, and when he turned on me with some asperity, without any warning my patience gave out. Perhaps I was a bit short of sleep. Anyway, I told him that he must not shout at me; that he was behaving foolishly. I left him before I said more.

*December 21, 1943*
'The Prime Minister continues to improve. The condition of the circulation is more satisfactory. The P.M. sat by his bed for an hour today.'

*December 22, 1943*

The P.M. said to me yesterday:

'Your arrangements at home must be in a mess. It looks as if this trip will keep us nearer two months out of England than the three weeks I planned.'

I answered without thinking, that the only thing that worried me at all was that I should miss John's[1] leave.

When I went to his room this morning he looked up from his book with a friendly smile.

'Charles, I don't want you to miss your boy's leave because of all this. I will arrange with the Admiralty for John to come out here by air for a few days. He could come with the courier.'

I am thrilled, but I am perturbed. I do not know the exact date of John's leave, and I am sure he ought to wait till he gets it in the ordinary way. I am worried that the Admiralty may take some action to please the P.M. I don't want anything done which will lead his mates on the lower deck to feel he is being pampered or favoured.

*Christmas Morning, 1943*

To Early Service with Mrs Churchill. It was held in a barn with a few officers and men of the Coldstream Guards as communicants. During the service a dove flew in and perched on a rafter. The men said it meant that there would soon be peace.

An officer asked me, a little wistfully, how long the war would last. They are out of it all for a week or two guarding the Prime Minister, but they must know that when they go back the odds are against them; that it is just a matter of time. These highly civilized young men, who are so meticulous in the discharge of their duty, feel the utter beastliness of war, though they never speak of it. They have been brought up by their fathers to think that there is no sense in war, that it brings the solution of nothing.

[1] My elder son John was at this time an ordinary seaman in H.M.S. *Belfast* with the 10th Cruiser Squadron in the Arctic.

*December 27, 1943*

We flew to Marrakesh this morning. I wondered a little if the P.M. would find himself short of breath in the air after his illness, but the pilot assured me we need not go higher than five thousand feet. I waited for Winston in the hall. When he appeared he was beaming. He called out to me:

'The *Scharnhorst* has been sunk by the *Duke of York* and three cruisers. One of them was hit.'

He wasn't sure which. It might have been the *Norfolk*. No, he couldn't be certain that it was not the *Sheffield* or the *Belfast*. I knew John was in the *Belfast*. Dorothy might hear it on the wireless.

'You are quiet, Charles. Why, we're beginning our holiday with good news.'

He had got back into his uniform and had a feeling that he was leaving behind him the bad luck which had dogged his steps since leaving England. But he is still feeble, and when he stepped out of the house and found a guard of the Coldstream standing to attention it was only very slowly and rather hesitatingly that he passed along the ranks. I was relieved when they helped him into his car. When we had been some time in the air the P.M. said to me:

'I don't like flying through these clouds, they may contain mountains.'

I looked out, but could see nothing but a white mist scudding past me. Presently he sent for the pilot and asked him what was the highest mountain anywhere near our course, and told him to fly two thousand feet above that level. I knew there was nothing for it but to await developments. However, none came, and when I saw that the P.M. was quite happy playing with his oxygen apparatus I fell asleep in my chair.

*

*Marrakesh*

The P.M. is gaining strength every day and seems well content with life here. Clemmie invited Max to come to Marrakesh to amuse him. She used to dread his influence on Winston, but when Winston became Prime Minister she resolved to bury the past. It was a wise choice for a difficult task.

Every day we picnic in the valleys at the foot of the Atlas Mountains. About noon cars appear, Winston leads with Max, and we tear after him over the red plain in clouds of red dust. I call it a picnic, but it is simply luncheon out of doors. Deck-chairs and hampers are piled on top of the cars, and the fare is adequate even for Winston's demands. Half a dozen Arab children gather round like sparrows waiting for crumbs, and when we are done, they greedily accept in their lean brown fingers what is left. But they do not eat it themselves, they put it in the hoods or pouches of their shapeless garments. Then, after luncheon, Winston, wearing an immense sombrero, slumps in a deck-chair and decides with Max that the Marconi case[1] was a squalid business. They go over once again how F.E.[2] and Carson[3] rescued Lloyd George, or Winston gets absorbed in *Emma*; so that when the sun has gone and the evening air chills, he becomes quite petulant when we press that it is time to go home.

One day we climbed into the mountains by a road which binds the side of a precipice like a rope. Duff Cooper,[4] who has no head for heights, became so uncomfortable that at last he got out and walked. Presently we came to our destination by a deep gorge, at the bottom of which there was a mountain stream. The P.M. insisted on descending this by a steep and rocky path. But when he came to the bottom he had no heart left for the climb back. At last, led by Diana,[5] we took the white tablecloth, folded it like a

---

[1] A complicated politico-financial imbroglio in 1912–13. It involved allegations, partly substantiated, of speculation in Marconi Company shares by some members of Asquith's Government, at a time when a government contract with the Company was under consideration. Churchill was completely cleared of any personal complicity.

[2] F. E. Smith, 1st Lord Birkenhead.

[3] Sir Edward Carson, later Attorney-General.

[4] Duff Cooper, British Representative with the French Committee of National Liberation.

[5] Lady Diana Cooper.

rope and put it round his middle. John[1] taking one end and the detective the other, they tugged him up while two of us pushed from behind, and a third carried his cigar.

Another day I left the house to walk in the garden and found Max and Monty sitting in the sun. Max called me to join them. He was in a mischievous mood. He took Monty up into an exceeding high mountain and showed him all the kingdoms of the world and the glory of them. And the rarefied air that he breathed on the mountain-top so suited Monty that he found nothing inherently improbably in all that Lord Beaverbrook said to him.

'Of all the soldiers, sailors and airmen in this war, you,' Max said, addressing Monty, 'are the only one the public knows.'

Monty faintly demurred.

'Oh, yaas, I tell you, it is so,' Max went on. 'The only one. There's nobody else who counts. After the war you can have a great political future if you like. You will appeal to all parties. You have no political past, only the glory of your victories, which has taken your name into every cottage.'

Monty sipped the heady wine. He made a few rather feeble, deprecating interjections.

'Isn't it so, Charles?' Max appealed to me.

I did not quite rise to the occasion, murmuring something about Cromwell. The introduction of Cromwell seemed to have a damping effect. The conversation languished.

As the P.M. grows in strength, his old appetite for the war comes back. The C.I.G.S. is in England, but the P.M. has a bright idea. He is organizing an operation all on his own. He has decided that it should be a landing behind the lines at Anzio. If the Chiefs of Staff are not available, there are plenty of lesser fry to work out the details. Hollis[2] is here to guarantee that they have been properly thought out, and there is Pug; he murmurs that it is the most important operation in which he has been concerned. Alex, too, is sympathetic. He sees that the Italian campaign may receive a great

---

[1] John, my elder son, was on leave after the *Scharnhorst* battle.
[2] General Sir Leslie Hollis, assistant to General Ismay.

fillip. Why, it may even shorten the whole war. The P.M. has become absorbed in his plans; twice the picnics have had to be sacrificed to stern duty. Councils of war have been held in Mrs Moses Taylor's pleasant villa. Hitler, I said to the P.M., seems not only to direct the policy of war, he even plans the details. 'Yes,' the P.M. answered with a smile, 'that's just what I do.'

# PART THREE

# Under the Shadow of Stalin

# CHAPTER NINETEEN

# Alex

*Seven months have gone by since the last entry in my diary. The Allies invaded France on June 6, 1944, and the Russians have advanced into Poland and the Baltic states.*

*August 4, 1944*
This morning, when I went to the P.M.'s bedroom, he did not bother to hide his cares. The fact is that he is no longer in good heart about the general situation, though he can still put up a bold show to the world. I tried to comfort him: I said that victory was following victory – the Third Army had crossed the Seine – and that some of the Americans were talking already as if the war were over. He merely grunted, as if I did not understand. In truth he is less certain of things now than he was in 1940, when the world was tumbling around his ears. It would have been wiser if I had kept my peace. He burst out:

'Good God, can't you see that the Russians are spreading across Europe like a tide; they have invaded Poland, and there is nothing to prevent them marching into Turkey and Greece!'

And then he made an impatient gesture: it was as if he said, What is the use of talking like this? How could I tell him where it would all end?

The American landings in the south of France[1] are the last straw.

---

[1] Operation 'Dragoon' was launched on August 15, 1944, when American troops landed near Toulon.

He can see 'no earthly purpose' in them: 'Sheer folly,' he calls them. He had fought tooth and nail, he said, to prevent them. If only those ten divisions could have been landed in the Balkans . . . but the Americans would not listen to him: it was all settled, they said.

The Prime Minister is distraught, but you cannot get him down for long. He has got it into his head that Alex might be able to solve this problem by breaking into the Balkans. Our troops are already in the outskirts of Florence. They would soon be in the valley of the Po. As he said this, his speech quickened, he sat upright in bed. He seemed to forget all about me. Perhaps, after all, the position was not as desperate as it seemed. He must see Alex without any delay. So we're off to Italy next week.

I dread the way he's banking everything on Alex. For four years Winston has kept his own counsel, sharing his secret thoughts with no man. The President seems to need a Harry Hopkins, someone in whom he can confide; the P.M., as far as I can tell, has never felt like that. In England, at any rate, there is no one to whom he opens his heart. Brooke is too cold and critical; he always seems to be doubtful of the P.M.'s facts and often throws cold water on his pet projects. There is Monty, of course; Winston admires him as a professional soldier, but he is put off by his boastfulness. Besides, Monty wants to be a king in his own right. But now something must be done, and Winston has a feeling at long last that he must unburden his soul to someone. Of course, he did not say as much, but when he mentioned Alex, he did murmur: 'Two heads are better than one at a time like this.' It is not at all like him, and, for the first time since he became Prime Minister, I believe that he feels a sense of isolation.

*August 6, 1944*
Now that we are going to Italy in August, there is the question of malaria. I had a presentiment that the battle for mepacrine[1] would have to be fought all over again.

---

[1] Mepacrine or hydrochloride atebrin is a synthetic anti-malarial drug, which was widely used for prophylaxis and treatment during the Second World War, when there was a shortage of quinine.

I determined to get my facts right – it avoids a massacre. I went for them to Millbank.[1]

'Whatever else he does in Italy,' they said, 'he must take mepacrine as a safeguard against malaria.'

As I made my way along the Embankment I could find no flaw in their arguments. I wanted to avoid, if I could, a pitched battle with the P.M. After all, he has enough trouble, without my adding to it. He will always listen to advice if the reasoning seems to him sound – it is futile, of course, to lay down the law – though I am careful to administer it in small doses and – this is important – I only give him the draught when we are alone.

So next morning I went to the Annexe soon after nine o'clock, knowing by experience that I was likely to find him alone at that hour. When I had said my piece, he glowered at me. Mepacrine, he was told, made people quite ill. And, anyway, he thought it was quite unnecessary. I stuck to my point, leaving him to think it over. When I had gone he telephoned Buckingham Palace, and the answer came back, 'The King knows nothing about mepacrine.' He hadn't taken anything at all when in Italy. Winston is just incorrigible. He has only to press a bell to bring into the room the greatest malarial experts in the world; instead, he turns his back on science and asks the King whether he ought to take mepacrine when he visits Italy. When the P.M.'s doubts were confirmed in this fashion he sent a telegram to Alex in Italy to elicit his views. I first heard of this when the P.M. sent me Alex's reply:

'Top Secret.
'Special Unnumbered Signal.
'7.0.0. 1025. 4th August.
'Top Secret and personal for Prime Minister from General Alexander.

'My doctors tell me that these yellow pills do not prevent malaria but only suppress it temporarily. They upset some people considerably. Whilst I cannot guarantee you immunity from malaria, I think you may

[1] Army Medical College, Millbank, London.

regard the risk as slight. Neither I nor my staff take pills and we have virtually no malaria at my headquarters. I suggest you tell the doctors to keep their pills. If you have Mess wellingtons or mosquito boots, bring them with you for evening wear.'

When I had collected ammunition I fired my gun at the Prime Minister. I began with figures. I explained that during the first two months of the Sicilian campaign last year we lost the effective strength of two infantry divisions from malaria. In the campaign in New Guinea half the force were evacuated sick in six months – 47,534 of 95,050 men, whereas there were only 3,140 battle casualties. Those in command agreed that this wastage from malaria could have been avoided, for if mepacrine were taken regularly there was little or no malaria. It was simply a question of discipline, of a drill for the administration of mepacrine. The principle was laid down that commanders would be held personally responsible for malarial wastage. As for Alex, when he proclaimed to the Prime Minister that neither he nor any of his staff set an example to their men by taking the pills themselves, he may not have known that it was a court-martial offence in the Army in Italy under his command to omit mepacrine drill.

The instruction of Winston is not without its own hazards, and I thought it prudent to close on a lighter note. The postscript to my letter read: 'General Alexander suggests the doctors keep their pills. I venture to wonder if General Alexander's views on medical matters have the same value as mine on military affairs.'

The P.M. lost no time in replying to this blast:

'Most Immediate.
'Secret.

'Telephone Message 6th August 1944 from the Prime Minister to Lord Moran.
'In view of your salvo, all surrender unconditionally and hoist the yellow flag.'

After that sally, how could anyone be out of temper?

*August 10, 1944*

Dorothy had been standing under a poplar tree for a long time. I went over to her to see what she was doing. 'Listen to the sound these leaves make in the wind. I'm trying to think what it is like. It is quite different from the sound other leaves make.' I wish in these harsh times that she had been built on coarser lines. One day, when John[1] was in her mind, she said: 'When a destroyer in an Arctic convoy is sunk, how long does one keep alive in the water?'

Dorothy drove me to the airfield at Northolt. We were stopped at the entrance, but the man on duty spotted me. We drove through two great hangars to the edge of the runway where the Skymaster was warming her engines. 'I don't think I'll wait for the P.M.,' said Dorothy. She did not want to be in the way. I knew she would stop the car on Western Avenue and wait until our great plane had gone over her head, roaring as it gathered speed and height.

*August 11, 1944*

After ten hours in the air we landed this morning at Algiers. Duff Cooper met us, and we drove straight to his house. Diana looks tired. Her bedroom, she told me, was 95° last night, so she slept on a balcony.

When a beautiful woman begins to lose her looks she needs something else to keep her afloat. Once I was called to the bedside of a woman whose beauty had been on many tongues. When it dawned upon her that her day was over and her reign had come to an end, she took to her bed, and, turning her face to the wall, presently snuffed out. The pathology of the business remained obscure, and for that matter no surgeon can tell me why he dreads to operate on a man who does not wish to live. When the time comes, Diana, who is still beautiful, will, I think, be saved by her character. Meanwhile she is one of the few women who are not intimidated by Winston.

After a pleasant break of a few hours we flew to Naples. The Villa Rivalta hangs over the Bay. I sat for a time looking across the

---

[1] John was now serving in a destroyer, H.M.S. *Oribi*.

water, turning things over in my mind. I had been talking to a young subaltern, who had been sent here for a rest. His three brothers have been killed, and he himself has been badly knocked about. He said, with a cheerful grin, that he liked his 'home comforts' and was in no hurry to go back to the line. He is not broken yet, but thank God it is not my job to return the poor devil to his unit. That was what the First War meant to me.

*August 12, 1944*

Tito[1] has been here all day. Winston is amused by a couple of fierce-looking bandits, bulging with pistols, who came as a bodyguard. Tito wanted to station them behind his chair during luncheon, presumably in case of treachery, but agreed as a compromise that they should be planted outside the door, where they looked like two Ruritanian figures out of a musical comedy. Winston makes great fun of Tito's gorgeous uniform, imitating the way in which from time to time he puts his finger between his collar and his neck to relieve the pressure of his blue-and-gold tunic. While Winston had readily accepted Wingate as a man of genius, he is only mildly entertained by Tito, who is, after all, playing for very high stakes. Surely the only excuse for these irregular practitioners of violence is that they should bring off their coups. Winston urged Tito not to let King Peter[2] down and expressed his conviction that Yugoslavia's international position would be stronger under a king than as a republic. One can but hope that Tito derived some benefit from Winston's homily on the blessings of a constitutional monarchy.

*August 13, 1944*

This morning I found ants in my bed; they were in great numbers on the floor, but my batman, a handy fellow, got four cigarette tins and raised the bed on these canisters so that the ants were defeated.

---

[1]  Marshal Tito, Yugoslav Resistance leader.
[2]  King of Yugoslavia. During the German invasion in April, 1941, King Peter had become a national hero, because of his courageous defiance of the Nazis.

While the P.M. bathed at Capri this morning, I climbed up to Axel Munthe's house. He was, I suppose, one of those doctors who trade on their personality and on drugs, though I am told that he had a strange gift of sympathy. The great charlatans – they are not all in medicine – have always fascinated me. When it falls to my lot to give the Harveian Oration at The Royal College of Physicians I shall choose as my subject 'Human Credulity.' It will be the story of the war with the quacks, which has gone on for more than four centuries. I shall give the P.M. some specimens of my script: I think it might be good for his education. Munthe claimed that *The Story of San Michele* was his autobiography; it was in fact a work of fiction that became a best-seller. Now I hear that he is staying with the aged King of Sweden; very nearly blind, he spends his days in a kind of helpless horror at the approach of death. A pathetic, decrepit figure, he cannot understand why the King does not seem to fear death and is not always thinking of it.

In the late afternoon I went with Attlee to see the Blue Grotto; it was pleasantly fresh crossing the Bay. Most of these politicians are cool customers, who have spent their lives dealing with human nature, but Attlee does not seem to have any self-confidence. He answered my questions in a quick, nervous manner, though he told me that he never worried about anything, he just did his best. I have a feeling, however, that there is a good deal more to him than this. Winston, I am pretty sure, underrates him. Anyway, I have made up my mind to find out more about him.

On our return to the Admiral's barge, we picked up Winston and then ran into a big convoy, which was on the point of setting out for the landing in the South of France. The P.M. directed our barge to go round the ships, while he stood in the stern waving and giving the V sign. Some of the men gathered on deck cheered, a few waved their caps. Twenty-nine years ago another armada left the harbour of Mudros for Gallipoli, and Masefield in a famous passage has given us the mood and temper of the men:

'All that they felt was a gladness of exultation that their young courage was to be used. They went like kings in a pageant to the imminent death. As they passed from moorings to the man-of-war anchorage on their way to the sea, their feeling that they had done with life and were going out to something new welled up in those battalions; they cheered and cheered and the harbour rang with cheering . . . They left the harbour very, very slowly; this tumult of cheering lasted a long time; no one who heard it will ever forget it or think of it unshaken.'[1]

I wanted to say to Winston that it made me sad to see these boys going to the war – many of them to their death – with but one thought in their heads, the futility of war. But I knew he would not see things like that.

*August 14, 1944*
The P.M. was in a speculative mood today.

'When I was young,' he ruminated, 'for two or three years the light faded out of the picture. I did my work. I sat in the House of Commons, but black depression settled on me. It helped me to talk to Clemmie about it. I don't like standing near the edge of a platform when an express train is passing through. I like to stand right back and if possible to get a pillar between me and the train. I don't like to stand by the side of a ship and look down into the water. A second's action would end everything. A few drops of desperation. And yet I don't want to go out of the world at all in such moments. Is much known about worry, Charles? It helps to write down half a dozen things which are worrying me. Two of them, say, disappear; about two nothing can be done, so it's no use worrying, and two perhaps can be settled. I read an American book on the nerves, *The Philosophy of Fate*; it interested me a great deal.'

I said: 'Your trouble – I mean the Black Dog[2] business – you got from your forebears. You have fought against it all your life. That is why you dislike visiting hospitals. You always avoid anything that is depressing.'

[1] John Masefield, *Gallipoli*, p. 35.
[2] Black Dog: Winston's name for the prolonged fits of depression from which he suffered.

Winston stared at me as if I knew too much. He went on to talk about the folly of repression. And then he spoke of asepsis and antisepsis. Turning to John Martin, who had come into the room with some papers, he said: 'You don't know the difference.' If John did, he held his peace, while the P.M. began to speak of the wonder of all the mind's activities being contained in a bit of brain the size of a hazel nut – 'the memories of a lifetime all in that little bit,' and his eyes dilated. He has a working idea of immunity, as of so many other things, and he asked all sorts of questions. Some of them made me think.

Watching the wear and tear of his life is, of course, part of my job. Is it because he is intensely interested about medical problems and wants to hear more about them that we go through this catechism? Is he aching to explore new ground? Or is he, perhaps, holding out signals of distress? Perhaps he is picking my brains and asking for help.

This afternoon Winston flew in Jumbo Wilson's Dakota to Corsica. There he will board a destroyer to see what he can of the American landing on the beaches somewhere near Cannes.

*August 16, 1944*
The P.M. came back from his trip in a querulous mood. He had only got within seven thousand yards of the beaches. He had not heard a shot fired. When I asked him what he had done, cooped up in a ship and cut off from everything, he answered that he had found a novel in the captain's cabin. Probably he did not mean this to be taken literally, for he rarely gets his nose into a book on our travels. I think he feels that it is wasting time.

*August 17, 1944*
We drove this morning, in great clouds of yellow dust, from Naples along 'Highway 6' to Monte Cassino. Winston dislikes other people's stories, and up to now I have respected his feelings. But as we stood in silence by the rubble of the old building I blurted out, on the impulse of the moment, how I had come to the monastery more than thirty years ago. Winston's attention was caught.

'You must tell me, Charles, why you became a monk.'

'Oh, it's a long story. It would only bore you. I was in a state of youthful rebellion against the wickedness of the world.'

Just then Alex came up and I moved away. It was soon plain to me that the minds of the soldiers were occupied by rather different thoughts, as with trained eyes they took in the scene. A glance at the battlefield brings home even to a civilian intelligence what our men were asked to do; it is impossible country in which to ask an army to fight a way forward. It is a mountainous land made for defence. I have no information that anyone has not got, but I should not be surprised if history is very critical of this Italian campaign, of opportunities lost (after Mussolini's fall, for example); it may happen that the campaign after the fall of Rome will be summed up as a pointless and stupid sacrifice . . . I fancy the Americans understand this and are all for cutting their losses.

After a picnic lunch we flew with Alex to his headquarters near Siena. The narrow streets of the old town were blocked by American cars, but we are quartered in a villa, in a peaceful spot, a few miles to the west. Tonight, when I was alone with Winston, to my consternation he said: 'I want you to tell me your story about the monastery. No. I'd like to hear it. I have always tried to understand the point of austerity' – a broad grin appeared – 'though I cannot claim that I have seriously practised it.'

This is the story I told him. It was before the First War, when I held the coveted office of Medical Registrar at St Mary's Hospital. There was then only one registrar, and the occupant of the post was, as it were, on approval for two years. If he passed the scrutiny, he was generally elected to the next vacancy on the staff and became a physician to the hospital, a full-blooded consultant. But, after a year in the office, I got it into my head – I was very young then – that some of my seniors were more concerned with their practices than with the students' training. It appeared a stuffy, material, and not very attractive existence, and I decided to send in my resignation. I did not give my reasons. It would sound priggish, I thought, if I tried to explain how I came to take such a suicidal step after all those years of apprenticeship.

As far as I can remember, I was not at all disconsolate that I had burnt my boats, irrevocably it seemed then. For some years my days had passed in the underground outpatient department of the hospital, lit even at noon by artificial light. I worked in a small room, like the inside cabin of a ship; it had no windows, and got very hot, and was full of microbes and of the sour smell of the human body. Then in the late afternoon, exchanging my white overall for a morning coat, I would don my top-hat and wind my way in and out of the vehicles and vans crowding the goods yard of the Great Western Railway, which then separated the hospital from the Harrow Road. For it was in that dreary street that I rented a single, shabby little room.

By coaching students for their final examinations I had been able to save a small sum of money, and this I planned to spend in travel – my resources would come to an end, I reckoned, in about a year.

It was in these circumstances that, in the spring of 1911, I found myself in Rome ready for adventure. One day I met a professor from Yale University, who told me he was going to Monte Cassino that afternoon. Whereupon I asked if I could go with him. From the wayside station we climbed in a creaking phaeton drawn by a dilapidated horse up what seemed like the side of a mountain. At length the driver, who had been encouraging his exhausted beast with curses and cracks of his whip, stopped at the gate of the monastery and rang a bell so violently that I felt abashed. A monk opened the door and spoke in Italian to the professor. He led us to a cell on the other side of the great stone building. That night I slept fitfully in my cell. Leaving my bed in the small hours, I wandered out into the long, deserted passages, until I found myself in a chapel where a monk was at prayer. I do not suppose that I was a very serious youth, but I got down on my knees and prayed. I waited for a long time until he rose to his feet. He left the chapel, and I followed him. He led me to a great terrace or battlement which looked down a wooded precipice into a valley far below. He had come to the monastery from Belgium to carve the screen in the chapel. Quite simply he told me, when I asked him, why he had given up the world. And then we stood in silence drinking in the utter peace of the place as the night left us.

When I had come to the end of my story Winston seemed abstracted. At length he said:

'I suppose you believe in another life when we die?'

When I did not answer he pressed me:

'You have been trained in logic. Tell me why you believe such things.'

I had a feeling that he, too, wanted desperately to believe in something, but from what he said he did not find it easy.

'You would have made a good monk,' he mused. There was a knock at the door. With an effort, Winston seemed to collect his thoughts. 'Tell me, Charles, did you never drink anything when you were with your battalion in France?'

*August 20, 1944*

I think I am beginning to get the hang of things here. If Winston came to Italy eager to see Alex, Alex is even more eager to see Winston. He has found that the preoccupation of the Americans with the invasion of France and their indifference towards the Italian campaign is wrecking his command. He knows that only Winston can stop the rot. When we landed at Naples, it did not need much acumen to see that the word had gone forth that the P.M.'s stay was to be made as pleasant as it could be made by taking thought and by remembering what he liked.

While I have been busy exploring the side streets of Siena, Winston has spent the sunny days working in bed. But at night Alex comes into the picture. Alex is particularly friendly; he also makes me feel an addition to the party. Indeed he makes himself so pleasant that I wish I did not feel that he was taking in the P.M. and the world. It is an astonishing instance of how a charming character with mediocre talents, a man whom the C.I.G.S. affirmed wasn't fit to command anything more than a division, should be floated successfully as 'one of the great captains of history'. If he has a grievance he is remarkably cheerful about it. Mark Clark may complain that a great chunk has been carved out of his Army and sent to France, but Alex says he is sure that there is a good reason for weakening his front. He knows that if the P.M. gets depressed nothing will happen. Only the timing, he thinks, is perhaps not very happy. Alex turned to me:

'The Prime Minister knows so much about our job that he was the first to see that we should soon be well on our way to Vienna if only the Americans would be sensible.'

P.M.: 'Glittering possibilities are opening up.'

Alex: 'There is still time to set things right. I am not at all pessimistic.'

A clock struck two, but the P.M. had no intention of going to bed.

It is not what Alex says that wins the day. He is not so foolish as to suppose that anyone has ever got his way with Winston by argument. Winston likes a good listener; he is always ready to do the talking. And Alex seems to wait on his words. He will listen attentively until half the night is over. Like a woman, he knows intuitively that listening is not just a question of keeping silent; it can be a means of communication of a more subtle kind. Besides, when Alex does open his mouth he is always so reassuring, always so sure that the P.M.'s plans are right, and that there will be no difficulty at all in carrying them out. That is what Winston wants; he dislikes people who are for ever making trouble. 'Anyone can do that,' he snorts impatiently. Soon he found himself confiding to Alex his most intimate thoughts.

'I envy you,' he said, 'the command of armies in the field. That is what I should have liked.'

When Alex told me of the P.M.'s confession I asked him whether Winston would have made a good general. At first I thought he was going to say 'Yes.' But he remained silent for so long that I added:

'Winston is a gambler. Marshall would make a big decision, but only after he had carefully removed every possible source of error.'

Then Alex, half to himself it seemed: 'Yes that's true. Winston is a gambler.'

The wooing of Winston has been deftly planned. Alex has promised to take him right up to the front line in the Adriatic sector, where he will receive the stimulus which danger always gives him. When Winston told me this he said: 'Before things happen I have a feeling of apprehension. But when things begin I feel almost gay. I get the same feeling at the tables at Monte Carlo.' And then, as if I were rebuking him for the risks he ran, he added: 'I cannot understand what is afoot unless I see for myself.' Yesterday Alex whisked him off to an American battery with a new nine-inch gun, where he was invited to fire the first shot – a very noisy performance which, however, gave him great satisfaction.

Alex not only thinks of the things the P.M. likes doing, he brings along the people Winston wants to meet. It was a happy touch to throw in General Mark Clark as a luncheon host. When Winston does notice anyone, he is usually attracted by male good looks and by a cheerful demeanour. Mark has both. After their first meeting the P.M. christened him the 'American Eagle': they were old friends. But there was a hitch in Alex's plans. Clark could not conceal his bitterness as he told his story: how a splendid instrument had been forged and then, when he was about to strike a shattering blow at the enemy, had been taken away from him and deliberately thrown into the sea. The P.M. was deeply affected by these words. He appeared to brood on them and went to bed last night grieved and forlorn.

When Alex learnt in the morning what had happened, he seemed to be put out. There was no purpose in sending the P.M. to bed in a bad temper, and he lost no time in taking steps to ease the tension. We got into a jeep, and for one and a half hours bumped down the very road up which the Fifth Army had painfully fought its way, foot by foot, crossing gorge after gorge on wooden planks because the enemy had destroyed the bridges. Alex knows his man. The P.M. never tires of playing at soldiers – the nearer to the real thing, the better. This grim expedition, he said, had helped him to grasp more clearly how we were winning the war. All day, whenever we passed Italian peasants by the roadside, they cheered and the P.M. gave them the V-sign. Tonight he remarked how friendly they were and that he must go again into the possibilities of more ships to bring them food.

Alex's little plot has been laid with great care, but in any case it was bound to succeed. The P.M. can never say no to Alex, whatever he asks; he keeps a place for him in his heart, apart from the others. Besides, both the P.M. and Alex have the same idea in their heads – they want to strengthen the Army in Italy. Already Winston stoutly affirms that he will not agree to any more divisions being withdrawn from the front.

### *Rome, August 21, 1944*

The P.M. is sorely perturbed about Greece. His mind is full of forebodings about what will happen when the Germans leave Athens. The Communists will seize power, and he is resolved to thwart their purpose. That is why we are here.

When the P.M. saw Papandreou, the head of the Greek Government, this morning he made no promises. Indeed, I gather that the Greek got little out of him beyond one of Winston's homilies on the advantages of constitutional government. But I fancy that the P.M.'s mind is made up, and from what he said today it appears that he is thinking of landing a small force in Athens, to strengthen the Greek Government.

Winston never talks of Hitler these days; he is always harping on the dangers of Communism. He dreams of the Red Army spreading like a cancer from one country to another. It has become an obsession, and he seems to think of little else.

### *August 23, 1944*

Winston was today received in audience by the Pope. When we left the Vatican, I asked him what had been the subject of their discourse. He replied that they had talked about the danger of Communism. Winston grinned. 'I talked about that with his predecessor eighteen years ago.' His eyes dilated as he declaimed a fine passage from Macaulay's essay on Ranke's *History of the Papacy*, setting forth how the Roman Church in the course of two thousand years had outlived all other institutions.[1] He felt that there

---

[1] On three different occasions Winston declaimed this passage to me.

must be something in a faith that could survive so many centuries and had held captive so many men. After his illness at Carthage he asked me rather abruptly: 'Do you believe that when you die it is the end of everything? Is there nothing beyond?'

*

Winston was not given to hero-worship of his contemporaries, and I was puzzled at the time by his affectionate admiration for Alex. It seems that Alex had been able to confirm what Winston had always felt about war. It is fashionable, of course, to subscribe to the belief that war is uncivilized, and Winston, like other politicians, had to make concessions to this popular sentiment. But he has an honest mind, and he knows that from the tremendous moment when he escaped from the Boers to the wonderful years of 1940 and 1941 the greatest thrills that he can recall have all been bound up with war.

To him it was a romantic calling, the highest man could embrace, but it was a game for gentlemen, which had to be played according to the rules. What he loved in Alex was that he had justified his own feelings about war, tried them out in the field and made sense of them. Alex had redeemed what was brutal in war, touching the grim business lightly with his glove. In his hands it was still a game for people of quality. He had shown that war could still be made respectable.

There were, of course, plenty of toughs in the Army, whose peace of mind came from a certain vacancy which had always passed for courage; in them freedom from fear was the outcome of the slow working of their minds, the torpor of their imagination. But Winston drew a clear line between Alex's gallant bearing and the blind courage of a man like Gort. 'Dainty,' 'jaunty' and 'gay' were the terms he chose for his knight errant as he flitted across the sombre scene. Here Winston's instinct was sound.

For my part I had come to think of Alex as a man without fear, until one day, when the war was over, I noticed that he had developed a facial tic or twitch, the certain badge of nervous tension. So he, too, was playing a part like the rest of us, only he was in more perfect control of his primitive instincts.

Winston loved to recount how Alex, when serving with a battalion of the Irish Guards in the First War, was reputed to bear a charmed life; his men, it was said, liked to tread in his footsteps when crossing no-man's-land, believing that they would share his good fortune.

*

The years that have gone since this was written have done little to settle finally the wisdom of the Italian campaign. Was the war in Italy a fiasco, as General Fuller thought, or was it a missed opportunity, a second Gallipoli? If the Americans had put their heart – and their landing craft – into the campaign, our first landing might have been in the North, perhaps in the Gulf of Genoa, as Smuts had pleaded. It might have changed the fate of Europe. At any rate, that is what Winston thought. He had no doubts about the merits of the high command. Once I asked him rather daringly: 'Was Alex a good general?' 'The best we had,' he answered at once, 'better than Monty.' Some of the serious people around the P.M. took a rather different view. They questioned the wisdom of the Italian campaign and Alex's handling of his army.

If Wavell is right, and there is not much in generalship beyond the knowledge of supply – logistics – then we may as well admit at once that Alex cannot claim a place among the great captains. But was Wavell's dictum meant to be more than a half-truth? Alex proved completely imperturbable in desperate circumstances – he brought up the rear in the retreat from Burma, and he was the last to leave the beaches at Dunkirk. There was indeed a singular serenity about the bearing of this man in battle. It is surprising that he could implant in his men the will to fight – and in this war that will depended more on leadership than sometimes in the past. It is absurd to say that these things do not count in the mixed business of war. To be clever is not everything.

# CHAPTER TWENTY

# Off the Rails

*September 5, 1944*

Dorothy had arranged to take Geoffrey[1] to Scotland to show him the mountains (a job I'd like) before he goes back to school, but our early return from Italy upset her plans, and she had to cancel sleepers and rooms. Then she learnt that we were off to Quebec and she could go to Scotland after all. However, the P.M. came to the rescue and suggested that they should travel on his train as far as Greenock. Geoffrey was thrilled. Early this morning I took them to Addison Road, which looked less like a station than usual; no one seemed to be about save two tramp-like figures in battered soft hats and Burberries, who turned out to be detectives. Winston arrived at the last moment and the train moved off immediately.

After about twenty minutes we slowed down and then stopped. It appeared that the P.M.'s spectacles had been left behind, and a message was sent back to retrieve them. At one o'clock we were summoned to luncheon with the P.M. After a little I peered down the table to see how Geoffrey was faring. I was reassured when I saw him engaged in earnest conversation with Peter Portal. Portal told me later that they had been discussing the efficacy of the Eton air-raid shelters.

At Carlisle we stopped. Apparently a message had been received that Hitler was rumoured to be suing for peace. So the P.M. had

[1] My younger son.

to speak on the telephone to Anthony Eden. 'I shouldn't be at all surprised,' someone said, 'if we all turned round and went home again.' Though no one was allowed on the platform at Carlisle, we could see eager and inquisitive crowds behind the iron barriers, to whom the P.M., who had been asked by the security people not to show himself, gave the V-sign.

It was after seven o'clock when we arrived at Greenock. The P.M. descended in the gathering dusk and began inspecting the guard of honour, drawn up on the platform, while Tommy[1] told Dorothy to wait for word from the Admiral of the Western Approaches. From the tender I could see them, a little forlorn now, on the deserted platform; then the Admiral's Flag Lieutenant, splendid in his golden ropes, appeared and took charge of them and their rather inadequate luggage and the two disreputable bicycles.

*R.M.S.* Queen Mary, *September 8, 1944*
It is just ten days since the P.M. landed at Northholt with a temperature of 103; for some days after that he was chesty, and the X-rays revealed a shadow at the base of the lung, a third dose, though a very mild one, of pneumonia.[2] There had been some doubt whether he would be fit to set off on another trip so soon. I decided at the last moment to ask Lionel Whitby[3] and a nurse to come with us. Winston has got it into his head that a pathologist is an essential part of the team to deal with an attack of pneumonia, and I thought it would comfort him to have one on board.

It was a happy thought. This morning when the P.M.'s temperature went up again he became thoroughly rattled and bad-tempered, until Whitby restored morale by finding that he had a

---

[1] Commander C. R. Thompson, R.N., Personal Assistant to Churchill.
[2] On September 1, 1944, Winant wrote from London to Hopkins: 'His (Churchill's) message to the President will have told you of his illness on arrival, which is only known to a dozen people here. Tonight his temperature is back to normal and he seems on the way to a quick recovery. But each journey has taken its toll and the interval between illness has been constantly shortened' (*The White House Papers*, Vol. II, p. 806).
[3] Sir Lionel Whitby, bacteriologist to the Middlesex Hospital.

normal blood count. The trouble is that Winston always has pneumonia at the back of his mind. Now the temperature has subsided and he is quite himself again.

*September 12, 1944*

I am stopping the mepacrine, though we were advised to take it for a month after leaving Italy in order to ward off malaria. The P.M. makes very heavy weather about the tablets; he ascribes to them his bad turn on the ship. Besides, mepacrine gives you a yellow cachectic look, as if you had cancer, and people like Brendan say to him: 'You ought to stop that stuff; it's making you ill.'

Dill came to me today. He is a sick man with a refractory anaemia; he asked me if I would come to his rescue if he needed me in Quebec. He then took out of his pocket a crumpled bit of paper and gave it to me. It was a report on the last two examinations of his blood. I saw at a glance that he was not reacting to treatment, and I doubt if he will last long. I wonder if he knows?

*September 13, 1944*

There was a men's dinner at the Citadel tonight; the President, the P.M., Morgenthau,[1] the Prof., Admiral Leahy,[2] Leathers,[3] Ross McIntire[4] and I were all seated at a round table. How to prevent another war with Germany was the only subject of conversation. The Americans were all for drastic action, maintaining that Germany should not be allowed ships or the yards in which to build them; what they needed could be carried in our ships. Morgenthau wanted to close down the Ruhr to help British exports, especially steel. The P.M. was against this. He did not seem happy about all this toughness.

'I'm all for disarming Germany,' he said, 'but we ought not to prevent her living decently. There are bonds between the working

[1] Henry Morgenthau, U.S. Secretary of the Treasury.
[2] Fleet-Admiral William Leahy, U.S. Chief of Staff to C.-in-C. (the President).
[3] Lord Leathers, Minister of War Transport.
[4] Admiral Ross McIntire, Personal Physician to President Roosevelt.

classes of all countries, and the English people will not stand for the policy you are advocating.'

I thought he had done when he growled:

'I agree with Burke. You cannot indict a whole nation.'

If the P.M. was vague about what ought to be done with Germany, he was at least quite clear what should *not* be done. He kept saying:

'At any rate, what is to be done should be done quickly. Kill the criminals, but don't carry on the business for years.'

Morgenthau asked the P.M. how he could prevent Britain starving when her exports had fallen so low that she would be unable to pay for imports. The P.M. had no satisfactory answer. His thoughts seemed to go back to the House of Commons and what he knew of the English people. In five years' time, when passions would have died down, people, he said, would not stand for repressive measures. There was a good deal of sentiment in all this and not much hard thinking. He harped on the necessity of disarming the Germans (as if most of this war's weapons will not be obsolete). This war, the P.M. wound up, could easily have been prevented. The P.M. is never less impressive than when he talks of the future. At that point one of the Americans intervened: he thought that Germany should be made to return to a pastoral state, she ought to have a lower standard of living. During all this wild talk only the P.M. seemed to have his feet on the ground. The President mostly listened; once he remarked that a factory which made steel furniture could be turned overnight to war production.

After three hours' discussion there seemed to be an absolute cleavage between the American point of view and that of the Prime Minister. The Prof., however, sided with the Americans. At last Roosevelt said: 'Let the Prof. go into our plans with Morgenthau.'

\*

My notes of the conversation at this dinner party bring out Winston's instinctive revulsion to Morgenthau's scheme. He hates cruelty, and the thought of a great nation starving shocked him. Plainly it was an emotional response. Within forty-eight hours I was bewildered by a sharp right-about-turn. Someone had said that the plan would not work. At this Winston lost his temper.

'Why shouldn't it work?' he demanded. 'I've no patience with people who are always raising difficulties.'

It was plain that the Prof. had got hold of him. Winston had changed sides.

Lord Cherwell was a very clever man, and he had learnt a good deal about Winston's mental processes during their long friendship. Later I bluntly saddled the Prof. with the responsibility for this particular decision. I asked him how he had managed to make the P.M. sign the plan. At first he tried to dodge my question, but when I pressed him he began to justify his action. 'I explained to Winston,' he said, 'that the plan would save Britain from bankruptcy by eliminating a dangerous competitor. Somebody must suffer for the war, and it was surely right that Germany and not Britain should foot the bill. Winston had not thought of it in that way, and he said no more about a cruel threat to the German people.'

As Lord Cherwell spoke, I could see him producing from his pocket one of his graphs, with that quiet, confident air that he was right. He explains the peaks to the P.M. At first Winston regards them rather blankly, and then he begins to ask questions and soon he is convinced. It is after all so obvious: if Germany were left without industries Britain must step into her shoes and take over her trade.

'They brought it on themselves,' he grunted.

The Prof. did not invent the plan. He borrowed it from Morgenthau, who was bursting with a scheme that would convert Germany from an industrial into a pastoral country. Morgenthau had no patience with half measures. He wanted to strip the Ruhr so that it could not in the foreseeable future again become an industrial area. He wanted to wreck the mines. The vanquished must be left without industries. The German people must, in future, live on the land.

As it happened, Roosevelt, like Winston, was in the mood to listen to Morgenthau. He had felt for some time before the

Conference that the Germans ought to be given a lesson that they would remember. His feelings, deeply stirred by their wanton conduct, were, too, fortified by a more practical line of thought.

'The real nub of the situation is to keep Britain from going into complete bankruptcy at the end of the war.'

For my part, I wonder how far Roosevelt's health impaired his judgment and sapped his resolve to get to the bottom of each problem before it came up for discussion. At Quebec he seemed to me to have lost a couple of stone in weight – you could have put your fist between his neck and his collar – and I said to myself then that men at his time of life do not go thin all of a sudden just for nothing.

Eden, arriving in Quebec the day after the President and the Prime Minister had signed the plan, flew into a rage when he learnt of the agreement. He had a heated discussion with the P.M. He asked him if he had forgotten that the Foreign Office had been working for many months on a plan which was to come into force when Germany surrendered. He reminded the P.M. that this plan had the backing of Molotov and that it had been sanctioned by the President himself. The P.M., however, was unrepentant; he instructed Eden not to take up the matter with the War Cabinet until he himself returned to London. He said that he was bent on pushing it through.

Morgenthau returned to Washington elated with his achievements. Mr Churchill, he said, had at first been violently opposed to the plan. The P.M. had bluntly demanded whether he had been brought to Quebec to discuss a scheme that would mean 'England being chained to a dead body.' But he was won over by the Prof., and in the end, according to Morgenthau, the plan was drafted entirely by Mr Churchill.

By the time that Roosevelt returned from Quebec to Washington, the mind of the Secretary of State had hardened against the course the President had taken. Cordell Hull lost no time in seeking an interview with Roosevelt, and told him that it was 'out of all reason' to condemn thirty million Germans to starvation. It was noticed that the President took little part in this conversation. He was plainly shaken, and when Henry Stimson[1] saw him alone on October 3 Roosevelt said that he had no intention of turning Germany into an agrarian state. Whereupon Stimson read out to him some of the memoranda of September 15, concluding with the words:

> 'Looking forward to converting Germany into a country primarily agricultural and pastoral in character.'

Stimson tells us that the President was staggered when he listened to this sentence. He had no idea, he said, that he could have initialled such language and confessed that it must have been done without much reflection. Those who were close to the President knew that the Morgenthau plan was dead.

We may well ask at this point how the Prime Minister came to Quebec without any thought out views on the future of Germany, although she seemed to be on the point of surrender. The answer is hardly in doubt. He had become so engrossed in the conduct of the war that little time was left to plan for the future.

In a long life, Winston had always done as he pleased. Military detail had long fascinated him, while he was frankly bored by the kind of problem which might take up the time of the Peace Conference. 'There will be plenty of time to go into that when we have won the war,' he would snap. The P.M. was frittering away his waning strength on matters which rightly belonged to soldiers.

My diary in the autumn of 1942 tells how I talked to Sir Stafford Cripps and found that he shared my cares. He wanted the P.M. to concentrate on the broad strategy of the war and on high policy. The P.M. played for time; he knew that a victory in the desert would silence his critics. No one could make him see his error. After El Alamein no one tried. The House of Commons and the country were reassured at the course of events, the crisis had passed and the P.M. was allowed to go his own way thereafter.

It seems that no one could stand up to him, either in the Cabinet

---

[1] Henry Stimson, Roosevelt's Secretary for War.

or in the House of Commons. Once he had made up his mind, nobody could make him change it. That was Norman Brook's[1] considered verdict after the war. When Chatham was in one of his paroxysms of gouty fury, it is said, no man could look him in the face. I could believe this when I saw the effect of Winston's overpowering personality on those around him. Mackenzie King told me that Winston bullied Attlee, and he likened the other members of the Cabinet to a lot of schoolboys frightened by the headmaster.

Nature, however, is not so easily stared out of countenance, and Winston was beginning to realize that he was the worse for wear. For the moment we were able to patch him up, but as time passed, and the war dragged on, his work began to suffer, so that those around him came to invoke my help. The office had been complaining for some time that the tin boxes by his bed were never empty. For hours, or so it seemed to him, he would devour the indigestible mass, but all the time a secretary kept coming into the room with an armful of papers to replenish the pile. Winston was conscious of a sense of oppression that he had not felt before.

This brings me to the Prof.'s graphs. They seemed to provide a short-cut to the mastery of a problem by peptonizing the facts. Almost at a glance, the P.M. could size up not only the problem but also the lines on which it might be solved. Sometimes these graphs appeared to serve a useful purpose, by fixing the P.M.'s attention on some pressing problem. More often they led him astray by over-simplifying the issue. One day Jock Colville[2] said to me:

[1] Norman Brook, succeeded Bridges as Secretary to the Cabinet in 1947. In a later essay, Moran records the following remarks by Brook about Churchill's role in 1940, 'If there hadn't been a Winston, I don't know what would have happened . . . There were a lot of jitters at the top'. Asked by Moran whether the Chief of Staff Brooke had given way to jitters, Norman Brook replied, 'No he didn't, but his staff did. The people who came back from France were particularly on edge. There was Rucker who had been Neville Chamberlain's secretary, and Bland the soldier and . . . these people ran into Winston and they found him with his jaw set, positively bristling with defiance. He stopped the rot.'

[2] John (Jock) Colville, assistant private secretary to the Prime Minister, on secondment from the Foreign Office.

'The P.M. is very tired. He insists on everything being boiled down to half a sheet of notepaper. It simply can't be done. He misses half the argument.'

Jock, of course, was right. As, year after year, I watched the P.M. doing the work of three men, I kept saying to myself that this could not go on for ever. 'Can't you do anything for this horrible feeling of exhaustion?' he demanded at Cairo. And then came his illness at Carthage. He never seemed to me to be the same man again.

Roosevelt soon woke to the fact that in signing the Morgenthau document he had done something that was foolish and even inexplicable, that might well have led to incalculable consequences. He was very penitent and much put out. Winston, on the other hand, was, as far as I could tell, not at all penitent. Anyway in Moscow he engaged in a serious discussion with Stalin about the future of the plan, a fortnight after the President had consigned it to the rubbish heap. Plainly Winston felt that it was still practical politics.

Why did Winston not admit that he had made a blunder? We shall have to turn back to the story of his early manhood for an explanation. Winston has never been at all like other people. No Churchill is. In his early days, as I have already recounted, he was afflicted by fits of depression that might last for months. He called them the 'Black Dog.' He dreaded these bouts and instinctively kept away from anyone or anything that seemed to bring them on.

Winston told me that when he was a young Member of Parliament 'a mistake would get him down.' It seemed to prey on his mind. The mere thought that he might trip up filled him with apprehension. When, for example, he made a speech in the House of Commons he would wake next morning oppressed with the fear that he had committed an irreparable error which might prejudice his political future. He had to school himself not to think about things when they had gone wrong, for he found that he could not live with his mistakes and keep his balance. This urge to obliterate had, in course of time, grown into a cast of mind in which he seemed incapable of seeing that he had been at fault. Of course, nothing of that kind could be absolute, and it is a fact that after his stroke in 1953, when death was round the corner, he did confide to me, not, however, without many qualifications, that he had been wrong about India. But the circumstances were exceptional, for his confessional was a sick bed. Of this need to forget, the Morgenthau plan is an apt illustration.

When, nine years later, the P.M. came to write the history of the Quebec Conference, he had to say something about the Morgenthau plan, and this is what he said:

'The so-called Morgenthau plan, which I had not time to examine in detail, seems to have carried these ideas to an ultra-logical conclusion. Even if it had been practicable I do not think it would have been right to depress Germany's standard of life in such a way; but at that time, when German militarism based on German industry had done such appalling damage to Europe, it did not seem unfair to agree that her manufacturing capacity need not be revived beyond what was required to give her the same standards of life as her neighbours.'[1]

It was, of course, no part of the Morgenthau plan, as Winston himself had drafted it, to give Germany the same standards of life as her neighbours. And the whole passage appears at first sight to be a little wanting in candour. Winston disposes of the plan in less than a page. It would be possible, I suppose, to dismiss the somewhat ambiguous sentences as no more than a good example of the political art of presenting a bad case in its least damaging form. I doubt, however, if this is the whole truth. So insidiously had this refusal to recognize a mistake grown on Winston, that it had become a habit of which he himself was probably not conscious, until it had affected not only his speech but actually his way of thinking. I am disposed to believe that his reluctance on this occasion to open up old wounds was but another instance of his drawn-out battle with the 'Black Dog.'

---

[1] Winston Churchill, *Triumph and Tragedy*, pp. 138–9.

# CHAPTER TWENTY-ONE

# At Sea

*R.M.S.* Queen Mary, *September 20, 1944*

After a train trip from Quebec, we left New York yesterday, shortly before midnight, and the P.M. will have nearly a week at sea to turn over in his mind what happened at Quebec. On these voyages he really gets going and talks himself out, but he has been taking stock in a sober mood. Looking forward, he sees the future in grey tones; the old familiar buoyant note is wanting.

Moran: 'Did you find this conference less tiring than the Cairo meeting?'

P.M.: 'What is this conference? Two talks with the Chiefs of Staff; the rest was waiting for the chance to put in a word with the President. One has to seize the occasion. There was nothing to tire me. I don't have to work out things. And if they are not in my head I'm very good at handing them on to someone who squeezes the guts out of them for me. But I'm older, Charles. I don't think I shall live long.'

Moran: 'You haven't lost your grip on things.'

P.M.: 'Oh, my head's all right. But I'm very tired. Can't you give me something to pick me up? I wish I could go to the South of France for two or three weeks at Christmas and get the sunshine. You, Charles, could send me. I'd tell them you ordered me a rest. I have a very strong feeling that my work is done. I have no message. I had a message. Now I only say "fight the damned socialists." I do not believe in this brave new world. Why, Charles, tell me any good in any new thing. That is' – and here he put his hand on my arm in a kindly way – 'excepting medicine.'

For a time the P.M. sat moodily surveying the papers on his bedrest. His cigar had gone out and lay beside his glass.

Tonight, after dinner, somebody said: 'Does the size and shape of your head tell whether you have any brains?'

Whitby: 'No.'

P.M.: 'Oh, yes. Take a line through my eyes; there's as much above them as below them. Look at Charles.' And then with a little chuckle, 'Of course it is exaggerated in his case by the loss of hair.'

*September 21, 1944*

The P.M. told how Theodore Roosevelt, on the outbreak of the First War, asked to see Woodrow Wilson. Wilson gave him an appointment, but received him very coolly. Roosevelt wanted to command something in the field. On going out, he met Colonel House and said to him: 'Wilson was very rough with me. After all, all I asked was to be allowed to die.' House (*in his silkiest tones*): 'Did you make that last point clear to the President?'

Winston made some gurgling sounds in his throat. 'Do you know the yarn of the man who was castrated?' More gurgling. 'A man called Thomson went to a surgeon and asked him to castrate him. The surgeon demurred, but when the man persisted and argued he eventually agreed, and took him into hospital. The morning after the operation Thomson woke up in great discomfort. He noticed that the man in the next bed was in pain and was groaning. He leant towards him over the side of the bed. "What did they do to you," he called. The man replied: "I've been circumcised." "Good Lord," Thomson exclaimed, "that's the word I couldn't remember when the surgeon asked me what I wanted done."'

The P.M.'s face screwed up into creases and he made some crowing, expiratory sounds in his throat as he did when really amused.

'I shall use that story,' he said, 'when they give me my degree. I'll bring it in by urging the importance of precision of language. Oh, they'll never report it. They couldn't.'

His stories are borrowed from the smoke-room, and are richly flavoured. Nevertheless, it is not, I think, unfair to Winston to say that he has more wit than humour. He has never been a detached spectator of life; he cannot laugh at the foibles of others. Nor, when things go wrong, does he find relief in that particular brand of self-mockery to which the English soldier turns in adversity. Humour has never protected him from the bruises of political life.

The P.M. has a good deal to say about the great figures of the past, but he does not often get under their skins. There is, of course, a good deal of repetition; the same actors are always appearing on the stage.

*September 22, 1944*

After breakfasting today on an omelette, grouse, melon, toast and marmalade, Winston ought to have been at peace with the world. But I found him militant.

'I'm distressed about France. I must not let de Gaulle come between me and the French nation. He is an enemy of the English people. I must not let him have the revenge of putting me wrong with France.'

And if de Gaulle is often on his tongue, Max is not far from his thoughts.

'Max is a good friend in foul weather. Then, when things are going well, he will have a bloody row with you over nothing. When he was most useful to me about supply, and was very bad with asthma, I wanted him to go up in an aeroplane and work there. It would have been worth the petrol.'

Tonight he began about Kipling.

'I liked him. He had a great influence on my life. But for years he would not speak to me.'

I asked why.

'Oh,' Winston answered, 'something I had said offended him, or he felt I was bitterly opposed to everything he believed in. Then we came together over the war graves in France. Somebody had spoken lightly of the wooden crosses, under one of which his son was buried, and Kipling was furious. I'm bound to say I agreed with him. Later India brought us together.'

He turned to Turkey. Why had she taken sides with Germany in the First World War? Commonly he addressed his monologue to no one in particular, but this question was plainly put to the First Sea Lord, who thought that the seizure of the *Agincourt*,[1] which was being built in England for the Turks, did a lot to put the Turks against us.

P.M.: 'Well the ratio in Dreadnoughts was only sixteen to ten, and two of these were in dock. I wasn't going to let a first-class ship be lost to England. I don't mind making decisions in a crisis and I said: Not a ship shall leave this country now war is declared. Besides, Enver[2] had already decided to join the Germans.'

Then Cunningham got into trouble.

'The United Nations will never be any use to anyone,' he said.

P.M.: 'I don't know why you say that; it is the only hope of the world.'

First Sea Lord, a little abashed: 'The idea is all right, but it will never work.'

The P.M., without further words, dismissed the subject as only he can, indicating by his attitude that it hardly came within the province of the Admiralty. But when all the others had gone and Winston was undressing he said to me:

'I like Cunningham very much. I'm very lucky to get such a successor to dear old Pound.'

As he settled into his pillow, he said:

'Well, you'd better get your bathing suit out. Good night, my dear.'

*September 23, 1944*

When he stands in the Map Room, gazing at the enemy submarines on the vast chart, I'm sure he sees the great ship torpedoed. He has too much imagination for these times. But the only thing he

[1] Just before the outbreak of the First World War Churchill, then First Lord of the Admiralty, was responsible for the requisitioning of two powerful cruisers which were being built in British dockyards for the Turkish Navy. One of these was later renamed *Agincourt*.

[2] Enver Pasha, leader of the 'Young Turks' and ruler of Turkey in 1914.

seems to dread is being taken prisoner. He'd much rather die, and
he says so. On the last voyage he arranged that a machine-gun
should be kept in the boat detailed to take him off if anything
happened. This voyage the same arrangement has been made.

'How long,' he asked the First Sea Lord, 'would the *Queen Mary*
take to sink after she was torpedoed; would it be a few minutes?'

First Sea Lord: 'More likely a few hours; she is well divided into
watertight compartments.'

\*

I remember Camrose[1] saying that he thought Winston had been a
little in awe of Asquith. 'Asquith, you see, kept conversation strictly
within certain limits; he had a sense of what was proper and relevant.' I thought of this when in the course of conversation during
luncheon I referred to Asquith's fine intelligence. I wondered what
the P.M. might say.

P.M.: 'Oh, he was more than a great brain. More than anyone
I can think of, he knew exactly where he stood in relation to things.
You could predict what he would do in certain situations, and you
would be right – more often than not. Margot[2] was a great woman,
impudent, audacious, a flaming creature. Asquith counted it his
greatest achievement when he pulled down this glittering bird on
the wing. Besides, she took him into a world different from the
bourgeois world he had known, and that counted for something in
those days.'

I was under the impression that Margot married Asquith and that
he was just a passive victim of her arts, until Desmond MacCarthy
assured me that Asquith was passionately in love with her. And, now
I think of it, this is the only time that I have heard Winston refer in
his conversation to women. He is not interested in them. Besides,
his chivalry forbids any dissection of them in public.

We hear very little of politics, and then Winston speaks darkly

[1] Lord Camrose, Chairman of the *Daily Telegraph* and a personal friend
of Churchill.
[2] Margot Tennant, wife of Prime Minister Asquith.

of the future. He dreads the financial consequences of the war. Even the housing problem depresses him.

'I am alarmed,' he said, 'at what would happen if peace was declared now. Some people – aesthetes,' he spoke with contempt, 'say the Portal house would deface the countryside.[1] As if the countryside isn't meant to live in. Nothing is more beautiful than smoke curling up above the houses, while' – with a grin – 'brats are made below. We may have to have Nissen huts. There must be somewhere for two hundred to three hundred thousand returned soldiers to live and get married. Builders can't do it in time. I have asked the Beaver, Brendan and Portal to prepare a plan by the time I get back. Portal told me he wasn't afraid the houses would not be ready, but what he did fear was, would roads be built, drainage and lighting turned on? I don't think there is much in this.'

He turned to me:

'Now, Charles, on which side are you about the Health Bill, the doctors' or the Government's?'[2]

Moran: 'The doctors'.'

P.M.: 'It's a free country and this ought to be debated out.'

Laski had written to him suggesting a monster subscription Churchill Memorial Fund to buy a million books.

'A very nice letter, fulsome even. If anything of the kind is to happen I'd like the houses of the poor people south of the River re-built and a great park, like Battersea Park, prepared for the kiddies, with lots of ponds full of sticklebacks and many fountains.'

Somebody criticized a Labour member of the Cabinet because he had once been a Liberal.

'A man who doesn't change his mind with new evidence is no use,' was Winston's verdict.

From time to time he spoke of the war, but when he did so he did not seem so much to be talking to us as arguing things out for

---

[1] June, 1943, Lord Portal, Minister of Works and Buildings, put forward a proposal to build 3,000 prefabricated cottages for agricultural workers.
[2] An early attempt in 1944 to put proposals for a National Health Service into statutory form. It was shelved and superseded after the war by the National Health Act, 1946.

himself. He seemed to want to clear his mind and straighten it all out for posterity.

I asked him about Lend-Lease and how it all began.

P.M.: 'I wrote a ten-page letter to the President putting our case. It was delivered to him on his yacht. I think it was among the Caribbean Islands. He sat on deck all day over the letter, and next day he saw no one. Then he came out with Lend-Lease.'

He mused. Then he began to talk of the First War.

'Stettinius Senior[1] came to see me. I rang a bell and three attendants came in, each bearing a big volume with details of all the alterations in factories, etc., so that I could go through the accounts week by week. Stettinius said: "What does it amount to?" I said, "Sixty millions." "Very well," he said. "But don't you want to go through the accounts? They're all here." "Oh, no," he answered; "if you say that's what we owe, that's quite all right."

'Sometime later I ventured to ask him if he had treated the French in the same manner. "Good Lord, no," he replied.'

At times – but not very often – Winston drew aside the curtain that had hidden his feelings at the time of some reverse.

'Anzio was my worst moment in the war. I had most to do with it. I didn't want two Suvla Bays[2] in one lifetime. I felt if we went back their field guns would command the beach and nothing could be landed. The heavier guns didn't matter.'

*September 24, 1944*

This is our last night at sea. Winston seems in better heart – no doubt the rest has done him good – and we were soon back in the Boer War. Lord Roberts[3] had three Dukes on his staff, and this had led to talk.

---

[1]  Edward Stettinius.

[2]  The landing at Anzio on January 22, 1944, was intended by Churchill to out-flank the Germans and secure Rome. It was not a success, and Churchill was criticized for his interference, which was compared with his conduct over the landings at Suvla Bay in August, 1915, during the Gallipoli campaign.

[3]  Lord Roberts, Commander-in-Chief during the Boer War.

'If I were Commander-in-Chief,' Winston said, 'I'd do what I damn' well liked, but Roberts was sensitive in such things. His A.D.C. said to Marlborough: "I fear you can't come up with us; we are going to leave you behind." Sunny was much upset and came to me. I said: "I am going off in another direction. Why not come with me?" We had an ox-wagon with four oxen and two good horses (the kind of animal that costs two hundred pounds). The whole outfit cost the *Morning Post* a thousand pounds. The wagon was full of Fortnum and Mason groceries and of course' (with a grin) 'liquor. We nearly lost the precious wagon fording a river, it just got across. One night we found a lot of geese on a pond. I threw stones at them and Sunny shepherded them my way. But they took fright and, half flying, half scurrying, rushed past me. I took a flying kick and winded one, and before it could recover I was on it.

'I loved it all: all movement and riding. I took a message from Ian Hamilton[1] to Roberts through Ladysmith, which the Boers were evacuating. I bicycled in plain clothes through the streets. There were odd Boers about, but I got through and met Roberts' column. It was explained to him that Winston Churchill had a message for him. Roberts had taken very little notice of me, though my father had got him his Indian appointment, which was his heart's desire, but now he sent for me and was very affable. I gave him a full account, while they brought me food and drink. I felt relieved I had got through. I had been a prisoner once, and I didn't want to be taken a second time. If you do a thing at once, when it's not expected, it's surprising what you can bring off.'

[1] Later General Sir Ian Hamilton.

# CHAPTER TWENTY-TWO

# Poles Apart

The P.M. had left Italy before Alex's summer offensive. I saw little of him during the few days that we were in London, but he was in good heart when we set out for Quebec early in September, and in his conversations at the Citadel[1] he made no bones about his plans: he wanted to forestall the Russians in central Europe.

On our return to London, towards the end of the month, I noticed that Italy had dropped out of the P.M.'s conversation. One day he owned to me that he was not so sure that Alex would be able to bring it off. He spoke his mind as he was getting into bed.

'Stalin will get what he wants. The Americans have seen to that. They haven't given Alex a dog's chance. He will do his best, but the cream of his army has been skimmed off.'

The P.M. got out of bed and began pacing the room. The advance of the Red Army has taken possession of his mind. Once they got into a country, it would not be easy to get them out. Our army in Italy was too weak to keep them in check. He might have to get his way with Stalin by other means.

All might yet be well if he could win Stalin's friendship. After all, it was stupid of the President to suppose that he was the only person who could manage Stalin. The President had a mad idea of getting thirty of the nations together and confronting Russia with one view about Poland. Of course Russia would take no notice. We

[1] The Citadel in the enclosed city of Quebec was used during the Second Quebec Conference.

could go to hell unless we were prepared to go to war. And no one will be prepared for that. Winston told me that he had found he could talk to Stalin as one human being to another. Stalin, he was sure, would be sensible. He went on to speak of this proffer of friendship to Stalin as if it were an ingenious idea that had just occurred to him, and while he spoke his eyes popped and his words tumbled over each other in his excitement. He could think of nothing else. It had ceased to be a means to an end; it had become an end in itself. He sat up in bed.

'If we three come together,' he said, 'everything is possible – absolutely anything.'

He appealed to the President to arrange a meeting with Stalin. The President's reply was brief and not at all helpful; he could do nothing before the Presidential election in November. The P.M. was unable to hide his irritation. The Red Army, he said scornfully, would not stand still awaiting the result of the election.

The P.M. decided at last that if the President would not play, he must 'go it alone.' One morning I found him in a rough mood. Without waiting for me to sit down he blurted out: 'I am going to Moscow.'

He said this as if he expected me to argue with him. When I said nothing he went on:

'The atmosphere there is quite different since we brought off the landings in Normandy. I shall take advantage of it to come to an amicable settlement with Stalin about Poland. That is why I am going.'

*October 8, 1944*
We left Northolt before midnight and landed near Naples at seven this morning. The 'York' is cold, and I was ready to get up when the P.M. sent for me half an hour before we landed. The man who called me had been put in charge of the oxygen cylinder. He said that the P.M. had been having oxygen throughout the night, although we had been flying no higher than 3,000 feet, adding that the P.M. had asked him to take his pulse. I found Winston dozing. The mask had fallen off his face into the bed, the oxygen was hissing

out while he held his cigar, which was still alight, in his hand. One day we shall all go up in flames. I was about to turn off the oxygen when the hissing stopped. He woke suddenly and lifted the mask to his face.

'What's happened to the oxygen?' he demanded.

'There is none left,' I said.

'What would have happened,' he asked, 'if others had wanted it?'

'They would have been told,' I said shortly, 'that they did not need oxygen flying at that height.'

When the P.M. teaches his soldiers and sailors how to do their own job it's their affair, but when he sets up as an apothecary it's time to take a stand. I took it. He accepted it meekly.

While the others held a conference at Harold Macmillan's house on the outskirts of Naples, I had a short talk with Alex and asked him how things had gone.

'Well, I must confess they might be better,' was his rather unexpected reply. 'We took some prisoners from the 90th Panzer Division. They were asked why they went on fighting when it was obvious that the game was up. They said: "You don't understand, or you wouldn't ask such a question. We belong to the 90th Division. As long as it is in the field we fight."'

Alex was determined that I should not miss the point. He wanted me to see what we are up against.

'They used to be a good division before they were mopped up in Africa. These fellows took on the old name, which was about all that was left. Now they in their turn have had an awful bashing, but they go on fighting. Pretty good, I call it.'

Alex is like Winston; his heart goes out to a good fighter.

The conference had broken up, the P.M. was in his bath, and Harold Macmillan as host kept the conversation going.

'The P.M.,' he began, 'has been told to keep off the grass as far as the King of Greece is concerned. We don't want him to commit himself to the Greek Prime Minister. Oh, he will, of course, whatever we do. He'll say: "You are the First Minister of the Crown. It is your duty to bring back the king." To Winston any king is better than no king.'

Macmillan smiled as he spoke of the P.M.'s wilfulness and of his romantic attitude to royal personages, to kings as kings, however impermanent their dynasties. At that moment Winston appeared. 'We are talking about kings, Winston.' The P.M.'s face brightened. He began to tell us about Edward VIII.

'Make no mistake, he had very engaging, crowd-compelling qualities, like his gaiety. He and Queen Mary exchanged very nice letters, but King George VI, when asked if he had a message for Edward, said: "I hope he is well and will make a permanent home in the U.S.A." The U.S.A.,' Winston repeated reflectively. 'Edward said: "England need not fear I am going to be a nuisance and settle in England."'

Eden: 'He was a wonderful host.'

It is the only time in four years that I have heard the P.M. refer to the Abdication. King and country, in that order, that's about all the religion Winston has. But it means a lot to him.

When we were alone the P.M.'s mood changed. Something had gone wrong. Before he saw Alex he had not given up hope that the army in Italy might be able to help. He was not prepared for Alex's doleful story. It appeared that our army was bogged down and that nothing could be done until the spring. 'Then,' the P.M. grunted, 'it will be too late.'

It was noon before we left Naples. The 'York' is very noisy; the P.M. addressed half a dozen observations to me during lunch, and I did not hear one of them. When I asked Eden, who was sitting next to him, to repeat a remark he told me that the P.M. had said: 'A good many people are abusing Charles, but I feel very well.' Eden added: 'More will abuse you when the news comes out at noon.' I took this to mean that I have been criticized in the Cabinet for allowing the P.M. to make these journeys.

*Moscow, October 9, 1944*

This morning the first thing I heard was Winston's voice above the noise of the plane.

'What do you take, Anthony?'

Eden: 'I always take a red. I think it's good stuff if you want to sleep on these trips.'

P.M.: 'I took two. I'm a hardened case.'

This house in the heart of Moscow, that has been set apart for the P.M., has been well chosen. Winston likes comfort, and he was in a cheerful frame of mind when Anthony came to talk things over. The Foreign Secretary could be obstinate, he must be told that there is only one course open to us – to make friends with Stalin. When the P.M. had said this he thrust out his chin.

Eden: 'How are you going to begin with Uncle Joe?'

P.M.: 'I shall say that the President and I have been like brothers, but I don't want the U.S.S.R. to feel it is just an Anglo-Saxon affair. I want them to know it's the three of us. That's why I've come. We can settle everything, we three, if we come together. If we don't there'll be years of diplomatic wrangling and suspicion. The President has illusions about China, and France is not on the same level as the three of us. Then I'll say there are some small matters to settle, but that will be easy if we work together.'

Eden: 'But, Winston, Poland is a big, not a small thing. It may spoil Anglo-Russian relations. If people feel that Russia is putting in puppets and that everybody who doesn't agree with her is an enemy of Poland they will be uneasy. Poland must be allowed to settle her own affairs.'

P.M.: 'We've agreed to the Baltic States[1] and the Curzon Line.'[2]

Eden: 'We've got to bring up this Polish question at once and tell Joe that Russia has enemies and they could make out quite a case against her in the last few weeks.'

Clark Kerr: 'They fear here that England will be soft over Germany.'

---

[1] Lithuania, Latvia and Estonia – these small states changed hands many times, and eventually in the spring of 1942 the Allies reluctantly agreed to the Russian claims.
[2] The much-disputed eastern frontier for Poland, proposed by Lord Curzon, the British Foreign Secretary, at the Paris Peace Conference, 1919–20. Following the Teheran Conference, it was agreed that the post-war frontier should follow this Line, despite the bitter objections of the exiled Polish Government in London. In July, 1944 the Russians set up a rival administrative body in Lublin which agreed to the adoption of the Curzon Line.

P.M.: 'I'm not a bit soft, but I can't stand for killing in mass. You need not accept a man's surrender, but if you do you mustn't kill him. The Russians would blot out their prisoners-of-war without a moment's hesitation.'

Eden: 'I'd like the Ruhr and Saar[1] to be permanently internationalized.'

P.M.: 'I would not give them to France. Of course, if the Ruhr were grassed over, our trade would benefit. I'm changing my mind about a list of war-criminals; we'd not carry it out. I'd like sixty or seventy of the people round Hitler shot without any trial, but I am against shooting all the German General Staff. Of course, Russia can do what she likes by force, but she would like sanction at the Peace Conference that her action was just and correct.'

Eden: 'Russia thinks England is hard on Bulgaria.'

Clark Kerr: 'He means praise by that.'

P.M.: 'Rotten people. They flogged our prisoners over barrels and left them in the sun to blister.'

The P.M.'s interest in the conversation was flagging. He got up and left the room.

*October 10, 1944*

The P.M. does not intend to allow anything to interfere with his plans, and anyone who raises difficulties gets short shrift.

P.M.: 'I must say I greatly covet that man's goodwill. How did things go, Anthony?'

Eden: 'Pretty sticky.'

P.M.: 'You really had a rough time?'

Eden: 'Not as bad as that. They were jocular. It was all in good temper. They don't want us to have any finger in Bulgaria. Why were we interested? It's a big issue for us. We might as well know where we stand.'

Clark Kerr: 'You were tough as well as charming, Anthony.'

---

[1] At Teheran Roosevelt had proposed the partitioning of Germany into five sections. In addition the Kiel Canal area and Hamburg and the Ruhr and Saar would become two separate areas under the control of the United Nations.

P.M.: 'I don't want you two to go after sticklebacks. If you get on to a bad patch I'd move on to another. There are a lot of things which don't matter.'

Eden: 'Bulgaria isn't one of them.'

The P.M. can say this sort of thing so that it is plain that he has exhausted the possibilities of the argument. He turned to me:

'Stalin looks much older. He wasn't a good colour. Ashen, yes, that's it. When he came to Teheran he came in a ship across the Caspian Sea and then by car. He didn't fly. You mustn't tell anyone that.'

Moran: 'If anything happened to him it would be a disaster.'

P.M.: 'God, yes. A catastrophe.'

The party broke up and I went with the P.M. to his room.

I asked him if the luncheon had gone well, and he repeated some of Stalin's conversation.

Stalin: 'Fear is a psychological factor. But it has very practical results. It was the fear of invasion that prevented the Germans transferring fifty divisions to the Russian Front in 1942. Those fifty divisions might have made the difference . . . I do not speak much, but drinking eases the tongue . . . I am a rough man and not much good at compliments.'

P.M.: 'But, after all, as I always tell the House of Commons, it's you Russians who have torn the guts out of the foul Hun.'

Stalin: 'Guts is the word.'

The P.M. went on to tell me that there had been a lot of talk of unpreparedness, but that Stalin had brought it to a head by asking: 'What is the moral? Only the aggressors can be prepared. Are all of us to be aggressors?' I thought the P.M. was going to bed, when Harriman knocked at the door; presently they settled down to play bezique and went on playing till three in the morning.

*October 11, 1944*

An enchanting morning, quite a hot sun in a blue sky. We feed at all kinds of hours. The P.M. breakfasted at eleven. But the food when it comes is excellent, though one meal is like the rest. Caviare with bread and butter; then smoked salmon on a long plate; then sucking pig. Even breakfast begins with those three courses; but at luncheon and dinner it is only a beginning; there follows soup, fish, some kind of meat, chicken or game, ice-cream with stewed fruit, and coffee. It sounds terrific to the underfed Briton, but it soon becomes a long-drawn-out, tiresome ritual, lasting two to three hours. You get tired of the plethora and long for an underdone steak.

I hear that Mikolayczyk[1] has been peremptorily summoned to Moscow. It appears that he gets savage when Stalin's name is mentioned. There is bound to be a row, for the P.M. is in no mood to listen to the Poles' strictures. I wish the meeting was over.

I would be quite happy here if I did not feel all the time that things at the College were going to pieces while I am away. The Abrahams and Miss Johnson of the Red Cross came to luncheon. I am sure that Clemmie had instructed Winston to be agreeable to them, but he is the poorest hand imaginable at small talk, or even at being polite to people who do not interest him.

\*

This afternoon I went sight seeing with the C.I.G.S. to a 16th Century monastery. He lives for the day when he can forget Europe and resume his country pursuits, especially photographing birds. He hates the war and all its ways, a little unusual in the senior soldier of his country in a world war.

The dinner at the Embassy tonight was rather tedious. People kept jumping up to propose toasts with turgid compliments (on our side), which all had to be translated. Winston's party manners were not at their best. The members of the English colony in Moscow, who were not asked to dinner, had been invited to a reception at the Embassy at eleven o'clock to meet the P.M. Poor things, marooned here, exiled in Moscow, they must be in sad need of a little excitement. At twelve forty-five we rose from the dinner-table and passed out into a great room, where those bidden to the reception awaited, with lively anticipation, the meeting with the legendary Churchill.

[1] Stanislav Mikolayczyk, Leader of the Polish Government in exile.

The P.M. gave one uncomprehending glance at the assembled guests, sent for a glass of champagne and then, without further ado, went into a side-room to confer with Stalin. He had forgotten all about the reception. The guests did not like to leave and stayed until nearly three o'clock in the morning.

Before the dinner I contrived to put in an hour at the ballet; a light to lighten the Muscovites in their grim, grey city.

*October 13, 1944*

As Maisky,[1] at the last moment, failed to produce the aeroplane he promised, I decided to go to Leningrad by a plane that was due to leave at nine o'clock in the morning. However, it was after one o'clock before I took my seat – a hard bench – in a small craft, with a drunken soldier, a woman and her baby. I was cold, for the derelict waiting-room was dirty and draughty, and most of the glass was missing from the windows. It was half-past four when we landed near Leningrad; a young woman who met me suggested that we should drive to the hotel, but I was bent on seeing the city while the light lasted. My guide, who had evidently determined to improve the occasion by adding to her stock of English and her knowledge of English ways, bombarded me with questions.

'*Lord* Moran . . . I do not understand. Then why *Mr* Churchill?'

At last I decided on a small counter-offensive.

'What will you do when Stalin dies?' I enquired.

She thought for a moment. 'Oh, I hope I shall die before dear Marshal Stalin.'

When I was ready to go to the Astoria, a palatial hotel, I found that they had reserved a suite of three sitting-rooms and a big bedroom, but the bath did not appear to have been used for months. The usual meal was brought, after the usual wait, but at five minutes to seven I proposed to my guide that we should abandon the rest of the banquet, as the ballet began at seven o'clock. She replied airily:

---

[1] Ivan Maisky, Soviet Ambassador in London, 1932–43.

'Oh, they will not start till we get there. We need not hurry.'

I found the great audience waiting patiently in their seats. If their drab poverty was in sharp contrast with the lovely scene on the stage when the curtain went up, they seemed to follow the technique of the ballet with the same understanding, the same approval, as our crowds follow the fortunes of the Arsenal or Chelsea football teams.

*October 14, 1944*
Back in Moscow, I found a rather disquieting mail from London. While I have been away a special Comitia at the College has discussed the White Paper on the new Health Bill, and the motion which the College officers put forward was lost. That means that, in my absence, my Government at the College has been defeated. There can be no doubt that my frequent absences from England, at a time when the medical services are being transformed, are exciting more and more criticism. Many Fellows of the College feel that I am so much away that the College has not taken a proper part in countering Willink's proposals.[1] I am always abroad, they say, when it is being discussed at the Ministry. There is a feeling, too, that I might be behind the White Paper and that I may indeed have inspired it. It is natural that this should be said, because I am always travelling with the P.M. We are bound to talk it over, people say, and it is inevitable, since the White Paper is anathema to most of the profession, that I am the target for adverse criticism. While many doctors are saying these things, a good many laymen are beginning to blame me because I allow the P.M. to go on these journeys. If I took a stronger line, they say, he would stay at home.

It is rather distracting, steering a course between my two

---

[1] The White Paper presented to the Commons in October, 1944, by Henry Willink, Coalition Health Minister. It was entitled 'A National Health Service' and envisaged a plan hardly less ambitious than that which Aneurin Bevan later introduced. Churchill supported the proposals with the words: 'Disease must be attacked in the same way that a fire brigade will give its assistance to the humble cottage as readily as it will to the most important mansion.'

conflicting loyalties, but it is plain that I must not abandon Winston, whatever happens at the College. After all, it is my job; the P.M. has enough on his plate without my adding my little worries. I am only sorry for Dorothy. She has to sit at home and watch the storm gathering. She asks: 'Can anything be done?' And the answer is, 'Nothing.'

If the P.M. really came here to make one final attempt to break down the deadlock between Stalin and the Poles the outlook is not very promising. It seems that Mikolayczyk, who arrived here two days ago, is agitated by the proposal to hand over half his country to Russia. This came out in the P.M.'s conversation. Good relations with Russia, he said testily, were more important than mapping frontiers. He is apt to lose his temper when Mikolayczyk thinks differently and cannot be persuaded that Stalin's intentions are honourable. The Warsaw underground,[1] Mikolayczyk declared, were deliberately incited to rise by the call to arms of Moscow Radio in July, and were then left to be annihilated by the Germans while the Russian Army stood by peacefully watching events. To Mikolayczyk the Russians' perfidy has been proven and he is impatient when he hears references to 'our great Eastern ally.' The P.M. sees, of course, that this kind of approach to Stalin leads nowhere. Squabbling between Stalin and Mikolayczyk will not help the Poles: it will only make Stalin more obstinate. They must be patient and leave it to him. The momentous meeting took place yesterday when I was in Leningrad, but from what I hear no good came of it.

\*

[1] As the Russians neared Warsaw, the inhabitants rose up to help evict the Germans from the city. The uprising began on August 1, 1944, and continued for two months, but the Russian forces did not relieve the city. Some 200,000 inhabitants, mostly young boys and girls, were killed by the S.S. troops during the fighting and on October 2 General Tadeuz Bor-Komorowski, the Polish commander, was forced to surrender. Thousands more were transported to Germany or expelled from their homes, and in order to wreak more revenge, the Germans began methodically to destroy the city. Warsaw was not liberated fully by the Russians until January 17, 1945.

In that bald sentence the meeting is dismissed in my diary. It was not till after the war, when I came across Mikolayczyk's own account, that I grasped the full significance of this encounter as a key to Winston's attitude to the Poles at that time. I give it in Mikolayczyk's own words.[1]

Molotov invited Mikolayczyk to speak first. The Pole did nothing to placate the Russians. He ignored the Lublin Poles, whom he regarded as Stalin's stooges. The P.M. spoke next. He supported Stalin.

P.M.: 'The Lublin Government should have a bigger share in the post-war Polish Government – the Curzon Line must be your eastern frontier.'

Mikolayczyk: 'I cannot accept the Curzon Line. I have no authority to leave half my countrymen to their fate.'

Molotov (*abruptly interrupting*): 'But all this was settled at Teheran.'

Mikolayczyk looked from Churchill to Harriman. They were silent. Harriman gazed at his feet, but the P.M. looked Mikolayczyk in the face.

'I confirm this,' he said quietly.

Mikolayczyk was shocked.

The revelation of what had happened at Teheran, in the absence of the Poles, only seemed to make the Prime Minister angry, as if he wanted to persuade himself that he was the aggrieved person and not Mikolayczyk. He demanded that Mikolayczyk should agree there and then to the Russian demands. The Pole would not give way.

P.M.: 'You can at least agree that the Curzon Line is the temporary frontier.'

At this, Stalin rose in his place. 'I want no argument. We will not change our frontiers from time to time. That's all.'

Churchill held out his hands, looked up to the ceiling in despair and wheezed. They filed out silently.

When later the P.M. saw Mikolayczyk with Eden the harm

---

[1] Stanislav Mikolayczyk, *The Pattern of Soviet Domination* (Sampson Low, Marston, 1948), pp. 104–13.

already done was not undone. The P.M.'s argument was sound enough. It was the manner in which it was advanced that gave hurt. He could have said with some reason to the outraged Poles: you cannot expect to carry us with you in a policy which threatens the unity of the three Allies by its unfriendly attitude to Russia. What he did say was quite different. Anders had said to the P.M. that he hoped the Allies when they had finished with Germany would defeat and destroy the Russians.

The controversialist in Winston seized on Anders' admission as the central theme of his attack on Mikolayczyk. It was as if a boxer, dancing round the ring, had seen a small cut above his adversary's eye and had rained his blows to keep it open. You would have thought that Poland was on the brink of war with Russia.

'If,' the P.M. shouted, 'you think you can conquer Russia, well, you are crazy, you ought to be in a lunatic asylum. You would involve us in a war in which twenty-five million lives might be lost. You would be liquidated. You hate the Russians. I know you hate them. We are very friendly with them, more friendly than we have ever been. I mean to keep things like that. I tell you, we'll become sick and tired if you continue arguing. We shall tell the world how unreasonable you are. We shall not part friends.'

This was not diplomacy. Nor did it intimidate Mikolayczyk. He was not going to be shouted down by anyone. He was furious and made no attempt to hide his feelings.

Winston told me the sequel with tears in his eyes. Mikolayczyk asked to be dropped into Poland, where he could rejoin the Underground Army. Winston in one moment forgot the obstinate peasant who had threatened our relations with Russia in his warm-hearted admiration for a soldier who is without fear.

Was Mikolayczyk a reliable witness? When Winston was recovering from his stroke in 1953 he was, for a short time, in the mood to listen to anything that I had to say, and I asked him if I might read to him Mikolayczyk's own account of his meeting with Stalin. When I had done, to my surprise he asked me to read it again. He seemed very sad. 'Does he exaggerate?' I asked. Winston hesitated: 'You see we were both very angry.'

*October 14, 1944*

It is plain that the P.M. has got the Poles on his conscience.

'I was pretty rough with Mikolayczyk,' he said this morning. 'He was obstinate and I lost my temper.'

Perhaps the P.M. was thinking of his own indignation when Chamberlain pressed Czecho-Slovakia to surrender a great part of her country in the interests of peace.

'It's a tragedy about these Poles,' the P.M. said tonight. 'All about one town surrounded in any case by non-Poles. Everything was signed, then Mikolayczyk said: "I cannot agree." I shook my fist at him and lost my temper. You see what will happen: the advancing Russians will be helped by the Poles. Then these villains will have them completely in their power. Whereas if the Poles are sensible I shall be able to help while they are bargaining with the Russians.'

\*

This evening there was a Command performance at the Bolshoi Theatre, first ballet and then opera, both in small doses. The Russians, according to Clark Kerr, had a suspicion that this was not exactly the P.M.'s native diet. In fact, Winston only came to life when Cossack dancers appeared on the stage and the Red Army Choir sang soldiers' songs. 'Are they going to sing the Volga Boat Song?' he asked. As we waited for the curtain to go up, Litvinov said rather excitedly: 'Almost anybody might come here in a few moments.' And then in a whisper: 'It's Stalin.' He had come in late by a side entrance and was with Winston in a box. The audience was looking in our direction, cheering. At the end of the performance I looked round, but Stalin had gone; he had slipped away as secretly as he came. I said to Winston that the applause was very vigorous and that I was surprised that Stalin excites such enthusiasm. He corrected me. 'There was passion in that outburst,' he said.

*October 15, 1944*

After breakfast I called on the P.M. and found that he had diarrhoea. He was, however, in good spirits, and very hopeful about the way things are going. This afternoon his temperature went up to 101. He is quite certain now that he is beginning another attack of pneumonia.

'I am in your clutches once more, my friend. What about getting Bedford? I wouldn't wait. The Cabinet will be getting fussed. Clemmie would like to come out, I am sure.'

He buried his head in his hands and moaned. Then Sawyers did something wrong and the P.M. flew at him. I fancy that his temperature is associated with the diarrhoea, but he won't accept this, because the diarrhoea stopped at noon, and now, seven hours later, the temperature is still up. Nothing is gained in such circumstances by arguing. If, on our journeys, I were to send for specialists and nurses every time the P.M. runs a temperature we might as well add them to our travelling establishment. However, I sent a message to Cairo asking Pulvertaft and Scadding and two nurses to stand by; it would take them twelve hours to get here. Time enough tomorrow to send a telegram to Clemmie.

*October 16, 1944*
The P.M.'s temperature is normal this morning. He has quite recovered his spirits, and we are on a level keel again.

Martin came in with a telegram. The P.M. smiled as he read it:
'Ha-ha, the F.O. making a bold gesture. They have told Tito that they are unable to understand the action of one of his officers. As if Tito cares a damn whether the F.O. understand! He has gone in with the Russians.'

I do wish that the P.M. would give himself a chance. I found him telephoning to Stalin. He wanted to see him this afternoon in spite of my protestations that the Kremlin was not a convalescent home. The P.M. went off at five o'clock, saying that he would be back in half an hour. He returned in two and a half hours in good form.

'You see, my half-hour became two and a half hours.'
'I had anticipated that,' I put in.
He smiled mischievously. 'Well, take my temperature. I don't think it's up.'

As he got out of his clothes he showed me a brooch with the flags of the two countries, and 'Liberty' underneath, in Russian, which Stalin's daughter was sending to Sarah. I said it was 'very nice.' 'Unique,' he corrected, a little excitedly. He was excited by this fresh proof of Stalin's friendship.

'I got nothing out of it,' he went on, but in a surprisingly good mood. 'There were two points only, and Stalin wouldn't give way over either. I am bound to say I think he is right in one of them; the Poles want to accept the Curzon Line only as the "demarcation line" between the two countries; the Russians say this means it isn't final; they want the Curzon Line as the frontier. The other point can easily be settled. It's the relations between the London and the Lublin Poles. Mikolayczyk says that if he goes any further he will be repudiated by his own countrymen.'

Whenever the P.M. sees Stalin he seems to come back in a good mood. He wound up:

'I said to Stalin: "Mikolayczyk is a peasant and very obstinate." Stalin replied: "I am a peasant too." I said, "You can be as obstinate as any of them."'

As far as I can tell, the P.M.'s plan is prospering. Stalin seems to meet him halfway. It may be that our stock has gone up or simply that Stalin is getting his own way in everything; at any rate, it is beyond question that the Bear, as Winston calls him, is more friendly, since we arrived in Moscow, than he has ever been. From time to time, too, Stalin strengthens the good impression left by his friendly advances by statements of an entirely reassuring character. Only yesterday he denied with great earnestness that Russia wished to convert the world to Communism, as many people feared.

'We could not, if we wanted,' he told the P.M. 'We Russians are not as clever as you think; we're simple, rather stupid. No one in Europe can be persuaded that England is either simple or stupid.'

Do these reassuring words mean anything to the P.M.? Does he trust Stalin? The trouble is that when the P.M. gets an idea into his head he lets his imagination play round it and will not bother to fit it in with the facts. At any rate he still makes his plans in the faith that Stalin's word is his bond.

There are relapses, to be sure, when the P.M. discovers that he is getting nothing out of Stalin.

'Of course,' he said today, 'it's all very one-sided. They get what they want by guile or flattery or force. But they've done a lot to get it. Seven or eight million soldiers killed, perhaps more. If they hadn't, we might have pulled through, but we could not have had a foot in Europe.'

Besides, he wants nothing except Stalin's friendship. I said to him this morning that Russia would have things all her own way in Europe after the war. He answered as if he were only half interested:

'Oh, I don't think so. When this fellow goes you don't know what will happen. There may be a lot of trouble.'

It seems incredible, but for the moment the red light has gone out.

While the P.M. was making friends with Stalin, I went over the Kremlin. An air of mystery hangs over the vast fortress. You feel it at once when the soldiers come out of the tower, which reinforced the defence of the wall in the old days, and one of them scrutinizes your pass pretty carefully – mistakes in Russia are expensive. The great wall, now that it has shed its camouflage, is like a lovely old garden wall, only three times the height. It's a bad simile, for the great wall *is* the Kremlin. There it stands for all that is secretive and sinister in the Russian character. Try to think of Moscow without the Kremlin, and what is left? Of the interior, the only part that comes to life is the old palace, built about 1400, where Ivan the Terrible and his kind lived in semi-darkness. Three or four rooms with low ceilings and hardly any windows lead to the Czar's sitting-room. Beyond, a bedroom with a four-poster, and beyond this, a small chapel, where Ivan lost his temper and killed his son. All these rooms, all small, dark and barbaric, were the living-quarters of the Czars until Peter the Great, wishing for a casement opening on Europe, migrated to St Petersburg. My guide smoked as he led me round, as if he would detach himself from all aristocratic folly, or perhaps just because he loved smoking.

As I drove from the Red Square I noticed that they were

repairing Lenin's tomb. He had been removed for fear he might be damaged by enemy action.

*October 17, 1944*

The P.M.'s temperature is still normal. 'You see, Charles, I did myself no harm. You oughtn't to fuss.' I asked him what were his plans for today. He replied:

'I shall not go out this morning. I've nothing till ten o'clock tonight, when I see Stalin.'

Moran: 'Couldn't 10 p.m. be altered to 6 p.m.?'

P.M.: 'No. Stalin specially said it would be more convenient for him at ten o'clock.'

Moran: 'You do all the travelling. Surely he could make this slight alteration?'

P.M. (*a little impatiently*): 'Stalin isn't as safe in his capital as I am in mine. When he came to the ballet it was all very secretive. I think we shall soon be on the move; the Poles' game is up; neither side will give way.'

*October 18, 1944*

Went to the P.M.'s room at ten o'clock this morning.

'Well,' he began, 'we got back at four-thirty this morning. But it was worth it; all very friendly. We went from the Kremlin to his private apartments. Stalin ate heartily, pork mainly. I picked at things. He dines at 1 a.m. as a rule, goes to bed at four and rises between noon and one o'clock, a relic of the days when it was safer for him to lie low during the day. Stalin is more friendly these days. The invasion and the number of prisoners taken by us have sent us up in his eyes. He talks freely to me.

'He told me stories of his exile in Siberia; he was a political prisoner with nothing to do in a forlorn place, with eight roubles a day to live on. He was there for four years before the 1914 war. Stalin told me how he caught a sturgeon. "With a rod and line?" I asked. "No," said Stalin, "I floated logs down the river with a hundred hooks on them, and with this contrivance I caught a big sturgeon; his length, from here to the end of the table where those seats are."

I asked him what emotions it caused him: joy, elation? "Oh, no, I was alarmed how in a small boat I could tow the big sturgeon in." Stalin put the sturgeon in a pool in which he had several smaller sturgeons. The sturgeon was half-dead, but it revived and ate some of the smaller fish. The colonel of the police said to Stalin: "We've had you three times in our power, and can never find anything against you, but we shall, and then you will get twelve years." Stalin spoke of all this without any bitterness. Then he was called up into the army.'

'Did he,' I asked the P.M., 'do much soldiering in the war?'

'Oh, no, he revolted.' The P.M. continued: 'Stalin's sense of humour is his strongest characteristic. He talked about my private war with Russia in 1919,[1] all in a friendly way. I said: "I'm glad now that I did not kill you. I hope you are glad that you did not kill me?" Stalin agreed readily, quoting a Russian proverb: "A man's eyes should be torn out if he can only see the past." We all made a move at three in the morning, but Stalin would not let us go and kept us till four. All the time he got more animated and expansive.'[2]

---

[1] As Secretary for War in 1919, Churchill was vehement in his denunciation of the Bolsheviks and made no secret of his belief that the Allies should support the White Russian armies. The Allied Supreme Council, while sympathizing with the White Russians, agreed to withdraw their forces from Russia in May, 1919. Churchill supplied and organized a volunteer force of 8,000 men to cover this withdrawal. Stalin was one of the leaders of the Red Army at the time.

2 Moran's papers have the following entry for October 20, 1944:
Churchill: 'We want nothing, we will take nothing. That will give us a strong position at the conference. America wants a lot, oil, bases. Russia wants a lot. It will be easier for them if England took something. Stalin asked what about the North African coast? But I stuck to my point; we entered the war for honour; we want nothing. That will put me in a strong position when they begin talking of the poor Hindhu.'

# CHAPTER TWENTY-THREE

# Athenian Interlude

At Teheran in December the Prime Minister had obstinately affirmed: 'We want nothing' – an attitude of mind not perhaps altogether appropriate to the transaction of business with Stalin. Whereas at Quebec, in the autumn of 1944, we find him more belligerent; he had been driven to the conclusion that the only way to save a country from the Russians was to occupy it. A month later, when Alex could not help, he was not so sure that such a policy made sense. He became certain that the only way to help the Poles was to make friends with Stalin. On his return from Moscow, the P.M. seemed to realize that he had got nothing out of Stalin and that Poland had been left in the grip of Russia. He lost no time in reverting to a more realistic policy.

Though there is nothing in my diary to account for this change of heart, I had come to connect these abrupt switches with Winston's physical state. I suppose I was at that time unduly preoccupied with his dwindling resources. I find this note in my diary under the date October 30, 1944:

'All this havering, these conflicting and contradictory policies, are, I am sure, due to Winston's exhaustion. He seems torn between two lines of action: he cannot decide whether to make one last attempt to enlist Roosevelt's sympathy for a firmer line with Stalin, in the hope that he has learnt from the course of events, or whether to make his peace with Stalin and save what he can from the wreck of Allied hopes. At one moment he will plead with the President for a common front against

Communism and the next he will make a bid for Stalin's friendship. Sometimes the two policies alternate with bewildering rapidity.'

Havering indeed! It reads to me now like the story of a fighting retreat that began in January, 1944, with Anzio, and only ended with his flight to Athens at the turn of the year – his stand in Greece was a kind of Battle of the Marne. If he appeared to haver it was because he was not strong enough to act. He was ready to act when he could.

The P.M. made his stand in the face of mounting criticism, both in America and in Britain. He seemed to be alone in his grasp of the danger to the liberty of the Greeks. But the bleak atmosphere created by this spate of criticism did not in any way deflect the P.M. from his purpose. He paid no heed to the clamour; his mind was sealed. He was grimly resolved that his timing on this occasion should come up to Stalin's standard. He would hold on to Greece – Stalin could have the rest of the Balkans. All his plans were made, and the P.M. felt a sense of relief that the time had come to act.

When the Germans marched out of Athens on October 2, only a few days passed before our troops, under General Scobie,[1] took possession of part of the city. The P.M. was ready, but the Communists, who were known to us as ELAS,[2] were ready too. It was not, however, until December 3 that civil war broke out.

When this was made known to the P.M. in London, he felt impelled to send a telegram to General Scobie in order to strengthen his hand and, in Winston's own words, 'to ginger him up a bit.' But before anything could be done, things must be put in their proper order, for, even in his most arbitrary moods, the P.M. was careful to conform to the usual procedure – that is, if it did not interfere with his set purpose. It was only right, he felt, that the steps he was about to take should be submitted to the

---

[1] Lieut.-General Sir Ronald Scobie, General Officer Commanding Greece.
[2] National Popular Liberation Army (military arm of EAM).

Foreign Secretary, who surely ought to agree that the time had come for our troops to intervene and, if necessary, open fire. Winston resolved to see Eden at once. So he was summoned to No. 10, where the P.M. set forth with unusual vehemence the case for action in Athens. The Foreign Secretary listened to this harangue in silence; he hated Winston's habit of taking over his job.

Winston himself has told us the sequel. About two o'clock in the morning of December 5, noticing that Eden was very weary, he said to him: 'If you like to go to bed, leave it to me.' When Eden had left the room, the P.M. began to draft a telegram to General Scobie, but it was not until a quarter to five that it was ready to be sent. I quote here only those words which the P.M. in his book put in italics as the pith of his message:

'Do not, however, hesitate to act as if you were in a conquered city where a local rebellion is in progress . . . we have to hold and dominate Athens. It would be a great thing for you to succeed in this without bloodshed if possible, but also with bloodshed if necessary.'[1]

Of this order Winston wrote in 1953:

'I must admit that it was somewhat strident in tone . . . I had in my mind Arthur Balfour's celebrated telegram in the eighties to the British Authorities in Ireland: "Don't hesitate to shoot" . . . it hung in my mind as a prompter from those far-off days.'[2]

Opinion in the United States was rudely shaken by Churchill's weakness for kings and by his seemingly blatant disregard for the will of the Greek people. The P.M. was much incensed by this criticism. Without waiting to cool down, he despatched a cable to President Roosevelt which, according to *The White House Papers*,

[1] Winston Churchill, *Triumph and Tragedy*, p. 252.
[2] Arthur James Balfour (1848–1938), Chief Secretary for Ireland (1887). He was an implacable opponent of Home Rule and earned the nickname 'Bloody Balfour,' because of his determined measures.

may well have been the most violent outburst of rage in all their historic correspondence. From the same source we learn that shortly afterwards 'relations between the White House and Downing Street were more strained than they had ever been before.'

At this point the P.M.'s order to General Scobie to act as if he were in a conquered city, which was in cypher and had been marked 'Personal and Top Secret,' was allowed by the State Department in Washington to leak out to the Press. The President felt the mounting public anger, and on December 13 he cabled the P.M. that he was unable to support his action in Greece.

The P.M.'s instinct was to press on with military operations until he could see light, but Alex, who was in Athens, was for once obdurate; he insisted on the necessity for a political solution. In this he had the backing of Leeper, the British Ambassador in Athens, who had revived the idea of appointing Archbishop Damaskinos[1] as Regent. This was the President's solution, and it found a strong advocate in Harold Macmillan. The P.M. still hesitated; he was not happy about entrusting absolute power to the Archbishop. Besides, the King of Greece was against this step, and it would therefore entail in the P.M.'s words 'an act of constitutional violence' to over-rule the King's veto. Something had to be done, and done at once. The day before Christmas the P.M. decided to fly to Athens, to see for himself what could be done.

*Harefield, December 24, 1944*

I was sitting over the fire in the cottage after tea, pondering how I could make Christmas amusing for Dorothy, who has had a dusty war, when the telephone rang. It was one of the secretaries at Chequers; he said that the P.M. wanted to speak to me. I held on, then the same voice said, 'Is Lord Moran there?'

'Charles?' the friendly voice was a little faint. 'I'm off to G. . . .

'When?' I asked.

The P.M. irritably: 'I can't hear.' With angry resignation. 'I can't hear a word you say.'

---

[1] Primate of Greece, 1938. Active leader of resistance movement.

I shouted: 'When?'

'Oh, tonight,' he answered.

When he had rung off I asked Dorothy where she thought G. might be. She suggested Gibraltar, 'but we must know because of clothes.' 'They won't tell us anything on the telephone; there's nothing for it but to drive over to Chequers and find out something definite.'

This morning the restriction on headlights was removed, so we joyfully stripped the black paper from the lamps of the car. We had forgotten what it felt like to sweep along a road thrown up by a searchlight instead of groping our way anxiously along the dark lanes around Harefield.

G. is Greece.

*December 25, 1944*

Our aircraft landed in the failing light at an airfield near Athens; from this we went in an armoured car by a coast road to a jetty, where a launch was waiting to bring us to H.M.S. *Ajax*,[1] a small cruiser which had been in the River Plate engagement. Eden told me with a wry smile that it was along that very road that he had passed through great crowds, wild with elation, only two months ago.

We dined on board with General Scobie, Harold Macmillan, Alex and the captain of the cruiser. The P.M. complained of the slow progress of Scobie's troops. Alex pointed out the difficulty of house-to-house fighting, of knowing, in such conditions, who was the enemy. He was soothing and cautiously optimistic. But the P.M. was not to be comforted. We were, he said, faced with two very forbidding alternatives: either to take on most of Greece with the growing disapprobation of the world, or to abandon our friends to be massacred. There had been a conference on the plane, and when the P.M. retired to his cabin Macmillan said that he had never seen him listen so patiently or so attentively.

---

[1] One of the four cruisers which were successful in forcing the German pocket battleship *Graf Spee* to scuttle herself at the mouth of the River Plate in December, 1939.

'The truth is,' he said, 'he has no solution himself.'

Macmillan affirmed that help was coming from the North, from Russia.

The P.M. joined us again. He blew up about the attitude of *The Times*; it was very badly informed. He grew vehement about some of his critics in the House of Commons, and promised that he would expose them on his return. I don't know whether it is that he is getting more and more restive under criticism or simply that he has taken a strong line over Greece and is not certain whether he can stick to it; anyway his language is pretty violent.

### December 26, 1944

We lunched on board and waited to go ashore for a conference with the Greeks at their Foreign Office. A shell or light mortar bomb fell somewhere near; we crossed the deck to see where it had fallen, perhaps sixty yards astern. As we stepped into a launch another shell came over, hitting a landing craft by the water's edge. At the jetty two armoured cars were waiting. The P.M. began to climb into the first, and I clambered into the other, where I found the Archbishop sitting patiently on a rough form. We had this car, which was like a furniture van, to ourselves, save for a security officer in the uniform of the 60th, who sat opposite me, fingering his tommy-gun. I could not talk to the Archbishop without an interpreter, so I stood looking through the one tiny peep-hole at the coast road. The great lumbering car swayed and turned clumsily around the sharp bends; suddenly we came round a corner on the top of some children. They scattered with a scream, all but one, and I was shocked that we did not pull up to see if the child was hurt. At last we stopped with a jerk, the door was drawn back and an officer appeared; he seemed a little fussed. He said that he wanted to get the P.M. into the Embassy as soon as he could. A woman had been shot dead a few yards down the street, just before we arrived. But the P.M. stood gazing up at the windows of the house opposite, giving the V sign to the Greeks looking out.

The great rooms of the Embassy were unheated, and in the dining-room the wife of the Ambassador, in a fur coat, was preparing tea for the typists, secretaries and cypher staff, who had been brought into the Embassy for safety. The back of the house was less safe from snipers than the front, and a small garden there was said to be particularly exposed. Into it the P.M. now went with the Archbishop, to pose before the photographers, whereupon an officer spoke to two soldiers, who proceeded to cover the upper windows of the adjoining buildings with their tommy-guns. The P.M. returned to the dining-room and made a graceful little speech to the staff around the long table, thanking them for their cheerfulness and fortitude.

We made the short journey to the Ministry of Foreign Affairs in our armoured car. I could not see if there was anybody in the streets. At the Ministry we were led by an old man with a haggard face to a room with an immense table and chairs; hurricane lamps flickered on the table, casting shadows in the dim light. Two soldiers drew down the shutters. The Archbishop took the centre seat; on his right sat the P.M. and beyond him Eden. On his left were placed Alex, and then Harold Macmillan and General Scobie. Opposite the Archbishop, M. Papandreou, the Prime Minister of Greece, and members of his Government sat uneasily. There was no sign of ELAS and it was decided to start without them. The Archbishop rose. His black head-dress added to his great height, and his flowing beard gave him a patriarchal aspect. His words of greeting were translated sentence by sentence by a young Englishman, as if it were his own speech. Then the P.M. rose:

'Your beatitude:

'Today Greece may march with the United Nations to victory, which is not far distant. But if all our efforts fail, we shall have to bend to our hard task, to secure the city of Athens from anarchy. We do not shrink from that task, but we hope for a happier issue . . .'

There was a knock on the door. The Prime Minister stopped speaking. A soldier half opened the door and spoke to someone on the other side. He closed the door again and whispered to an officer who had approached him. The officer went and spoke to the P.M., who announced that the representatives of ELAS had arrived. Three men filed in, led by M. Partsalides.[1] He had a grey waterproof and brown muffler over his British battledress. In the dim light I could not see how the other two were dressed, but they were muffled to the ears, like pilots coming into the mess from a winter flight. Without further greeting they took the chairs nearest to the door.

I glanced involuntarily at the members of the Greek Government. M. Papandreou did not look at the Communists; even when their leader spoke he kept his eyes fixed on the other side of the room. He appeared ill at ease, while the Greek on his right had the aspect of a sick man. A long tendon stood out in his scraggy neck, and I noticed that he kept swallowing. These members of the Greek Government were lean cattle, who looked as if they had not been outside their houses for months and were now blinking at the pale light of the hurricane lamps. The Communists had the look of men who had spent their lives in the open air and were always making decisions on the spur of the moment. They sat very still and upright in their chairs, all keyed up, as if they were waiting for something to happen. The suppressed vitality of ELAS contrasted strangely with the gaunt, grey, weary faces of the Greek Government. Someone dropped his spectacle case on the floor. It made a clatter, very distinct in the silence that had fallen on everything.

The British Prime Minister began his speech again:

'I trust,' he said, 'that the representatives of ELAS will not feel that we misunderstand their point of view and their difficulties. We came here because we were invited by all parties in Greece. We cannot leave until we have brought this matter to a good conclusion. We want nothing from Greece, not an inch of her territory. We must, of course, ask acceptance of General Scobie's terms. But we hope this conference may restore Greece again to her place among the Allies.'

I was sitting a little behind and to the right of the Communists and had scarcely taken my eyes off their faces, which were alert and yet expressionless. Nothing that the P.M. said was reflected

---

[1] Leader of ELAS.

in their looks. M. Partsalides was listening intently, but his intelligent face revealed only his concentration. Siantos's sharp, foxy features, preceded by a full moustache, were equally without expression. He had put on spectacles and was now busy making notes. I moved my chair that I might be able to see his face. He was stroking his moustache, and, as the P.M. continued, he shaded his eyes with his hand.

When the Prime Minister sat down, the Archbishop asked if there were any questions; Mr Churchill, he said, was willing to answer them. At this ELAS began whispering among themselves. At last M. Partsalides rose. He spoke at first as if he was not certain of himself or of his audience, but after a little his right hand began to pound the air with a slow piston movement, and his voice grew more confident.

'I take this opportunity of expressing sentiments in common with the Archbishop. I am,' he said, 'expressing the feelings of the Greek people,' – here M. Papandreou made little restless movements with his hands, – 'on behalf of EAM,[1] for the efforts of the Prime Minister of our great ally, England. Despite the fact that we find ourselves face to face with exceptionally tragic circumstances, we are convinced that the clashes between the Greek people, and between them and the British troops, will not shake the traditional relations of the Greek people with the British people. The Greeks rose as one man because they believed in the destruction of Fascism, in the right to live free upon the basis laid down in the Atlantic Charter.'

The other two representatives of ELAS might have come from a camp in the mountains, with red hands, and this was their sleek-faced lawyer, with white hair brushed smoothly back from his delicate features.

'We thank Mr Churchill,' he ended, 'for taking the initiative, but inasmuch as it is a conference of our political parties, we feel that the party of EAM should also have been called, EAM, which commands the living forces of the nation, which was the first to

[1] EAM, National Liberation Front.

rise in support of the great struggle which the British people waged alone.'

Eden rose to point out that the conference could invite anybody they wished to attend the meeting.

Winston said: 'We would now like to go. We have begun the work; make sure you finish it.'

Everyone rose. The P.M. passed down the side of the long table, shaking hands with the members of the Greek Government, until he came to the Communists, when he paused. He had vowed that he would not shake hands with these villains. What was he going to do?

'Who,' he asked, 'will introduce these gentlemen to me?'

He then shook hands with each of them in turn. And now for the first time the expressionless features of ELAS came to life, and a look of pleasure crossed their faces. They wrung Mr Churchill's hand with slight, stiff bows.

As we returned in the armoured car to the ship the P.M. said that the Communists did not seem as bad as they had been painted; they were a different lot of people from the Lublin Poles. They had wrung his hand on parting. This had impressed him. He felt that if the three Communists could be got to dine with us all difficulties might vanish.

After dinner the P.M. again argued that the fighting was very slow. Couldn't, say, twenty tanks go one way and twenty another, with say twenty in reserve? And then the area between the two lots of tanks could be cleaned up. Alex repeated that street fighting was a slow business. Men of ELAS in civilian clothes infiltrated behind the lines. He pleaded for patience. Of course, Germans or Russians would soon have liquidated the affair, blowing up houses and exterminating those who resisted, but we could not do that.

The P.M. said that he would not, of course, presume to give a military opinion, but he wanted them to know the political aspect of the matter. If the fighting dragged on, difficulties might arise with America and even with Stalin; the affair ought to be finished off as quickly as possible. Finally, he said that Parliament would be meeting on January 12, and he asked Alex if he thought the military situation could be cleared up by then. Alex thought it could. The P.M. then said:

'I don't want you to alter your plans to suit me or Parliament.'

*December 27, 1944*

As I was waiting for breakfast Eden passed through the cabin on his way to see the P.M., who had apparently sent him a message that he was going ashore forthwith to see the Archbishop.

Eden, a little wearily: 'I do wish he'd let me do my own job.'

Presently the P.M. came out of his cabin and, seeing Alex and Scobie talking to me, sat down.

'I'll stay two days here,' he began, 'but you must find something to amuse me. I'd like to go to some forward observation point and see the problem for myself. It helps me to see things . . . I'm not doing this for amusement.'

He went out on to the deck.

'I hope,' said Scobie to me, 'he won't go ashore; it isn't safe. I simply can't compete if the P.M. will keep going ashore in the next two days.'

Last night the Admiral harped on the same theme.

'I was horrified,' he exclaimed, 'to hear that the P.M. is going ashore. These Communists have their duties and he has his – and his is to keep alive. It's as simple as that.'

The P.M. came into the cabin and sat down; the launch had not come back from the shore.

'I shan't see the Parthenon this time. The last time I was here before the war I spent eight days there with my paintbox; sandwiches were sent up to me. I didn't really paint. I just loved it. The faint pinks and blues. Have you been to the Acropolis, Charles? You haven't? Oh, we must remedy that.'

We were sitting at luncheon with the Ambassador and his wife when there was a knock at the door. It opened and a paratroop officer saluted and stood to attention.

'I have come,' he said, 'for Lord Moran.'

It was all like an incident in one of Sean O'Casey's plays, where some wretched man is taken for a ride and bumped off. Alex turned to me:

'Where are you going, Charles?'

'The Acropolis, I suppose.'

'Can I come with you?'

No armoured car was waiting, but a local touring car. We were apparently to see the Acropolis with an armed escort of two paratroop officers. When we got to the Parthenon Alex went to speak to a machine-gun section stationed in a position to command the entrance. One of the paratroop officers came up to me.

'It's a lovely spot,' he said. 'We have got all Athens in our arc of fire.'

As we left, Alex said: 'I propose we send the car away and walk. I want a little exercise. What about it, Charles?'

Halfway to the Embassy, Alex stopped. 'Do you see that little temple there?' pointing to a small building about a quarter of a mile from the road. 'I have never been there; let's go and have a look at it.'

We started off, but one of the paratroop men came up. 'I don't think, sir, you ought to go there. There was a man killed there this morning; there are some snipers overlooking it.'

'Oh, nonsense,' Alex broke in. 'If we go that way' – pointing to a short detour – 'it's quite all right.'

Our guard made one more attempt a little further on to dissuade Alex, but to no purpose. We loitered in the little temple for some time.

*

To a man of my calling, the bald record in my diary of events in the weeks immediately preceding the P.M.'s arrival in Athens reads like a bulletin issued at the crisis of a protracted illness. It was in this parlous state of mind and body that the P.M. was confronting the growing hostility of public opinion in the United States, which found expression in a press campaign of some virulence. This was echoed in the British Press: even papers like *The Times* and the *Manchester Guardian* were, in their demure way, full of lamentations over the

P.M.'s 'reactionary' policy. Intervention in Greece was his own idea, and he had to defend it practically single-handed.

It is one of Winston's engaging qualities that he will never say 'I told you so,' yet two years later the temptation must have been compelling, for his policy was taken over, lock, stock and barrel, by the United States.

'A Communist-dominated Government in Greece would be considered dangerous to United States security.'

That was part of the evidence given on March 21, 1947, by Mr Dean Acheson, the Acting Secretary of State, before the Foreign Affairs Committee of the House of Representatives.

Once again Winston had spoken before his time: he had given a lead to the English-speaking peoples, and before they had fallen into step he had saved Greece from the fate of Czecho-Slovakia, leaving it a free nation.

# CHAPTER TWENTY-FOUR

# Yalta Diary

*London, January 29, 1945*

Greece is, after all, only a fragment of the P.M.'s problem. What is to be the fate of the rest of Europe? What is to happen to Germany? Will Stalin help to knock out Japan? These are the issues to be settled at Yalta.

The P.M. has decided on the spur of the moment to fly to Malta tonight. There is bad weather coming in from the Atlantic, and snow is expected at Northolt. This might make taking off difficult, so we are to be in the air by nine o'clock. The idea is to fly before the gale.

*January 30, 1945*

I turned in soon after we were in the air to get some sleep, as we were to land at Malta between four and five in the morning; an hour later Sawyers pulled my curtain back and said that the P.M. had a temperature – a good beginning to a winter journey of three thousand miles. The P.M. blames my sulphaguanadine tablets, which he has been taking during the day. As they are not absorbed from the gut, they could not be responsible, but the P.M. has views on everything, and his views on medicine are not wanting in assurance.

He was restless, and I soon gave up any attempt to sleep. He asked me if I would like to send for Whitby, the pathologist, and what about Clemmie? – the Moscow performance over again. He has developed a bad habit of running a temperature on these journeys.

It is not the flesh only that is weaker. Martin tells me that his work has deteriorated a lot in the last few months; and that he has become very wordy, irritating his colleagues in the Cabinet by his verbosity. One subject will get in his mind to the exclusion of all others – Greece, for example.

Winston stayed in bed in the plane till noon, when he was taken to H.M.S. *Orion*. He rested until the evening, when Harriman came to dinner. Only this morning he was in the doldrums when, turning his face to the wall, he had called for Clemmie. Surely this bout of fever should put sense into his head. But Winston is a gambler, and gamblers do not count the coins in their pockets. He will not give a thought to nursing his waning powers. And now, when it was nearly midnight, he demanded cards and began to play bezique with Harriman. Damn the fellow, will he never give himself a chance?

*H.M.S.* Orion, *Malta, February 1, 1945*
When Sarah began talking about palmistry today I explained that there was a perfectly simple anatomical explanation of all the lines in the palm of the hand, which had been invested for commercial purposes with such portentous significance.

'You think there is nothing in it?' There was an air of disappointment as she traced the line of life and the heart line in my hand. I thought it wise to change the conversation to hands in general, telling her of a dinner-party given by Macready, the grandson of the actor, who is Major-General on the Q. side,[1] and his Polish wife, at their flat in Washington. I was tired and only ticking over when the woman on my right said without warning: 'Why are your hands so much younger than your face?' Winston looked up from his work; he had been listening. 'Let me see them,' he demanded, and went on: 'You must have watched complete strangers walk into your consulting-room one after the other, for how long? Forty years? Now, Charles, did you really look at their hands? Did you learn anything from them?' I had landed myself and had to say something. 'I think it was after I read what Gorky wrote about Tolstoy's hands that I got into the way of looking at people's hands.'

---

[1] The Army administrative side.

'What did he say?' Sarah broke in.

'He has wonderful hands – not beautiful, but knotted with swollen veins and yet full of the singular expression and power of creativeness. Probably Leonardo da Vinci had hands like that. With such hands one could do anything. Sometimes, when talking, he would move his fingers, and gradually close them into a fist, and then suddenly opening them, utter a good full-weight word.'

I wanted to tell Winston about Dudley Pound's hands, which were like a navvy's, very muscular and insensitive, but he had taken up his work. Winston has small, white hands – misleading hands; they give one the impression they have not been used.

*February 2, 1945*

This morning the *Quincey*, with the President on board, passed slowly by us. The President, in a cloth cap, sat scanning our ship for Winston, who was on the quarter-deck raising his hat in salutation.

After tea the P.M. appeared. He said that the President had been very friendly.

'He must have noticed the candle by my bed when we were at the White House, because there was a small lighted candle on the luncheon table by my place to light my cigar. The President's very friendly,' he repeated, half to himself.

Winston would normally never notice anything like that.

*February 3, 1945*

All night planes have been taking off from the large airfield to carry our party of seven hundred across the Aegean and the Black Sea to the Crimea, fourteen hundred miles away. There, after a flight of seven hours, we made a bumpy landing on Saki airfield, from which the snow had been swept, leaving an icy runway only just long enough for our craft to land on. Molotov, Litvinov,[1] Vyshinsky[2] and Pavlov[3] – the usual people – met us.

---

[1] Maxim Litvinov, Soviet Vice-Minister for Foreign Affairs.
[2] Andrei Vyshinsky, Soviet Deputy Foreign Minister.
[3] Marshal Stalin's interpreter.

The P.M. walked over to the President's aircraft, the 'Sacred Cow', and stood while he was helped out by Mike Reilly, his body-guard, and deposited in a jeep, which then proceeded to move slowly to another part of the airfield, where a guard of honour and a band were posted. The officer commanding the guard stood frozen to attention. He held his sword straight in front of him like a great icicle. The P.M. walked by the side of the President, as in her old age an Indian attendant accompanied Queen Victoria's phaeton. They were preceded by a crowd of camera-men, walking backwards as they took snapshots. The President looked old and thin and drawn; he had a cape or shawl over his shoulders and appeared shrunken; he sat looking straight ahead with his mouth open, as if he were not taking things in. Everyone was shocked by his appearance and gabbled about it afterwards. While this was happening, one of our party decided to explore the three big tents on the aerodrome. He was well rewarded for his curiosity. The Russians had done things well: caviare, smoked salmon and every kind of drink. But he was the only man in the tent.

When the band had worked off the three national anthems we were packed into cars; the P.M. called me to his car. I could see that we were crossing a snow-covered moor before we began to climb into the mountains. All the way I caught glimpses of sturdy girls, dressed like Russian soldiers, and carrying tommy-guns, who stood rigidly to attention as each car passed. I must have dropped off to sleep, when we pulled up with a jerk at a house on the outskirts of a village, where luncheon was set out on great tables. It is always the same. Caviare, smoked salmon, sucking-pig and the rest, with their sweet champagne. I looked on this collation doubt-fully, for we had already lunched on sandwiches, but the P.M. likes good food and he soon got into form, making some rather daring remarks.

'I don't think much of the Lublin Government,' he confessed, 'but I suppose they are the best you can get.'

The short winter day was closing in before he rose from the table. For a long time we went uphill and downhill, flanked as long as we could see by mountains. The light had gone when we stopped.

As I got out of the car, I noticed how mild and balmy the air was after Saki. We followed the P.M. into the great hall of a palatial house. I went to his room after dinner to see how he had weathered the journey. I found him talking to Anthony and Sarah. He made me sit down, though it was nearly midnight and I was weary. He was in great form, protesting that he could easily make the same car journey now, and – raising his voice – make a speech at the end of it.

The P.M. began talking about the Poles – we were in for a late night. A message had come from Roosevelt suggesting a start at four o'clock tomorrow afternoon.

P.M.: 'If the President is only going to be here for five days, we mustn't waste time like this. We must begin with the political part of our programme, the Poles in particular. After all, I can't tell the Russians how to advance more quickly in the East. Stalin must realize that the people in England who are keenest on good relations with Russia are most worried over Poland. Our future good relations with our ally are at stake. We can't agree that Poland shall be a mere puppet state of Russia, where the people who don't agree with Stalin are bumped off. The Americans are profoundly ignorant of the Polish problem. At Malta I mentioned to them the independence of Poland and was met with the retort: "But surely that isn't at stake."'

When the P.M. begins to talk of the Poles, I know what is coming. I could prompt him if he faltered in his piece. I slipped off to bed.

*February 4, 1945*

Breakfasted with the C.I.G.S. I said jokingly he must hurry up and finish off the Germans, or I should have to make a separate peace. He replied quite solemnly:

'You cannot be more weary of the war than I am. It's becoming a damned nightmare.'

To get out of uniform, to turn his back on London streets and to return to a country life – this is the sum of his ambitions.

When I left the C.I.G.S., I went to find out where everybody was. At the end of the nineteenth century this part of the coast, which is blessed with the mildest climate in Russia, became a fashionable watering place. After the Revolution the palatial residences of the Czar and his Grand Dukes were converted into sanatoria or rest homes for Russian workers: the 'star' workers are given free railway tickets to Yalta, and lodge at the Government's expense, but they have to bring their own beds. When the Germans occupied the Crimea they looted everything and destroyed the buildings. But this immense castle where we are staying, which was built at some fabulous cost for a Prince Vorontsov, Ambassador to the Court of St James's in 1837, was left undamaged because Hitler gave it to Mannstein[1] to be his summer home when peace came.

It is a curious mixture of Gothic and Moorish art. Passing through a great Moorish archway, I descended a wide flight of steps, flanked by six marble lions, to the garden, which falls in terraces to the Black Sea. There are two fine cypresses in the courtyard, and rare subtropical plants are scattered through the garden. The house is sheltered by mountains, which are clothed with vineyards on their lower slopes, and higher up there are dark pine trees. When I returned to the house I found that the reception rooms are what might be expected from the gentleman who was responsible for the lions, but the plumbing and sanitary arrangements are elementary.

Down a dozen stairs, there is a passage, off which perhaps a score of small bedrooms open, as in an hotel. These must once have been the servants' bedrooms; they are now full of Air Marshals, Generals and Admirals. This morning I found them hunting for a tin to wash in. If anyone had any success in the search he promptly secreted it in his own room so that he could get a wash without lining up for the two communal basins, which have no plug and where only the cold tap works. There are two baths in the castle, so I shall take a tub in the middle of the afternoon, when there is a lull in the demand.

Nor is plumbing the only thing missing in our stately home. The Russians have done their best, but their task has not been easy;

[1] Field-Marshal Erich von Mannstein, Hitler's adviser on military affairs.

for, if the Germans spared the building, they removed everything in it. All the furniture and pictures and food and wine, even the waiters, have been brought for our entertainment from Moscow, which is nine hundred miles to the north of Yalta. These waiters are really the only people I recognize when I revisit Russia – apart from Stalin himself, Molotov, Litvinov and the immense fellow who is head of the Security Police – and all my Moscow friends seem to be here in their white coats; their faces are glum, and there is a furtive air about them, but they, at least, look the part and sometimes seem to be the only links with the old Russia of the Czars.

The Russians thought nothing of converting the eighty miles of snowbound mountain road which connects Saki with Yalta into a good surface for a car; they lined the road all the way with troops, but in the end they were defeated by the common bug. In this palace, with its gilt furniture, its lashings of caviare, its grand air of luxury, there is nothing left out but cleanliness. The P.M. sent for me this morning because he had been bitten on the feet. A more thorough assault had been made on Sawyers, while Dixon,[1] Eden's right-hand man, had been eaten up by bedbugs in the night. While thinking out a line of action, I was asked to go to one of the two sanatoria where the rest of our party are lodged, to see one of the Foreign Office people who was running a high temperature. I found seven officers in a room, with the most elementary bedding arrangements, spread out on the floor, and bugs in all the bedding. Give the Englishman real discomfort, and he becomes cheerful, but it was plain something must be done. I telephoned the Americans, and found they were in trouble too. They lent me a couple of their sanitary squads, and we began going round all the beds with an instrument which squirted D.D.T. But I haven't unpacked my suitcase, and I have no intention of doing so.

Stalin called after luncheon. He stayed only a short time, visiting the map-room before he went. I had a talk with Bridges[2] this afternoon. He does not exactly radiate geniality. His steady, appraising

---

[1] Mr Pierson Dixon, Principal Private Secretary to the Foreign Secretary.
[2] Sir Edward Bridges, Secretary to the Cabinet.

gaze behind thick spectacles seems to register disapproval; and when I used to run into him at No. 10 I thought he took unnecessary pains to frown on a stranger. Now I find this is only a mask. His uncompromising integrity, his dislike of intrigue of any kind and his rugged honesty are known to everyone. That is why he is Secretary of the Cabinet, and also head of the Civil Service. But what I've seen since we left England is quite new to me: his eagerness and his unspoilt pleasure in sightseeing – the Isles of Greece brought him out of his bunk in the 'Skymaster' at five o'clock in the morning. I have seen a good deal of him while we have been here, and I like what I have seen. He has a good headpiece and thinks for himself. He is very loyal to the P.M., but, evidently, thinks the present régime unusual in more than one respect. He feels that you can influence Winston up to a point, but that it is useless trying to do so beyond that. 'People,' he said, 'criticize me, I know, for not doing more, but I'm sure it's no good.' Of course, he is right. The P.M. will listen so far; after that he becomes antagonistic. Archie Sinclair[1] does not seem to realize this; he will go through his whole piece independent of the effect on the P.M. Portal tells me he feels sometimes he must nudge him but that he has not got as far as this yet. Bridges thinks very highly of the C.I.G.S. He feels that Brooke has shown great judgment in his dealings with the P.M., giving his own opinion firmly and independently, but without making it too assertive. In response to my doubts, Bridges admitted that he, too, is dubious about the next fifteen years.

Livadia Palace, where the President is housed, is about a mile from Yalta; it was the summer home of Nicholas II. The Czar had a number of bedrooms on the first floor, for it was his custom to sleep in a different room every night – sometimes he would even change his room during the night. Stalin said, with a grin, that the only place where one could be certain of finding the Czar was in the bathroom first thing every morning. Probably Stalin felt that the Imperial security technique was rather an amateur business.

Here, in the Grand Ballroom, at five o'clock today, the first

---

[1] Sir Archibald Sinclair, Secretary of State for Air.

formal meeting of the Conference was held, and developed into a three-hour discussion about the military position. Stalin expressed pleasure when he heard our main drive was planned to begin in a month's time. But what we do or do not do is no longer vital to the Russians.

Dined next to Portal. He led me on to talk of medical matters, cancer research, cerebral localization and the possibility of lengthening the span of life. Then I started him on the selection of men. He began:

'Someone maliciously said that the P.M. will fight to the last ditch but not in it. He does not like making decisions.'

Alex broke in: 'And he will not listen to evidence.' This remark, coming from Alex, surprised me.[1] It was not in character. Alex went on: 'Winston is not really interested in those around him.'

I told Portal my impression of the President when we were in Washington after Pearl Harbour: that he doesn't like thinking things out, but waits for situations to develop and then adapts himself to them. His face brightened.

'That is the exact truth,' he said. 'I never thought of putting it like that.'

There was a good deal of talk after dinner about the conference at the President's house. Everyone seemed to agree that the President had gone to bits physically; they kept asking me what might be the cause. I first noticed his loss of weight at Quebec. It was not only his physical deterioration that had caught their attention. He intervened very little in the discussions, sitting with his mouth open.[2] If he has sometimes been short of facts about the subject under discussion his shrewdness has covered this up. Now,

[1] In a handwritten notebook (PP/CMW/K4/2) Moran remarks that Churchill 'likes Alex more than any soldier or sailor'.

[2] Was Roosevelt properly briefed for Yalta? J. F. Byrnes, Director of Office War Mobilization, writes: 'So far as I could see, the President had made little preparation for the Yalta Conference . . . Not until the day before we landed at Malta did I learn that we had on board a very complete file of studies and recommendations prepared by the State Department . . . I am sure the failure to study them while en route was due to the President's illness.' (From *Speaking Frankly*, p. 23.)

they say, the shrewdness has gone, and there is nothing left. I doubt, from what I have seen, whether he is fit for his job here. Stalin doesn't seem to be taking advantage of the situation. Cadogan said he feared Stalin would say: we've done our bit, we can't do much more, but that was not what happened. Stalin said the allies had not asked him to commit himself to any military plan. He had done this offensive in a comradely spirit. He meant it for the end of January, but had put it forward because of events on the Western Front. In spite however of the putting forward of the date the offensive had gone better than he expected. Now he wanted the allies to tell him how he could help. He would like to discuss the summer campaign.

Cadogan told me he did not think Stalin liked the P.M.'s theatrical style. He had noticed him looking at Winston when he was making gestures with tears in his eyes. I wonder if this only means Cadogan himself doesn't like this particular style of oratory.

Roosevelt blurted out to Stalin: 'We always call you Uncle Joe.' Stalin did not appear a bit amused; he said he ought to have been told this before or not told now. Byrnes attempted to pacify him by saying that Uncle Joe was no worse than Uncle Sam. But Stalin was not mollified. He demanded how much longer he must remain at the dinner, and Winston, on the other side of the table, said: 'Half an hour.' When the P.M. told us about this someone asked if Stalin has a sense of humour. Winston said at once that he had, but that he was not always as amused by our jokes as he was meant to be. You could not be certain how he would take things.

*February 5, 1945*
Winston was in great form at the President's dinner last night. He told me about it while he disposed of a substantial breakfast. 'In the White House, I'm taken for a Victorian Tory.' I broke in: 'It isn't fair. You never were a Tory.' He looked at me as if he would like to know what was behind my remark. When I was silent, he went on: 'Stalin and the President can do what they like, whereas, in a few months' time, I may find myself in the street.' Then he began trumpeting. He counted up on his fingers the number of

elections he had fought. He likes them. They were fun. All the same, I fancy that it will irk him when he has to go to the country for orders. It is the first time that I have heard him mention the election, though he must know that it is bound to come when the Germans surrender.

All morning the P.M. has been losing things.

'Sawyers, Sawyers, where are my glasses?'

'There, sir,' said Sawyers, leaning over his shoulder as he sat, and tapping the P.M.'s pocket.

At last, when the P.M. was getting ready for his afternoon sleep, he cried out irritably:

'Sawyers, where is my hot-water bottle?'

'You are sitting on it, sir,' replied the faithful Sawyers. 'Not a very good idea,' he added.

'It's not an idea, it's a coincidence,' said the P.M., enjoying his own choice of words, and without a trace of resentment.

There was a sharp discussion today on whether France should be given a representative on the Allied Control Commission for Germany. For Stalin, France is a country without an army; he measures nations in his practical way, by the number of divisions they put into the field during the war and how they fought. By that test Poland and Yugoslavia have done more than France for the Allied cause. Stalin made no bones about the matter; he could not see the Prime Minister's point. Perhaps the P.M. did not say plainly what was in his mind. He was thinking of the future, when the Americans would have gone home and Britain would be left alone to contain the might of Russia. The President sides with Stalin; he likes France, but de Gaulle gets on his nerves. However, Hopkins is backing the P.M.; he has the good sense to see that a stable Europe is impossible without a strong and virile France. France, in Eden's words, is a geographical necessity.

Hopkins is, of course, a valuable ally, particularly now, when the President's opinions flutter in the wind. He knows the President's moods like a wife watching the domestic climate. He will sit patiently for hours, blinking like a cat, waiting for the right moment to put his point; and if it never comes, he is content to leave it to another time. The battle is not lost yet, but I wish Harry was in better fettle.

When the P.M. told me Stalin's words it was clear that he was puzzled.

'Do you suppose Stalin reads books? He talks of France as a country without a past. Does he not know her history?'

The P.M. did not expect an answer. He loves France like a woman. When Stalin said that he did not know what France had done for civilization he felt bewildered. In Winston's eyes France is civilization.

### February 6, 1945

'The next war,' the P.M. said to me while breakfasting in bed, 'will be an ideological one.'

'Between whom?' I asked.

The P.M. shrugged his shoulders and made a gesture with both hands, but did not answer.

'I do not think that Russia will do anything while Stalin is alive. I don't believe he is unfriendly to us.'

That is as far as he would go.

The discussion on the United Nations Organization[1] today threw some light on the difference between the mental processes of Stalin and Roosevelt. In American eyes the first purpose of this Conference is to lay the foundation of an international peace organization. It appears that Byrnes was quite put out when he discovered that, two months after Washington had sent Stalin a proposal about voting in the Security Council, he had not even read it. As Hopkins puts it: 'That guy can't be much interested in this peace organization.'

Stalin can see no point in vague sentiments and misty aspirations for the freedom of certain small nations. He is only concerned with the borders of Poland, with reparations and with what he can pick

[1] The Declaration of the United Nations was signed by twenty-six states on January 1, 1942, and set forth the aims of the Allied Powers. A United Nations' conference met at San Francisco on April 25, 1945, when the Charter was drafted, and signed on June 26, 1945.

up in the Far East. These are tangible things that he can get his teeth into. He said yesterday: 'We are interested in decisions and not in discussions.' Roosevelt would like to prescribe for the world, Stalin is content to make clear what the Soviet Union will swallow.

*February 7, 1945*
Drove with Jumbo Wilson, Alex and the Chiefs of Staff to Sebastopol. We got out of the cars after leaving Balaclava, when the C.I.G.S. pulled out a map, which he studied attentively for some time; then he gave it back to his A.D.C. and pointed to the valley below us.

'That's where the Light Brigade charged.' But I noticed that no one was paying any attention to his discourse; they were all looking intently at a skull, a thigh bone and some ribs scattered on the ground. One of them touched the skull with his foot.

'Can you,' he whispered, 'tell if it is a Russian or a German skull?'

To a doctor's eye, the President appears a very sick man. He has all the symptoms of hardening of the arteries of the brain in an advanced stage, so that I give him only a few months to live. But men shut their eyes when they do not want to see, and the Americans here cannot bring themselves to believe that he is finished. His daughter thinks he is not really ill, and his doctor backs her up.

The day before we left England, I received a letter from Dr Roger Lee of Boston.[1] He wrote:

'Roosevelt had heart failure eight months ago. There are, of course, degrees of congestive failure, but Roosevelt had enlargement of his liver and was puffy. A post-mortem would have shown congestion of his organs. He was irascible and became very irritable if he had to concentrate his mind for long. If anything was brought up that wanted thinking out he would change the subject. He was, too, sleeping badly.'

Winston is puzzled and distressed. The President no longer

[1] Dr Lee had been President of the American College of Physicians and also of the American Medical Association.

seems to the P.M. to take an intelligent interest in the war; often he does not seem even to read the papers the P.M. gives him. Sometimes it appears as if he has no thought-out recipe for anything beyond his troubles with Congress. Nevertheless, though we have moved a long way since Winston, speaking of Roosevelt, said to me in the garden at Marrakesh, 'I love that man,' he is still very reticent in criticism. It seems to be dragged out of him against his will. And with half a chance he will tell over dinner how many divisions the Americans had in a particular show against our handful, and how their casualties in that engagement dwarfed ours, and things of that kind.

*February 8, 1945*

Drove with Alex to see Chekhov's house. The dining-room was a grim little apartment with a piano, a big photograph of the author, a print of Leighton, and a life-size painting by Chekhov's brother of a young woman sitting distractedly trailing a very shapeless hand. His sitting-room was less forbidding: the window looked down on a valley and the room looked as if it had been lived in; there was a small bronze figure of Tolstoy on the table, with paper-cutters, half a dozen pencils, some books, two small black elephants in ebony and Chekhov's small wooden stethoscope.

I went to see Hopkins, who is in a poor way. Physically he is only half in this world. He looked ghastly – his skin was a yellow-white membrane stretched tight over the bones – but he began to talk with all his old verve. He was full of the Russian claim for two additional votes in the General Assembly, one for the Ukraine and one for Byelorussia. The President seems to have no mind of his own. He came to Yalta apparently determined to oppose any country having more than one vote, but when the P.M. came out strongly in favour of Stalin's proposal Roosevelt said he, too, would support Stalin at San Francisco.

*February 9, 1945*

Stalin's dinner-party did not break up till two o'clock this morning. The P.M. was sentimental and emotional. I asked Clark Kerr bluntly if he really thought much came out of the Conferences. Couldn't it all be done without the Big Three? The Russians were realists; they would toe the mark as long as it suited their purpose. The Ambassador had no need for reflection. He said at once:

'No, these meetings have helped, I think, quite a lot. Stalin has got an impression of the P.M. as a broth of a boy, full of guts and determination – what Stalin calls his "desperation." And that helps.'

Stalin's speech last night in proposing a toast to the P.M. had made a great impression on the Ambassador. He went on quoting it while I scribbled down his words:

'Without the Prime Minister's guts – the interpreter didn't say guts but that's what he meant – England could not have stood up to Hitler. She was alone; the rest of Europe was grovelling before Hitler. Do you know what Stalin said? He said that he could think of no other instance in history where the future of the world depended on the courage of one man.'

Clark Kerr is an earthy creature, with his feet planted firmly on the ground, and he has had opportunities in Moscow of sizing up Stalin. When he says Stalin respects the P.M.'s guts it rings true. Whereas it is plain that Stalin can make nothing of the working of the President's mind. But it is typical of Stalin that he does not let his feelings count if it does not suit his book. During the Conference he has been quite rough with the P.M. All the same, when I look through my diary I am left in no doubt about Winston's feelings of friendship and respect for Stalin. He is thinking already of Stalin's place in history.

At other times Winston's eloquence is less usefully employed. When the British Empire is mentioned he indulges in histrionics, which do no good. There was rather a sad scene this afternoon. It all began with a report by Stettinius on the appointment of trustees for colonies. I have not been able to check Hopkins's account and he, like the President, seems to lose his balance when colonies are discussed; they might be back in the War of Independence, fighting their English oppressors at Yorktown. It seems that Stettinius had hardly got under way when the P.M. shouted his disagreement. According to Harry, Winston spoke so rapidly that he could hardly follow what he said. He would not have the British Empire run by a lot of bunglers. He would refuse point-blank to countenance such folly. He spoke with heat. Stettinius, it appears, was a good deal rattled by the violence of this outburst, and hastened to explain that what he was saying did not apply to the British Empire. The P.M. appeared a little mollified. He would not argue if they were only thinking of enemy territory. After the P.M. sat down he kept mumbling: 'Never, never, never.'

There was a general feeling of relief when Mr Churchill at last agreed to the American formula. This sort of thing does harm, of course. When Winston talks big about the British Empire the President gets very restive; he has a bee in his bonnet about our colonies. Besides, it is all so unnecessary, for the P.M. could, without all this diatribe, have found out from Stettinius that the principle did not apply to the British Empire. If only he would listen occasionally!

And yet, I wonder if I am fair to Winston. When the Prime Minister announced, 'I have not become the King's First Minister in order to preside over the liquidation of the British Empire,' it was not just bravado. He was affirming a faith for which he was prepared to give his life. The President knows this side of the P.M., but he cannot leave the Empire alone. It seems to upset him, though he never turns a hair when a great chunk of Europe falls into the clutches of the Soviet Union. I don't think he has ever grasped that Russia is a Police State in which freedom is more at a discount than in Hitler's Germany. He appears to be happy to seek the advice of his confidants, Stalin and Generalissimo Chiang Kai-shek, about how best he can secure the freedom of small states.

*February 10, 1945*
The President has changed his mind again. But nobody appears in the least surprised. He has now agreed with the P.M. that France should be a member of the Control Commission. Stalin made it plain at once that if this was the President's wish he would accept it. One cannot help noticing Stalin's deference to the President's opinions throughout the Conference. This frame of mind does not

come naturally to Stalin. It must cost him a great effort. What is behind it all? As far as Stalin has a steady policy and as far as his actions are not governed by mere opportunism, I believe his one purpose is to drive a wedge between the two democracies. If this can be done, the rest must seem simple.

Whenever the future of Germany is discussed the Russians bring up the question of reparations. That is what interests them. It is, at any rate, something they can get hold of, and Maisky, their expert on reparations, has a firm grip on the facts. The little man, with his slanting eyes and pointed beard, asked for his pound of flesh as if he were addressing the students of the London School of Economics. I watched, once, a farmer being sold up. I remember the anguish of his wife, as, with tears rolling down her cheeks, she saw a hard-faced woman bearing away to her car as much as she could carry between her hands and her chin. The Russians have, of course, no reason to feel compassion for the Germans; they hate them with a cold ferocity for the savage scorching of their land, and this combination of greed and venom is frightening.

I tried to explain to Hopkins that the P.M.'s mind is full of what happened at the end of the First War. He thinks the Russian demands are madness. Who, he demanded angrily, is going to feed a starving Germany?

Then Stalin spoke. Harry brought it all to life. How Stalin rose and gripped the back of his chair with such force that his brown hands went white at the knuckles. How he spat out his words as if they burnt his mouth. Great stretches of his country had been laid waste, he said, and the peasants put to the sword. Reparations should be paid to the countries that had suffered most. While he was speaking no one moved.

When Harry had given me the story I made the mistake of arguing with him. He flared up and said bluntly that he had advised the President to support the Russian proposal, whatever course the British took. The Russians had given way a good deal at the Conference. It was our turn to give something. We could not expect them always to climb down. The President took Harry's advice. Once again, as over France, he changed his mind. The Reparations

Commission, he said, should take, as a basis for discussion, the suggestion of the Soviet Government.

When Winston told me about the discussion he spoke as if he felt very sad about the greed and folly of the Russians. And I noticed a grey look about his gills which I haven't seen before. I never think of him as an old man who is past the span of life given to us in the Psalms.

*February 11, 1945*
Found the P.M. moody when I went to him after breakfast. He gave me a sour look.

'The President is behaving very badly,' he said. 'He won't take any interest in what we are trying to do.'

I interjected that I thought he had lost his grip on things. The P.M. replied that he thought he had. I suggested that the President had been a passenger at the Conference. I think the P.M. felt this was going too far. He spoke gloomily of reparations, and said he was worried about Poland. 'With the Red Army where it is, isn't it too late,' I ventured, 'to try to bargain? Wasn't the damage done at Teheran?' The P.M. did not seem to hear. He picked up a document rather wearily, and I left the room. Hopkins tells me that the President does not want to fall out with Stalin. He is quite sure that Russia will work with him after the war to build a better world. He does not see that he has invented a Russia which does not exist.

In the passage I ran into Clark Kerr.

He told me that the P.M. is obstinate about the President staying one more day. Winston had got on his sulky look and meant business.

P.M.: 'But Franklin, you cannot go. We have within reach a very great prize.'

President: 'Winston, I have made commitments and I must depart tomorrow as planned.'

Then Stalin said he thought they might have difficulty in completing the business without more time. Roosevelt answered that he had three kings waiting for him in the Near East. Stalin, however, stuck to his point, and the President, after a little, gave way.

'Why,' Clark Kerr exclaimed, 'they haven't yet got down to an agreed communiqué.'

Sarah came up. Yesterday, she said, had been a bad day. The P.M. had an appointment with the President, but he left the villa half an hour late and went and saw Stalin.

'Probably he forgot all about the President,' she said with a smile.

Anyhow, he was an hour late when he stalked into the President's room and found him sitting patiently. Left to himself, the President would not harbour resentment, but the little people around him work him up. Sarah dined with Roosevelt's daughter, who said the President had appointments which he must keep.

'As if,' said Sarah, 'the Conference isn't so much more important than anything else.'

This afternoon, at half-past four, as I was going for a walk, the P.M. swept into the house.

'We leave at five o'clock. Where's Tommy? Sawyers!' His voice rose, 'Sawyers! Where is everyone?'

Apparently there is bad weather approaching, and we must get off before it. It was half-past five when we left, and two hours later the car drew up on the jetty at Sebastopol. We were to dine and sleep in the *Franconia*. The P.M., who has been in a vile mood throughout the Conference, irritable and bad-tempered, is now in tearing spirits.

'I'm so relieved to get this bloody thing off.'

The bloody thing was the agreed communiqué.

'Anyway,' he growled, 'that's done with and out of the way.' He is trying to forget that he has achieved little. He is playful, smiling, mischievous.

'Charles,' he said, 'is silent, kindly and grave, but make no mistake, when the occasion comes, he lashes out like a horse.'

He put his hand affectionately on my knee.

'He demolished the President of the other College[1] in *The Times* without any mercy.'

Twice he sang (very flat) snatches of old songs, 'The Soldiers of

---

[1] Royal College of Surgeons.

the Queen' and some ditty I had not heard before. This during dinner. Then he gurgled:

'Grand to get back to English fare after the sucking-pig and the cold fatty approaches to all their meals.'

The P.M. moves among words as a friend. His precision in their use is helpful at these Conferences, where sloppy thinking may lead to recrimination later. When he had given his blessing to the revision of the Montreux Convention[1] about the Dardanelles, and Stalin was in a relaxed mood, he gravely enquired of the President what he meant by 'Freedom from want.'

'I suppose the word "want" means privation and not desire.'

And when there was agreement about the joint communiqué, and everyone was smiling happily, he persuaded the President to cut out 'joint':

'The word "joint,"' he said, 'means to me the Sunday family roast of mutton.'

The Americans pitch their song on a higher note. They are leaving Yalta with a sense of achievement, they feel they are on top of the world and that while other conferences had been concerned with proposals of policy, Yalta has been the scene of important decisions that must influence the future of the world. Harry Hopkins, lying on his sick-bed, is firmly convinced that a new Utopia has dawned. He says the Russians have shown that they will listen to reason, and the President is certain that he 'can live at peace with them.'

I do not know what decisions they have in mind. It was plain at Moscow, last October, that Stalin means to make Poland a Cossack outpost of Russia, and I am sure he has not altered his intention here. He has, too, been given the additional votes he demanded, and he seems to have secured the President's support for a policy of greed in reparations which must bring plenty of trouble in the days to come. It is the story of Teheran over again. Stalin fights

[1] Signed July 20, 1936. It established a new international régime of the Turkish Straits, replacing that of the Lausanne conferences, 1922–3. At Montreux the International Commission of the Straits was abolished and its functions were handed over to the Turkish Government. The latter was also authorized to remilitarize the zone.

for and gets what he wants. Then, at the banquet, which brings the proceedings to a close, he thaws and is polite.[1]

Only a solid understanding between the democracies could have kept Stalin's appetite under control. The P.M. has seen that for some time, but the President's eyes are closed. What is more remarkable – for Roosevelt is a sick man – the Americans round him do not seem to realize how the President has split the democracies and handcuffed the P.M. in his fight to stem Communism. They cannot see that he is playing Stalin's game. As at Teheran, he has been at some pains to see Stalin alone. Hopkins boasted this morning that the President had gone out of his way to inform Stalin that there had been disagreements between Winston and himself about the zones of occupation of Germany and the general policy to be followed where France was concerned. Roosevelt went further: he repeated to Stalin what he had said at Teheran: that Hong Kong should be given back by Great Britain to the Chinese. One can almost see the grim old gentleman from the Kremlin rubbing his hands with glee, in Hitler fashion, as we play his game. He purrs when anything like this happens.

The Americans are saying that the relations between Stalin, Roosevelt and Churchill have never been so close. Alas, it is far from the truth. Winston's emotional nature, to be sure, has been deeply touched by the faithful manner in which Stalin has discharged his undertaking not to interfere in Greece. He has stuck to his bargain to the letter. The P.M. put it like this tonight:

'Stalin has only referred to Greece once, when he asked me what was happening there. He said: "I don't want to criticize anything,

[1] Looking back on this, it is difficult to see what could have been done to save Poland's independence. A strong line, with all its consequences, might perhaps have induced Stalin to change his mind. But Roosevelt's ineptitude at Yalta made that impossible. He saw no reason for a strong line. Indeed he went out of his way to inform Stalin of his differences with the British Prime Minister. He did everything he could to convince Stalin that America did not mean business if it came to a 'show down'. He even told him that America might keep troops in Europe for two years, but certainly no longer. Stalin, a little incredulous, listened attentively to the President's discourses. There must be, he was sure, some crafty plot which had not yet come into the open.

nor to interfere. I'm quite content to leave it to you."'

When Winston had said this he seemed to go over the past in his thoughts, then he went on:

'Stalin isn't going to butt in in Greece. In return, he expects a free hand in Bulgaria and Rumania. The fifty-fifty plan[1] arranged at Moscow is working out in his favour. He'll let his people be beaten up in Greece for the sake of his larger plans. I find he does what he says he will do. It isn't easy to get him to say he will do it, but once he says something, he sticks to it.'

The P.M. spoke once more of the disaster it would be if anything happened to Stalin. His humour, understanding and moderation, on many occasions, had made a deep impression on him.

'When Stalin had a strong case – so strong that I was supporting him – he would say: "We attach importance to this, it means a good deal to us, but if the President feels it will conflict with his plans, I'll withdraw it."'

But, if Stalin and the P.M. are working together more smoothly than ever before, it is quite another story where the President and the P.M. are concerned. The storm of criticism in America for his actions in Greece had partly prepared the P.M. for what has happened here. The President's decrepitude has filled him with grief and dismay. All the same I do not think he realizes how ill he is. The P.M. has for some time been thinking of the outcome of the war; and he can see that the map of Europe will be redrawn in red ink. Far more than at Teheran he is conscious of his own impotence.

---

[1] At his meeting with Stalin in Moscow in October, 1944, the Prime Minister said to Stalin; 'Let us settle about our affairs in the Balkans . . . don't let us get at cross-purposes in small ways.' While his words were being translated the P.M. wrote out on a half sheet of paper the predominance of Russia and Britain in percentages.

| Rumania | Greece | Bulgaria | Yugo-slavia and Hungary |
|---|---|---|---|
| Russia 90% | Great Britain 90% | Russia 75% | Russia 50% |
| Others 10% | Russia 10% | Others 25% | Others 50% |

This Stalin blue-pencilled as a sign of agreement. *Triumph and Tragedy*, p. 198.

*February 12, 1945*

A parcel came to my cabin addressed to me in both English and Russian. When I opened it I found a big tin of caviare, and ten small boxes of Russian cigarettes – a present from Stalin.

In this ship of 20,000 tons, which had been acting as a troop-ship until at a moment's notice it was painted and furnished and reconditioned so that our delegates to the Conference might use it if the accommodation at Yalta proved to be inadequate, we are comfortable to the point of luxury and wonderfully over-fed. The chef of the *Queen Mary*, borrowed for the occasion, produces perfect food, and the white rolls take one back to times of peace.

For two hours this morning Alex and I wandered through the rubble of Sebastopol. This afternoon when we asked the Russian soldier sitting in front with the driver to take the P.M. to Balaclava he shook his head; he had never heard of the village. He did not know what we meant by the Crimean War. After a short drive we got out of the cars and walked through the streets of Balaclava. The P.M. pulled up short: 'I have been studying their faces, Charles. There is pride in their looks. They have a right,' he added, 'to feel proud.'

Sarah was giving chocolates to some children, when a Russian soldier waved the children away, and, turning to Sarah, said that their children did not need feeding.

The P.M. asked his guide if the Russians were short of glass, and he answered that they were, and used plywood in its place. Stalin had told Roosevelt that all they lacked in Russia was tin, rubber and pineapples. The P.M. explained that we, too, were short of glass: two million houses in England had been hit, ten per cent were made uninhabitable.

On our return from Balaclava I said, without thinking, that a hill on our left was like the Berkshire downs. Bridges said he could not pass that remark: the contours of hills of stone and hills of chalk were quite different. But later, when someone said the Russians were not demonstrative, and I had interjected that if they were they would not fight as well as they do, he grunted: 'There speaks the expert.'

*February 13, 1945*

No one has any idea where we are going when we leave tomorrow. The plans have been changed half a dozen times, till even the mild Martin thinks our vacillations and inability to make up our minds must make a bad impression on the Americans, who are making the flying arrangements. First, the P.M. was to fly to Athens and go from there to Alexandria. Anthony did not like this plan; he wanted to go to Athens by himself. Last night, it was decided that the P.M. would fly to Alexandria, while Anthony would go to Athens. This morning, Athens is on again. Anthony is piqued and avoids the P.M.

Before dinner I found Pug waiting outside the P.M.'s cabin. Winston had promised to address the ship's company, and they had already been drawn up waiting for him for more than half an hour. 'It's very naughty of the P.M.,' Pug said in a low tone. 'It's this unbridled power. The heating throughout the ship has all been cut off because his room seemed too warm for a moment.'

I had dinner in the *Franconia* with the P.M., Eden, Clark Kerr and Pug Ismay. The P.M., as usual, did most of the talking. He spoke at great length of the Greek situation, arguing vehemently for firmness in dealing with ELAS. When he went to Athens at Christmas the situation at home was very uncertain, and the truce was made largely because of that feeling. It was a mistake. We ought to teach the Communists a lesson. They were getting quite cheeky again since the truce. He wouldn't shake hands with them again after the exposure of the atrocities they had committed. Leeper had been very weak. The P.M. wanted to visit Athens to ginger up the Greek Government and the Archbishop so that they might take a firmer line. Usually he is magnanimous to a fault, but the opposition to his policy and the way public opinion has been stirred have entered into his soul. Someone suggested he had had a great moral victory, but he was not satisfied with this. He would plainly like to beat up the Opposition at home, and he is prepared for more shooting in Greece.

No one had the temerity to change the subject. It was only when the P.M. had exhausted the topic of his crusade against Communism in Greece that he reverted to the natural conversation of old age, with its dislike of change. He bemoaned the passing of ritual. He had not really forgiven the King and his family for allowing the eight cream ceremonial horses to disappear. They could not be replaced now. The breed was extinct, or at any rate, since they came from Holland, and Holland was in a turmoil, their successors could not be bought. Black horses would draw the coach of state in future; they were well enough, but – well, they were not the same thing.

The P.M. had had a battle (including an acrimonious debate in the House of Commons) to get the Guards back into scarlet after the last war. Northcliffe had talked of the waste of money; he said that was why the income tax was so high. The P.M. had arranged with the King to put the sentries at Buckingham Palace into scarlet when this war came to an end. He wanted the bands of other regiments to resume their formal dress.

Then the inevitable Max came up. Leaning across the table to Eden, the P.M. said:

'Don't underrate Max. He is one of the most remarkable men, with all his faults, I've met in my long journey through this world. He made Bonar Law[1] Premier. Walter Long[2] was a mediocre man, but the Tories didn't want a Liberal Unionist, like Austen,[3] being elected Leader of the Party. The strength of both factions was about the same, there was nothing in it. Austen always played the game' – Winston smiled – 'and always lost it. Austen said, if it helped towards the unity of the party, he would stand down, and Walter Long had to do the same.'

It all sounded to his audience, who, apart from Anthony, were politically unconscious, as if a voice out of the past was talking about Peel and Stafford Northcote and the worthies of a bygone age. The talk, however, still stuck to politics.

Winston: 'I have not lost one night's rest in the war, but,' turning to Eden, 'when you resigned in 1937—'

Eden: 'It was early in 1938.'

---

[1]  Andrew Bonar Law, Prime Minister, 1922.
[2]  Walter Long, Tory politician in running for leadership.
[3]  Austen Chamberlain, Tory politician in running for leadership.

Winston: 'Yes, in 1938, I didn't sleep from the time I put the light out till dawn. I was too excited. It was a grand thing to do, but I never felt it was done in the right way. More could have been made of it.'

The P.M. was kept awake when Anthony resigned because he could not help wondering if any advice he had given to Anthony had influenced his fateful decision. He is, of course, a little *naif* when he preens himself on not losing a night's sleep in the war; he forgets that he takes precautions each night to prevent such a mishap, in the shape of a red tablet.

The difficulty in remembering the names of members of the House came up.

Eden: 'I think it's bad to say: the Member who has just spoken. One ought to say: the Member for Salford.'

P.M.: 'One ought to spend an hour a day in the smoke-room.'

Eden: 'But you only meet there the members whose names you already know.'

P.M.: 'Your P.P.S.[1] can bring other members along.'

Eden: 'I suppose so, but I don't like it.'

P.M.: 'Harold Macmillan has done very well. I like him very much. I had thought of him for the War Office.'

Eden: 'He wants the F.O.'

P.M. (*dryly*): 'There isn't a vacancy at the Foreign Office.'

The P.M. wandered on and the conversation became a monologue. There would be a general election at the end of the war. The P.M. said he would use the Greek business against those who had attacked him. His eyes became more prominent, his voice rose: 'I'll say: You went about maligning British troops in Greece, and what' – the voice became louder still – 'were *you* doing at that time?'

The 'you' was almost spat out.

Then we went back to the Boer War – the P.M. always goes back to the Boer War when he is in a good humour. That was before war degenerated. It was great fun galloping about. Alex agreed. Modern war, he said, was not fun; he was the only officer

[1] Parliamentary Private Secretary.

in his battalion to come out of the Somme. To lose, say, two out of twenty, was a sporting risk, but after the Somme there was no mess and no mess servants. That wasn't really fun.

The P.M. spoke of Monty. It was a great blow to him to have an Army taken away from him just before the great advance in Normandy.[1] The P.M. had made him – he corrected himself: recommended that he be made – a Field-Marshal as a solace. But when Monty was given back the Army, after the Germans had broken through in the Ardennes, he made such a cock-a-doodle about it all that the Americans said that their troops would never again be put under an English general. The P.M. made a fine, flamboyant gesture as he quoted Monty's words: 'I flung in the British Army.' The facts were, the P.M. added with a grin, that we had five hundred casualties and the Americans sixty thousand.

The P.M. contemplated his plate for some time. Then he told us about Esmond Harmsworth's two brothers, who were killed in the last war. The elder, who had blue eyes and fair hair, was a good fellow. Harold (Lord Rothermere) was eaten up with love of this boy, and one night, when the P.M. called at the Ritz, where Rothermere lived, he said the boy was on leave, and took the P.M. up to his room. They entered on tiptoe. It was very late, and when Harold opened the door he could see him sleeping like a child. Rothermere asked Sir John French[2] if his leave could be extended, and it was. But the boy got restive and wrote to his battalion in France to ask for him. He went. The P.M. thought he was gassed and died from the effects. He was a good fellow, the P.M. repeated, half to himself.

For three hours last night Anthony kept on saying he would not

[1] General Eisenhower, the Allied Supreme Commander in Europe, assumed the role of Ground Force Commander on September 1, 1944, in order to conduct personally his broad-front strategic policy in the military offensive against Germany. General Montgomery had held this role since the D-day landings and now returned to command his own Army Group. From then on he commanded British 21 Army Group and temporarily ceded all direction of American forces.
[2] Sir John French, Commander of the British Expeditionary Force in France, 1914–15.

go to Athens if the P.M. did. The P.M. didn't trust him to finish off the business. It weakened his position. The trouble is that he doesn't like playing second fiddle to anyone.

As I was about to turn the light out in my cabin in the *Franconia*, Alexander Cadogan put his head in. He had finished his packing.

'I never bargained,' he said in his quiet, dry way, 'to take Tetrazzini and Melba round the world together in one party.'

### February 14, 1945

We left the *Franconia* at nine o'clock this morning and, after bumping for three and a half hours on a bad road, arrived at Saki airfield, which was covered with a thin layer of snow. A bitter wind blew across the open space, and I grew anxious as we stood shivering for twenty minutes while the band went on playing and the guard of honour marched past. There were some new ceremonial trumpeters, who greatly pleased the P.M. with their precision. He said their movements in bringing the trumpets to their mouths were heraldically correct. They might have stepped out of the Moscow ballet.

We crossed the Black Sea, flying over Turkey and past Lemnos, Samothrace, Mount Athos, names with long echoes. It was pleasant coming from the bleak, snowy Saki into the blue skies and sunshine over the Isles of Greece, and there was a feeling of security with an escort of six fighters.

On landing, we went in cars straight to the Royal Palace, through streets lined with cheering Greeks. In the vast square the crowd was packed so tightly that they could just throw up their hats without much chance of recovering them. The size of the crowd and its noisy enthusiasm impressed the P.M., who is apt to assign more significance to these mass demonstrations than should be given to them. At the Embassy he came eagerly up to me:

'Were you there, Charles? I have never seen a greater or more demonstrative crowd. If we'd been wrong that wouldn't have happened.'

I remember when we went in cars to Leghorn, how impressed the P.M. was by the plaudits of the Italians we passed by the roadside. At the end of the day he took quite a different view of the

Italian people. Now it was the turn of the Greeks. Ought they, after all, to have more food sent to them? Perhaps we could spare the ships. I was glad when we got him safely into the Embassy; some of the crowd had the look of brigands.

The 'Mosquito' has brought the mail to Athens, and it was waiting for us at the Embassy. I found a small parcel addressed to me. It was my book, *The Anatomy of Courage*, bound and ready to be launched on its precarious voyage. The binding, print and paper are better than I had expected. How many years has it been on the stocks? I have wanted to do this job as well as I can – more, I think, than I have ever wished to bring off anything else in life, and now, when it is done, and I ought to be on tenterhooks how it will be received, it is hardly ever in my mind. The thing is done and it can't be undone. What fun it has been in the writing! What a constant source of comfort and interest when things were going badly in the competitive world in which I live. It has been my child, and now it has thrown off all parental control and must face the world on its merits, if it has any.

This evening, in failing light, I went to the Acropolis, and when I got back I found them still sitting at the dinner-table. The P.M. was still speaking of Greece. He told us what he had said in the House about *The Times*, which had attacked his policy.

'Never have I heard louder cheering, from all parts of the House, at any rate since the last war. Barrington Ward was in the gallery. Members looked up at him. The proprietor of *The Times* was also in the House.'

The P.M. said that Barrington Ward had done well in the last war; he had been given two decorations. It was a little like the judge saying the little he could for the prisoner in the dock before passing sentence.

'*The Times*,' the P.M. went on, 'had no policy between the two wars; it drifted.'

They spoke of E. H. Carr[1] and his influence. The P.M. said that during the debate the Speaker had been very weak, and his shuf-

---

[1] E. H. Carr, Assistant Editor of *The Times*.

fling when one Member called another a liar was a sorry business.

Winston went on: 'His Beatitude said to me that he hoped the ancient claims of Greece to Constantinople might be remembered.' I retorted: 'Dismiss those dreams from your mind.'

Randolph broke in to ask what was the effect on the Archbishop of these words.

The P.M., with a smile: 'He dismissed them.'

Once more he spoke gloomily of England's financial position after the war, when half our food would have to be paid for by exports. The P.M. had sat down to dinner at a quarter to nine. It was now a quarter to one. For nearly four hours a figure out of history had talked to us without reserve, and yet those who heard him appeared half asleep.

*February 15, 1945*

Flew from Athens to Alexandria to take leave of the President before he departs for the United States. And so by air to Cairo. The dreary story of de Gaulle's gaucherie came to its melancholy climax today. He has sent a curt message to Roosevelt that he will not come to Algiers to meet him. It appears that the communiqué issued after Yalta contained no reference to him.

*February 16, 1945*

The P.M. has spent the day in a series of conferences, first with the Emperor of Ethiopia, then with the King of Egypt and after that with the President of the Syrian Republic.

*February 17, 1945*

This morning, shortly before noon, we set out across the desert for L'Auberge du Lac, fifty miles from Cairo, where the P.M. will act as host to the King of Saudi Arabia. Two jeeps, each with four military policemen in their red caps, followed by three policemen on motor bicycles, with white tin hats, like basins, escorted a string of cars, as they bumped in single file through the desert. Trees and a green field marked the oasis where the hotel had been built on the shores of the lake. The setting provided by the hotel was an inadequate background for the ten Sheiks with their brilliant robes and curved swords. The King, Ibn Saud, himself appeared, wearing ceremonial robes, gold and brick red; he has a fine face with brown, benevolent eyes, a high, hooked nose and expressive lips. The party included the King's sons and brothers; his Ministers; the King's physician; Magid Ibn Kalayella, Astrologer, Fortune-teller; Abdul Rachman Djuez, the chaplain who leads the Palace prayers; the Commander and Adjutant of the King's Guards; Mohamed Abdul Djither, Chief of Communications and Radio Officer; Mahsoel Effendi, Radio-supervisor of the Nejd; Siraq Dahran, official Foodtaster and Caterer; Abdullah Al Hadrani, Royal Purse-bearer; with the Chief and Second Servers of Ceremonial Coffee. There were also ten guards, with sabres and daggers, who had been chosen from the principal tribes, three valets, and nine miscellaneous slaves, cooks, porters and scullions. During luncheon the Food-taster stood behind the King, holding a glass of water, a grim, dark-faced figure. On his left, the interpeter stood, leaning forward with animation to interpret what the P.M. said to the King and what the King said to the P.M. Behind the interpreter stood two armed guards, who looked the part. Their faces were unpleasant and contrasted with the open, intelligent countenances of many of the Sheiks. Before luncheon began, the P.M. retired for a conference with the King. It may well be that the exchanges were of some interest, for Ibn Saud is made after the pattern when kings were kings. He has led armies in the field with unfailing success and is the master of the Arab world; he was not in the least overawed now by his English visitor, whose Zionist sympathies were no doubt known to him. I do not suppose that either the King or the British Prime Minister had much success in persuading each other. But the gestures were not affected by this.

After luncheon presents were handed to our party, who had been graded into three classes: the first was confined to Mr Churchill and Mr Eden. The P.M.'s sword was inlaid with jewels and his dagger was also embellished in this fashion. There were two ropes of pearls – no one present felt capable of valuing them – marvel-lous robes for Mrs Churchill, one purple and gold, each more splendid than the last. Thrown casually into the box containing these was a small box containing a diamond, valued later at eight hundred and fifty pounds. I fell into the second class and received a parcel in a red cloth like a cushion, which proved to be an Arab's ceremonial robe with a dagger. The third class received wrist-watches. The choice of a present for the King had been left to Tommy, who is a little parsimonious in these matters. He produced some scent, concentrated essence of amber, musk, mimosa and jasmine. The P.M., with great presence of mind, sensing the munif-icence of the King's gifts, told him that, if he would accept it, he was sending him a motor car. The P.M. talked about returning the more valuable of the gifts, but was told this would cause offence. He is very punctilious in such matters, and they will all be reported to the appropriate quarters. The warning that no one may smoke or drink in the King's presence had induced in the P.M. a mood not particularly receptive to this visit, but he was favourably impressed by the King, and the story has a happy ending.

### March 1, 1945

Lunched with the P.M. The C.I.G.S. sat between Herbert Morrison[1] and Dorothy. He has a great capacity for looking straight ahead of him and can do so for quite a long time on end without any feeling of embarrassment. I don't think he has any time for Herbert. Anyway he didn't waste any small talk on him. Basil Brooke[2] was on my left. He was bothered by the prospect of unem-ployment in Ulster with a probable election in June. The closing down of a big aircraft factory threatened to throw a large number of men out of employment. Morrison supported him and the P.M. was sympathetic and would see what could be done in the way of redress. So encouraged, Brooke said that the social services which were being instituted in Ulster on the same lines of those in England, with the higher wages, were going to attract a lot of labour from the Free State and that there was a real danger that Ulster in

[1] Home Secretary.
[2] Prime Minister of Northern Ireland.

a short time would lose its political colour. He advocated some measure of exclusion. The P.M. agreed and said it ought to be done now, during the war. The P.M. dilated on Ulster's services to the Empire – she had left her foot in the door so it could not be closed. If all Ireland had belonged to the Free State, the entrance to the Mersey and the Clyde might have been impossible. We had run it pretty fine as it was. The P.M. had said to Neville Chamberlain[1] that if Ireland did close our ports and if it really became a matter of life and death, then he, Winston (then 1st Sea Lord) would have to come to Neville and ask him to let him use force in opening up the ports. Neville replied that if Winston had to do this he would back it. The P.M. said there was very strong feeling in England against the Free State though it was never mentioned. They would not be present at the Peace Conference, they had made an awful mess of things.

The P.M. said that when he was at the Home Office, the decision whether a murderer should be reprieved was a very unpleasant part of his duties. He was not then accustomed to loss of life as he had become during the war, and it got on his nerves. Morrison agreed but the P.M. pointed out that in his day at the Home Office there had been no Appeal Court and that now sheltered the Home Secretary. Morrison is not impressive. He is not, as Ernest Bevin is, a man of the world. That is perhaps not the expression most people would use for Bevin, but I think it is a just distinction.

I said to the C.I.G.S. after lunch that when all this war business was over he and I would have to find something to do. He said his first task would be to write up his diary. He had often only made headings at the end of the day and one's memory does not improve, he added, as one gets older.

[1] Neville Chamberlain, Prime Minister, 1937–40; at this time Lord President of the Council.

# The withered garland

*April 1945–July 1945*

O wither'd is the garland of war,
The soldier's pole is fallen: young boys and girls
Are level now with men: the odds is gone.
And there is nothing left remarkable
Beneath the visiting moon.

ANTONY AND CLEOPATRA

# PART FOUR

# Fall from Power

# CHAPTER TWENTY-FIVE

# The Prime Minister
# Loses his Touch in Politics

After Yalta there is a break in my diary until April, 1945, the month in which President Roosevelt died, when, with an election in sight, I began to take down again what Winston said to me. The entries for the next two months are a brief record of the lonely processes of his mind. The war had exaggerated the isolation in which he had dwelt apart during his political life.

'Winston,' Clemmie said to me, 'has always seen things in blinkers.'

She held up her open hands at the level of her eyes, so that they were a foot apart, to illustrate the cutting off of the field of vision.

'His eyes are focused on the point he is determined to attain. He sees nothing outside that beam. You probably don't realize, Charles, that he knows nothing of the life of ordinary people. He's never been in a bus, and only once on the Underground.' She smiled. 'That was during the General Strike, when I deposited him at South Kensington. He went round and round, not knowing where to get out, and had to be rescued eventually. Winston is selfish; he doesn't mean to be, he's just built that way. He's an egoist, I suppose, like Napoleon. You see, he has always had the ability and force to live his life exactly as he wanted.'

Clemmie went on: 'Winston is non-party; he makes up his mind on questions as they strike him. He said to me yesterday: "If I were ten years younger I might be the first President of the United States of Europe."'

If Winston did not at any time find it easy to follow what other people were thinking, when war came he appeared to give up the attempt altogether. As early as the autumn of 1944, Gil Winant, the American Ambassador in London, came to me because he was worried about Winston, who had become so engrossed in the war that he had lost touch with feeling in the country. Winant told me that there was a good deal of disquiet in the Labour Party, which would have been more vocal if Ernest Bevin had not exerted a moderating influence. Even as it was, some of the big trade unions had passed resolutions critical of the Prime Minister's handling of the troubles in Greece. That Winston might lose the election had never crossed my mind. After all, it could not be easy for an American to say how labour would vote. I had forgotten how close Winant was to the leaders of the Labour Party. He pressed the point. He asked me very earnestly whether anything could be done. I had to explain to him that the P.M. did not turn to his doctor for political guidance.

In the spring domestic politics could no longer be put on one side; the war was on its last legs, and an election was in the minds at any rate of the Labour members of the Government. Neither Max nor Brendan, his advisers, were wise counsellors, and the P.M.'s political judgment – it had never, perhaps, been his strongest suit – was always threatening to get him into trouble.

The P.M. did not even follow what his colleagues were thinking. One day, late in April, he spoke to me about Ernest Bevin,[1] who was 'rather putting his weight about.' Bevin had attacked the Tories in a speech at Leeds, and the P.M. could not understand why he had broken the Party truce. I confess that I was worried by this development, and I wondered if Bevin's health was making him difficult. He was already a very sick man, suffering from alarming attacks of heart-block, in which he would lose consciousness. But full of guts, he was determined to do his job and would not give in.

One evening at a sherry party at the Russian Embassy I was asked if I could stay until Bevin left the house. I was told that he had had a heart attack just before the party. When most of the

[1] Ernest Bevin, Minister of Labour and National Service, 1940–5, Foreign Secretary, 1945–51.

guests had left the Embassy I found Bevin in a small room drinking with Molotov. Bevin was tossing back vodka, while Molotov sipped a red wine – an unequal contest. I sensed that things were not going well. I think that was why Molotov beckoned me over, for I hardly knew him. He called on me to propose a toast. When I stood with a blank face he appealed in his wooden way to Winant. Winant stood gazing vacantly over our heads for some time, but nothing happened. Bevin was rather the worse for wear, and when at last I got him away he told me that he was lunching with Reggie Purbrick[1] in the country next Sunday.

When Bevin entered the dining-room of Purbrick's house he stopped at the door to take in the lovely Georgian silver laid out on an exquisite lace centrepiece. A great grin spread over his untidy features as he rubbed his hands together.

'I always like,' he said, 'to return to the atmosphere of the proletariat.'

During lunch Bevin drank a great deal and became very talkative. Beaming on the company, he rattled on, and soon began to talk about what he wanted for 'his people.' After the war seventeen million would get three weeks' holiday every year with pay. He had a plan with an architect to build a thousand flats at Hastings, where working people could go for their holidays and get a bath and a bed. He was going to have circular glass shelters on the Front so that they could sit by the sea, even in winter. Someone blurted out: 'What's wrong with the working classes?' Bevin gave a great guffaw. 'Well, they aren't here,' he snorted.

When we rose from the table I asked him about his speech at Leeds. Bevin answered very seriously:

'We have a political Rasputin (Max) who very thoroughly and scientifically has been putting it about that I was going to be another Ramsay MacDonald.[2] I was asked about this, even by a large trade union. I didn't want to do it. I hesitated for a long time,

[1]  Reginald Purbrick, M.P., Australian industrialist.
[2]  Ramsay MacDonald, Prime Minister of the Coalition Government, 1931.

but when I had made the speech my stock went right up.'

Bevin held up his hand to illustrate the point.

Bevin had played a man's part in the war and supported Winston loyally, but that wasn't going to do him any good when the war was over and the Tories were once more the enemy. He knew that his position in the Party was at stake.

The P.M. did not follow the workings of Bevin's mind. In the Labour Party when a man falls out of favour he is politically dead; he cannot retire for a season to Chartwell to write the life of one of his forebears. He does not know, perhaps, who they are. Bevin broke the party truce to save his skin. In this sense Winston has led a sheltered life, and for all his prestige, this complete detachment from the tooth-and-claw business in politics has been a big handicap.

*April 27, 1945*

At the Annexe this morning I ran into Jock Colville, who informed me with a seraphic smile that he was in a Bolshie frame of mind; the P.M. had not gone to bed till 5 a.m. A bit of paper with 'Resting' on it was still pinned to his door. Sawyers said that he had been given orders not to call him until 10.30 a.m. When he was awake the R.N.V.R. sub-lieutenant from the Map Room took him the news and a big map; then I went in with his breakfast. He made no attempt to tackle it, but, picking up a paper, read me a letter from Stalin, which he said had given him a lot of pleasure.

'Himmler' – he stopped and looked up at me – 'this is very secret, has proposed surrendering to us, but going on fighting the Russians. I sent the whole correspondence to Stalin. I told him we should insist on unconditional surrender to all the three great powers. Stalin, though lately he has called us all the names under the sun, wrote, "Knowing you, it is what I should expect from you."'

The P.M. leant over to the table by the side of the bed and put down the papers.

'A more friendly letter than he has written yet,' he added. 'Their suspicions and their sense of inferiority have made things difficult up to now.'

The P.M. ruminated moodily. He read me some of his reply to

Stalin. His heart is still in the war, and he cannot put his mind into the election.

*May 7, 1945*
When Winston woke this morning Pim[1] took him the news of the German surrender.

'For five years you've brought me bad news, sometimes worse than others. Now you have redeemed yourself.'

And yet the P.M. does not seem at all excited about the end of the war.

*May 8, 1945*
The Government's warning to housewives to lay in bread for VE day has not worked according to plan, and there were bread queues everywhere as I made my way to the House of Lords this morning to hear the P.M.'s broadcast on victory over the enemy. There was not a seat vacant in the Library; I found partial support against one of the ladders which served the upper shelves.

At three o'clock the loudspeaker gave us the Prime Minister's speech from Downing Street. It was a short, factual statement, arranged by a man of letters, though the ending had a tinny sound.

'Advance, Britannia. Long live the cause of Freedom. God Save the King.'

The peer next to me (I could not put a name to him, for all sorts of unfamiliar faces turned up for the occasion) thought it strange that there was no allusion in the speech to God. There was, however, no doubt in Winston's mind to whom the credit was due.

I asked John Masefield[2] what he thought. 'I'd rather,' he answered, 'have the honest utterance of Winston than the false rhetoric of a lesser man. Lloyd George might have gone in for this rhetoric.' Lincoln, I argued, would have struck a deeper note. Masefield agreed; but added that he was a man of deep piety.

---

[1] Captain Richard Pim, R.N.V.R. In charge of the Prime Minister's map room.
[2] John Masefield, Poet Laureate since 1930.

*May 20, 1945*

Went to see the P.M. at a quarter to ten, but he was still sleeping. I returned at half-past ten and found that Sawyers had just called him. 'He's keeping dreadful hours, sir, these days.' Rowan, too, spoke to me about it and asked if I could do anything; on four of the last eight nights it had been between three and four o'clock in the morning before he went to bed. He seemed tired.

P.M.: 'I wrote a letter which Attlee took to Blackpool. He hoped to persuade the Party to let their Ministers stay in the Government until the war with Japan is finished. A.V.[1] was very keen on this and Bevin agreed. But they wouldn't look at it. Boiling with hate.'

So the election will be in July.

The P.M. has tried to keep the Government together. He has failed. His thoughts turned wearily to the election. To have had arbitrary powers for five years, to speak for Britain without anybody's leave or question, and then to wait, cap in hand, on the doorstep, irks him. 'There are two opposing ideas in the country,' I said to him. 'There's pretty universal gratitude to you, and there's a notion about that you aren't very keen on this brave-new-world business.'

Winston answered: 'The desire for a new world is nothing like universal; the gratitude is.'

I did not argue the point.

The P.M. seems too weary to think out a policy for the restoration of the country after the havoc of the war. This morning he sent me that part of the Conservative Election Manifesto which deals with the new Health Service. He asked for my comments, though it is printed and ready for circulation. I found the manifesto full of platitudes: 'Liberty is an essential condition of scientific progress,' and other resounding phrases of that kind. It is all politics. No attempt is made to face the facts. Poor people have come to dread the expense of illness. They want their doctoring for nothing, and the party which gives them this will be on a winner.

[1] A. V. Alexander, First Lord of the Admiralty.

Unhappily this is not the kind of thing that stirs Winston's imagination. As for the rest of the Party, they ought to come out of the smoking-room of the House of Commons and plot a little less and feel a little more. I sat down and wrote a short criticism of the manifesto, and after lunch I took it to the Annexe, where I found John Anderson and Ralph Assheton, the Chairman of the Conservative Party, closeted with the P.M. Anderson left, but Assheton remained. The P.M. read what I had written in grim silence. My quips did not seem to amuse him. He did not really want my help, he only wanted my blessing for his plans. He looked up and scowled.

'The doctors aren't going to dictate to the country; they tried to do that with Lloyd George.'

I did not answer. I wondered who had put these ideas into his head.

'It isn't bad really?' he demanded. I answered that the manifesto, where it dealt with health, was feeble stuff; like the coloured water some doctors prescribe for their patients, it would do no harm if it did no good. He asked sharply how I would alter it. I answered that Health Centres ought to be in the manifesto, not a few experimental centres, but a thought-out scheme. To my surprise he agreed. Then he went off into a little harangue, all about the great advances medicine had made; doctors could not make use of these working as individuals, they must come together in these centres and have the necessary means and equipment. He turned to Assheton, and in his arbitrary way said: 'Get them to put it in.'

As the British Medical Association has dug in against my zeal for health centres, I thought I ought to warn the P.M. what might happen, but it was plain that he had exhausted the possibilities of the centres and indeed of health generally. When I said that the health proposals in the manifesto would not bring many votes to the Party he said testily that he was not after votes; he wanted to do the thing properly. He was in a bad temper.

The P.M. told me that the B.B.C. had asked him to take twenty minutes only for his first election broadcast. 'I insisted on at least half an hour.' This is a sign of the times. While the German War lasted he could wander on as long as he liked. Now things are different. Presently he will be treated like other men. It is going to be a big drop to earth. It will hurt him. He will hate it.

*June 4, 1945*
I am staying at Professor Wynn's house in Birmingham, where I have come to examine students, and we were checking the marks in the papers when Wynn proposed that we should break off to listen to the Prime Minister's broadcast. 'It's the kick-off in the election campaign.'

When it was done I glanced round the room. It was plain that it had not gone down with anybody. Cloake thought it was all negative, just abuse of the Socialists; Wynn felt that it was out of tune with the forces that are trying to plan a better world: his daughter considered it 'cheap.' No one agreed with the line that Winston had taken. He scoffs at 'those foolish people' who want to rebuild the world, but beneath this bluster he is, I believe, less certain about things. He has a feeling that he is back in the thirties, alone in the world, speaking a foreign tongue.

And so he falls back on vituperation. He was brought up on that, and well it has served him in the Commons, where he could demolish the Stokeses and Shinwells. But now his blows seem to miss the mark. The war is over and the public are tired of strife, they do not want bickering. They want to get on with things.

*June 5, 1945*
Attlee, the 'poor Clem' of the war years, did his piece tonight, and did it well. Perhaps his years in Bermondsey have brought home to him that politics are more than a game. At any rate, as I listened, it became plain that one ounce of Gladstone's moral fervour was worth a ton of skilled invective. And this in spite of the handicap of Attlee's delivery. It is clear that the P.M. is on the wrong tack; Max and Brendan are his advisers, and he will not learn from anyone else. For the first time the thought went through my head that he may lose the election.

*June 14, 1945*

Told the P.M. about Eden's illness. I think he misses him. He glanced at me as he said: 'I expect you liked my second broadcast better than the first.' He looks on me indulgently as 'rather red.' He added that he was going to do two more. 'Everybody listens and you get your message home.' He does not realize that after each broadcast he has lost ground.

Miss Watson, one of the staff at No. 10, met me in the passage. She feels that neither of the two broadcasts is the true P.M.; there was no 'vim' in them. 'You know, Lord Moran, his heart isn't in this election.'

It appears that Winston is now resigned to the election. Only, if the play must come to an end there ought at least to be a curtain; but as he stands there in the wings, waiting for the call, the theatre is emptying. I urged him to take a holiday in France. He is toying with the idea. He puts off a decision; he hates making decisions.

*June 22, 1945*

I am counting the weeks until I can take the P.M. away for a rest. It seems that he cannot make up his mind about anything. He is still sleeping at the Annexe, and had not breakfasted when I called this morning. I ran into him as he crossed the passage to his bathroom. He beamed, and was obviously in a very different mood. 'I shan't be a moment,' he said. 'Go to my room.'

When he rejoined me he began at once in a cheerful voice:

'I have been quite rattled. I showed my broadcast to Max and to Margesson.[1] They said it wasn't good. I don't like other people doing things better than I do.'

It was his old, very personal, way of looking at everything.

'There's usually something in the well which I can fish up at any time. It was very unlike me. I did ten thousand words before I got the eighteen hundred I wanted. With an audience I can tell how things are and what they will take. But speaking into a microphone, you don't know what's there. I stayed in bed for four days. They

[1] Viscount Margesson, Secretary of State for War, 1940–2.

brought me papers and documents, but I sent them away. I didn't want to work on them with this damn' business hanging over my head.'

I asked him how he was. His face flickered into a smile. 'The appetite is good,' he replied with mock solemnity, surveying the substantial breakfast set out on the bed-rest. The smile vanished. 'I am worried about this damned election. I have no message for them now,' he said sadly. In the war, compared with other members of the Cabinet, he understood what his soldiers and sailors were after. Now, men who did not count then, Attlee and Morrison, are coming to the microphone and seem to know better than he does what people are thinking and what they want. The vision of a better world, at which he has so often jibed, seems the only thing that interests them. 'If things come out pretty level, they will think of another coalition,' he said, 'but without Max.'

He was now half talking to me and half reading the headings of the newspapers spread on the bed-sheet. On Monday he is setting off electioneering. He will sleep in his train. 'Oh, no, I can use it, because I shall get back to it in the evening and do my office work there.' And then, confidingly, as if he was at last addressing me and not just ruminating: 'I feel very lonely without a war. Do you feel like that?'

# CHAPTER TWENTY-SIX

# Suspense

When a man begins to grow old his future becomes guess-work. His faculties may be unimpaired, his health by all appearances sound, yet any day, without warning, a coronary thrombosis may strike him dead, or leave him an invalid, who remains a tenant of this world only by courtesy, well knowing that another arrow from the same quiver will get him in the end. Winston was in his sixty-sixth year when in the spring of 1940 I was first asked to see him. I could find no evidence in mind or body of the corroding effects of a long and arduous existence; it was not until the last years of the war that I began to notice intimations of mortality.

The Prime Minister was slow, even then, to heed any warning or remonstrance. He had taken on a job; he was determined to see it through. His whole being was in the struggle.

But now the General Election had brought home to him that his resources were nearly spent, and when I pressed him again to take a short holiday before the Conference at Potsdam he said quietly that he had made up his mind to go to the South of France for ten days.

Ten days' rest would not repair the hurt done by the prodigious strain of the last five years, but patchwork was better than nothing. Moreover, if peace of mind was the first necessity, Hendaye had been well chosen. He could get busy there with his paint-box, and there was good bathing, which he loved when the water was warm.

*Hendaye, July 7, 1945*

The château of Bordaberry is a white manor house on a tongue of land at the mouth of the Bidassoa River, which separates France from Spain. It stands in a place apart, about a mile from the sea, where the P.M. is not bothered by the curious; but he has only to go down into Hendaye to excite the friendly and indeed affectionate interest of the inhabitants. The P.M. is too most fortunate in his host. General Brutinel is intelligent and contrives to interest the P.M. That is an achievement at any time, but in his present mood it is more: it is a certificate of the General's tact. He is not frightened of his guest; he seems to know intuitively that Winston, though not interested in other people's opinions, is curious about facts, and the General serves these up with a wise economy of words. The P.M. wished to know when the Germans first showed signs of clearing out of these parts; he had wanted to attack Bordeaux when Normandy was invaded, but expert opinion had been against any dispersal of the forces available. Winston seemed pleased when the General told him that in August, 1944, the Germans in these parts wished to surrender, and overtures were made to our Military Attaché in Madrid, who was then in France. But the officer commanding the F.F.I.[1] intervened; the Germans were beaten, he said, and ought to surrender to the F.F.I., and General de Gaulle backed him up. The Germans, however, would not surrender to the F.F.I., and so possession of Bordeaux was denied to us for another nine months. The P.M. listened to Brutinel closely, nodding his head from time to time in agreement.

'Another example,' he grunted, 'of de Gaulle's folly.'

The General went on to tell him in detail how the Germans who were billeted in his house had behaved. The P.M. confessed that he liked detail, he wanted the picture filled in. If our host gives

---

[1] Free French Interior forces. Admiral Meyer refused to surrender to Colonel Adeline, commanding the Bordeaux Forces of the Interior in September, 1944, and instead withdrew to entrenched positions at Royan and the Graves peninsula, on either side of the Gironde estuary. Meyer was able to effect a partial blockade of the port of Bordeaux until forced to surrender by the Americans six months later.

the P.M. the facts he wants, he also displays sagacity in selecting subjects for conversation which are congenial to him. He spoke today of the gratitude of humble folk to the P.M. Before the whisper went round that the General was to be Mr Churchill's host he could get no one to do any work in the house, charwomen were unprocurable; but when his agent was told that the P.M. was coming, four charwomen volunteered. His words only confirmed Winston's own convictions. As he drove up from St Jean de Luz this morning, some of the friendly inhabitants, mostly women and children, cheered.

'I believe,' the P.M. said, 'I could go to any country in the world and be received with cheers from humble folk.'

If he loses the election he will miss this heady wine. Wherever he goes, too, people say acceptable things, selecting what they think will be most gratifying to him. The General, an astute man, goes one further and brings him books which show him in a light he will like. 'This book,' Winston said, holding up *La Verité sur L'Armistice*, by Albert Kammerer, 'is very fair to me.'

And that, too, does not go on for ever.

## *July 8, 1945*

'I'm very depressed,' said the P.M., walking into the room before luncheon and flopping into an armchair. 'I don't want to do anything. I have no energy. I wonder if it will come back.'

The election festers in his mind.

'Nothing,' he says, 'will be decided at the conference at Potsdam. I shall be only half a man until the result of the poll.[1] I shall keep in the background at the conference.'

He seemed very doubtful whether he had enough energy to paint. But after luncheon he got up suddenly as one gets out of bed.

'Come along, Charles, and watch my preparations.'

---

[1] Polling had taken place on July 5th. In order to allow time for the collection of votes from the Services, three weeks were to elapse before the declaration of the result of the poll. The conference at Potsdam was due to open on July 17.

Clemmie was trying to sleep, but he stumped through her bedroom on to a balcony where the paints had been set out on a small table; his feet brushed the floor as if he were too tired to lift them off the ground.

'Where are the other paints?' he demanded impatiently of Sawyers as he surveyed those before him with displeasure. 'I've no reserves here' – his voice rose in anger – 'you've left a lot behind. Why did you do that? Who told you to bring only these?'

Sawyers bluntly disclaimed responsibility for the paints.

'Where is the cobalt?' The P.M. spoke with great irritability and vehemence. 'You ought not to have left everything at home. Ah, here it is,' he murmured, in subdued tones. 'Get me a stool. I must sit.'

When he had done I followed him back to his bedroom.

'I'm going to relax completely. I'm not going to look at any papers. Only twice in my life have my knees shaken under me when speaking; at Edinburgh and on Richmond Common, when I was speaking for Harvie-Watt.[1] I imagine one is nearly all in when that happens. Take my pulse, Charles.'

During dinner the P.M.'s mind went back to Moscow. One night he was dining with Stalin and Molotov – they were alone save for the interpreters – when Molotov told of a visit to Berlin in the winter of 1940, before Germany attacked Russia, and how Ribbentrop had taken him into a safe place during a heavy raid. Ribbentrop had suggested that after the war Germany and Russia should agree to share the spoils. Molotov had asked what about England, but Ribbentrop replied England didn't count. Molotov retorted: 'Why, if England doesn't count, are we where we are? Whose bombs are falling, anyway?'

The P.M. went on to speak of the Russian purges. Beneš[2] told him that he had warned Stalin of the plot of high Russian officers to make an alliance with Germany. The plans passed through the

[1] Sir George Harvie-Watt, Parliamentary Private Secretary to Churchill, 1941–5.
[2] Dr Eduard Beneš. Led exiled government of Czechoslovakia from London.

Russian Embassy at Prague. So Stalin acted, and four thousand or so officers in the Russian Army, whose rank was above that of Colonel, were liquidated.

'Stalin was thoroughly justified,' the P.M. added. 'These officers were acting against their country.'

When Clemmie and Mary had gone to bed the talk drifted to medicine. At last I said:

'We have been talking about the advances medicine has made in curing diseases of the body, but in the future the doctor must find out more about how the mind works.'

The P.M. said at once: 'As long as you keep this psychiatric stuff out of the Army I don't mind.'

I suppose I had forgotten that nothing could come of a discussion on morale with him. Anyway, I allowed his antiquated approach to the vagaries of the mind to irritate me into an argument. I was sufficiently ill-advised to quote Wilfred Trotter[1] on the herd instinct. He flew at me:

'You are ascribing to instinct the noblest motives of men. War broke out and people spoke to each other in buses. Well, that wasn't herd instinct. It was men coming together for a common purpose.'

His words followed each other with gathering speed, his voice rose. He ended with a great outburst against Herbert Morrison:

'He is a loathsome creature with a warped mind; he was a "conchy" in the last war, he would not let boys drill, and he even opposed conscription. I shall never speak to him again.'

In such a mood you cannot reason with him; you can only listen.

*July 9, 1945*

All morning the P.M. has been painting a sea piece with the hills beyond. As he left, a crowd of smiling women and children pressed into the open gateway to greet him, and a photographer dodged from one point to another. The P.M. called him and asked him to photograph the scene which he had been painting, that he might study the composition.

---

[1] Wilfred Trotter, author of *Instincts of the Herd in Peace and War*.

He is thinking a lot these days of the election. One moment he sees himself victorious; the next he pictures himself beaten. If he wins, he will work out plans which would make Communism unnecessary and distasteful; if he loses, well, that would release him from a crazy world. He would feel the British public had treated him ill, but that would pass. He would take long holidays, appearing from time to time in the House and intervening perhaps in debate.

He finds this state of suspense unpalatable, and turns for comfort to other thoughts. In three years, Winston told us, he had lunched more than two hundred times with the King. No servant was present; they waited on themselves. If the P.M. rose to get something for His Majesty, the King in turn got something for the P.M. No subject had ever been so honoured. He wanted no other reward.

Tonight he spoke of France: 'As long as there is a kick left in my carcass I shall support France's efforts to re-establish herself. She must have a great Army; France without an Army is a cock without a comb.'

He went on to talk of the destruction of the French Fleet – the best since the fleets under the Kings of France.

'It was a terrible decision, like taking the life of one's own child to save the State. Our admirals were very loath to act, they were very sad; it was necessary to give them the most precise orders. I accepted full responsibility. I was determined to prevent the French ships falling into German hands. If this had happened, then with the German, Italian and Japanese ships, a formidable challenge to democracy might have been thrown down.'

The P.M. told us of England's offer of common citizenship to France, when she was on her knees.[1] There was a Cabinet on a

1 Following the withdrawal of the British Expeditionary force from Dunkirk at the end of May, 1940, and the decision to reserve our fighter aircraft for the defence of Britain, the War Cabinet evolved a Declaration of Franco-British Unity, which included plans for common citizenship and joint organs for defence, foreign, financial and economic policy. It was hoped that this unprecedented offer would help Reynaud, the French Prime Minister, to carry a majority of his Cabinet for a move to Africa and the continuance of the war. The offer was rejected, and Reynaud resigned on June 16.

Sunday. All sorts of improbable people were there, Corbin,[1] de Gaulle, Margesson. Neville Chamberlain put the suggestion to the P.M. Winston described the scene:

'That rough Cabinet,' he said, turning to General Brutinel, 'to which men had come by so many different ways, was carried off its feet. It was like a religious revival. It was a *cri de ceur* from the rough heart of Britain.'

There were tears in the P.M.'s eyes. The recollection was to him profoundly moving.

He marvelled at America's disinterestedness. She had come into this war and 'cast away her wealth for an idea.' If his father as well as his mother had been an American he was not certain that he would have advised her to come into the war.

(This was an emotional outburst rather than a considered verdict. America came into the war because Japan attacked her.)

The P.M. had been speaking with great animation. The vast brow, which mounts straight above his eyes, was puckered, so that a deep line passed up vertically from his nose. The eyelids seemed pressed down on his eyes by the weight of his brow, the thin lips were pursed together, pouting. At the summit of his forehead two wisps of hair went their several ways, and gave an impression that he had more hair than was actually the case. He became silent and no one spoke. At last he looked up and laid bare where his thoughts were:

'I hear the women are for me, but that the men have turned against me.'

Clemmie reminded him how bitterly he had opposed the vote being given to women.

'Quite true,' he mused.

At that moment Jock came in and gave me a telegram. It was from Lübeck. There had been an accident and John had been shot through the knee.

[1] André Charles Corbin, French Ambassador in London.

*July 10, 1945*

The P.M., during luncheon, recalled 1918, when he was hard at work on his plans for the 1919 campaign.[1] He had an entirely new conception to break the enemy front. He talked it over with Foch,[2] and then came the 'bloody peace.'

There was a pause. I said that when we heard in Washington of the fall of Tobruk it was the worst moment of the war. The P.M. retorted at once:

'Oh, no, it was painful like a boil, but it was not a cancer. I was miserable because thirty-three thousand men had laid down their arms; even now we don't know why. It was a muddle, but all war is a muddle. The two critical moments in the war, when everything was at stake, were the Battle of Britain and the submarine attack.'

Once more he told how the German submarines gripped us by the throat. When the Germans held Brest and could fly over Southern Ireland to the mouths of the Mersey and the Clyde they could report to their submarines and then go on to Norway.

'It was touch and go. Yes, it was life and death. Our food supply was balanced on a knife-edge.'

When Winston was First Lord he had told Neville Chamberlain that he would never ask him to use force against Southern Ireland unless the safety of England was at stake.

Once again he speculated on the chances of success if England had been invaded. It was as if he wanted to say: 'Do you quite realize how near you came to defeat? Has it gone home how narrow a squeak you have had?' He stopped abruptly:

'Mary,[3] you oughtn't to drink spirits at your age; it isn't becoming.'

Mary, demurely: 'I can't do anything right.'

[1] Churchill was Minister for Munitions during the period July, 1917 – January, 1919, and was most concerned that we should break through on the Western Front by reason of our superior technical and mechanical equipment.
[2] Marshal Foch, Generalissimo of the Allied Armies on the Western Front, 1918.
[3] Mary Churchill, youngest daughter of the Prime Minister, serving in the A.T.S.

The P.M., affectionately: 'You do very little wrong.'

After Clemmie, Mary, Jock and Tommy had left the luncheon table the P.M. talked till four o'clock struck. His mind wandered back to his boyhood.

'I think,' he said, 'I gained a lot by not overworking my brain when I was young. I never did anything I didn't like. I used to write essays for older boys. I would dictate to them. But presently the master became suspicious. The stupid Jones was raising quite interesting points. Jones was invited to elaborate the points he had made. But Jones had nothing to add to what he had said in his essay. I got kicked,' the P.M. added ruefully, 'for landing him in this position.

'Two things have disappeared in my lifetime. Men no longer study the classics. It was an advantage when there was one common discipline and every nation studied the doings of two states. Now,' with a sniff, 'they learn how to mend motor cars.'

'The other thing is— Can you guess what I am thinking of ?' he asked the General. 'No? Why, the horse. We have lost a good deal in these two things.'

He did not know which he would hate more: leading the Government with a small majority in a sick world or guiding the Opposition. I thought he had done when he said:

'I don't want anything. I've had five years of continuous excitement.'

Of course, it is not true that he is satisfied. He keeps stamping into the Secretaries' room from habit. 'Any news come in?' And when Jock, for the sixth time, assured him that there was none he became petulant:

'I won't have it. Telegraph to Leslie that I must have more regular reports.' To Jock, severely: 'It's your business to keep me informed.'

*July 11, 1945*
The P.M. disclosed during luncheon that he had had reassuring reports both from Ralph Assheton,[1] and from Max, which

---

[1] Ralph Assheton, Chairman of the Conservative Party.

confirmed Margesson's earlier estimate of a majority of a hundred. I said Max had set his heart on winning this election. The P.M. turned to me and said:

'Do you think his support is a liability or an asset?'

He described him as a remarkable man.

'There is no one like him. He has unmade several Governments in my lifetime. It's better to have his support than his opposition. The *Express* has a circulation of between three and four millions.'

I expressed doubts about whether those who read such papers necessarily voted as they were told. He looked unconvinced, but said nothing. He had put Max into the Cabinet when things were very bad and no one had liked to say anything. Then Max wanted to resign and pressed his point until the P.M. had to let him go. But when some time had passed and Max was ready to rejoin the Cabinet the P.M. sent his name to the King without a word to anyone. The King, according to the P.M., was very reluctant to accept his advice. Max didn't trouble to attend important Cabinet meetings. Then he would get hold of some idea and champion it fiercely.

I hummed something out of *The Mikado*; the P.M.'s eyes brightened, he began to sing refrain after refrain from that opera. He sang, with great gusto, 'A Wandering Minstrel I.' He loved the words and the tunes. And Mary in her eager way joined in. Then I asked him about some game they had played at Chartwell, and soon we were saying, 'I have a cat,' to be asked by one's neighbour, 'What kind of cat?' Whereupon one had to find adjectives beginning with the letter chosen, a tame cat, a timid cat, a troublesome cat, a tabby cat and so on until no more adjectives would come into your head and you were counted out, and only those with a full vocabulary were left in. Winston searched his storehouse of words as earnestly as if he were writing for posterity. This went on until ten minutes to four, when the P.M. went off to the Nairns[1] to paint.

---

[1] Bryce Nairn, British Consul at Bordeaux, and his wife, an artist.

*July 12, 1945*

The P.M. woke with indigestion, which he confidently ascribed to his painting.

'Where is the General?' he demanded angrily. 'Send for him at once.' When he came, the P.M. wanted to know why Nairn was fussing him to see de Gaulle. De Gaulle would love to hand out a snub to him. Besides, the time could hardly be more unpropitious for any advance to him; just before the Potsdam Conference, from which de Gaulle was excluded. General Brutinel waited patiently for a lull, then, when the P.M. had subsided, he explained that he only wanted to approach de Gaulle to suggest he should come to see the Prime Minister. Winston would have none of this; he complained that de Gaulle had sent a telegram to Roosevelt asking for assistance. He could trust America not to take France's colonies; he could not trust Britain.[1] And this, said Winston scornfully, at a time when we were pouring men into France for her relief. No, he would not see him. General Brutinel was puzzled. After all, it was the Prime Minister who had begun the whole business; it was he who had suggested breaking his journey to Berlin at Paris in order to see de Gaulle. Then, on second thoughts, it occurred to him that he might be snubbed. If, the P.M. ruminated, it had been the other way round, if, for instance, de Gaulle were in Scotland, he would have sent him a telegram to welcome him and to ask if he could do anything for him. No such telegram had come from de Gaulle when the P.M. came to France. So, after many hesitations and endless preambulations, he decided to do nothing till Duff Cooper[2] arrived in the afternoon.

He got up, very grumpy, to go bathing, but returned completely renovated and almost hilarious. No, he would not have a bath; he would leave the salt on him. It did good.

Our pilot came to luncheon. The navigator of the Skymaster

[1] In an undated section in PP/CMW/K4/2, Moran quotes Churchill saying, 'Roosevelt wanted to take Indo-China from France, but I argued we didn't go into the war to rob other countries of their own lands and goods.'

[2] Duff Cooper was at this time British Ambassador in Paris.

has been offered a job in Washington; he wanted to go. It meant promotion. The P.M., however, does not like changes. Had the pilot anyone else in view? The pilot had. Was he a good navigator? Was he as good as the man who was leaving us? He, the P.M., did not want to find himself over the Atlantic when he ought to be crossing the Pacific. He might be heading for the Pacific presently, he added reflectively.

The P.M. asked who was in the aeroplane that was taking Attlee to Berlin. His eyes twinkled; a smile hovered not far away.

'We don't know whether we are on speaking terms until we meet at Berlin.'

The General, overnight, had asked Tommy Thompson whether the P.M. could lunch early so that the servants might be able to attend the Basque games and dancing. Tommy promised to do something, but it was after three o'clock before he mildly suggested to the P.M. that they might make a move to let the servants clear the table. The P.M. said he must be allowed to drink his coffee. Clemmie brought him downstairs at a quarter to four. He squatted like a child who is a little out of temper.

'Why do they bring me down so early?' he complained petulantly. After a pause: 'Is there anything I can do in the meanwhile?'

Clemmie said that his boots, which were done up with a zip fastener, were very shabby.

'Are they your best?' she asked.

'No, but they are the most comfortable, and' – with a return to good humour – 'I have reached a time of life when I allow that to count.'

The Mayors of Biarritz and St Jean de Luz and other local potentates arrived and were presented to him. They gave Basque bowls and flowers and walking-sticks to him, to Clemmie and to Mary. Then we filed to the great court lined with French folk in their holiday clothes, where there was an awning to shield a few of the most important guests and spectators from the powerful sun. The proceedings opened with a Basque game, like fives. Soon after the game began the P.M. rose from his place in the front row and stalked out, followed by Tommy and myself. I thought for a moment he felt ill, but he was only bored. To Tommy he said impatiently:

'I don't know why they arranged this, they know I hate all games.'

Jock came into the sitting-room looking for the P.M. He found him in a very bad temper.

'I have come as an ambassador to ask you to return. They were very much upset by your leaving.'

'Go to Hell,' was the P.M.'s unpromising response.

Jock is not without courage, and is the only one of the secretaries to say this sort of thing. About three-quarters of an hour later Winston returned to the court with Duff Cooper, who had just arrived. There was a lot of Basque dancing, and games. When it was all over the P.M. made a short speech in his most Churchillian French, and we dispersed.

The P.M. came up to me: 'It would have killed me if I had stayed all the time.'

I said it was pretty stuffy.

'Hot and boring,' he corrected me.

When Winston had gone to his bedroom he said to me that he thought that General Brutinel was a very agreeable man and very well informed. He asked me his age. I fancy he must be thinking of using him in some way. *La Verité sur L'Armistice* and his carefully selected remarks had done their work.

### July 14, 1945

Went after breakfast to find out if the P.M.'s indigestion had gone.

'I've just thrown the reins on the horse's neck and let things rip,' he said. 'I've never done it before.'

This is true. He has hardly read a document or dictated a letter since we came here. Whether this is nature demanding a let up or the absence of any interesting news, I cannot say.

In all the P.M.'s ruminations about the election he has been concerned with how it would affect him, but this morning as we came back from bathing he said the election had done a lot of harm.

'You mean abroad?' I asked.

'No, they take my re-election for granted, but at home one section of the Liberal Party cannot say too poisonous things about the other section, and there has been a great stirring up of feeling and strife.'

Whether this point of view was present in his mind during the election campaign, when something might have been done by example to soften the discord, is open to doubt. Anyway, it is a little late for a death-bed repentance. Probably, once an election was unavoidable, much bitterness was inevitable. But many think things would have been different if the P.M. had said at the outset: 'I have worked with these men as colleagues, we have been through pretty tough times together, and whatever they do I cannot bring myself to exchange hard words with them. The German War is over. We have had a miraculous deliverance. The only fitting way to make a thank-offering for our escape is to turn our hands with the same single purpose to prepare our country as a proper habitation for a people which has endured so much. I mean, if you still trust me – and I have never promised you what I could not carry out – to get the houses which are needed, to see everyone has work and food, and to ask that all kinds of people, from every class, who have worked together to save England, should continue to plan as one man for the betterment of all. I can say no more.'

When we were leaving the sands Jock sought out Monsieur to pay him for the tents and deck-chairs which we had hired from him, but he would not hear of it. Five times Jock tried, five times it was refused with growing emphasis. He would take nothing from the man to whom France owed so much. Last night at Hendaye when we arrived for the fireworks the crowd were so friendly and even affectionate that when the P.M. came to speak and said only, 'Vive la France,' it seemed just right. Mrs Nairn, wife of the Consul, tells me that it is like this all through France.

She paints with the P.M. – she was a professional artist before she married – and advises him. A wise little woman, with a quiet, sympathetic manner, she has succeeded where so many have failed in breaking down the formidable ramparts of indifference which he presents to women generally, and to his hostess in particular.

All the same, I doubt whether she could have done this without her paints.

The maid brought coffee and we sat round the table listening to the P.M., who had some difficulty in keeping awake. He nursed his head in his hands, and for a time seemed oblivious of the company. Then he looked up.

'Tommy, could you get me some brandy?'

They brought books and photographs, which he autographed, and some caricatures, which he refused to sign, as is his habit. Then he went to prepare his last attack from the land front on the house of the Black Prince, which he has been painting and repainting for three days. There is no light in the water, or on the house, or in the tree tops which surround the house, as he has painted it. But he has stuck to it. One day he painted for nearly four hours on end. It brought on an attack of indigestion. He would not be defeated. He had the house photographed and compared it with his picture. Mrs Nairn, too, put on canvas her impression of the scene, and he stood for a long time in silent scrutiny of the two pictures. The P.M. is a determined man; if organization could have produced a painting all would have been well.

# CHAPTER TWENTY-SEVEN

# Too Late

We are waking up to the fact that Roosevelt's death has changed everything. He was always flat footed about France; he would have no truck with de Gaulle (partly this was personal), but apart from this he never acted on first principles. Indeed he rather avoided the big issues. Sufficient unto the day is the evil thereof.

But if he had no plan for the settlement of Europe, (out of his own country he seemed to avoid the big issues) he was determined not to repeat the same mistakes of President Wilson after the first German war. So that he was resolved not to enter into any commitments until the war was over. Even when there had been agreement at Tehran and Yalta it was never allowed to crystallize into anything on paper which might have been binding on America. So when Roosevelt died his successor found that he had not inherited any commitments, but he discovered too that the democracies had no policy. If Roosevelt had any plans for the future of Germany or the fate of Europe generally, he had taken them with him to the grave.

This was not all. The President was convinced that even if he could not convert Stalin into a good democrat, he would be able to come to a working agreement with him. After all he had spent his life managing men. Once more the fortunes of the world, after a war involving five continents, were in the hands of a President of the United States who was inspired by a lofty idealism, which had cast adrift from the facts of human nature. In his talks with Stalin, Roosevelt was handicapped by his complete ignorance of the Russian character but with his natural self-confidence he was so sure he was right that he took no heed of other men's warnings. Not even when they came from the Marshal himself, for Stalin, in his cups and outside them, made no attempt to conceal his aims. Indeed he had so often blurted them out . . . that I sometimes fancy that I knew more of his mind than I do of Roosevelt's . . . I suppose that may be because Stalin always knew exactly what Russia wanted. And you could guess what that was since he had only one policy, the interests of Russia. Every other country, Stalin supposed, was like that, only the Americans and the British were hypocrites and wouldn't say so . . . Churchill saw clearly what Stalin was after. 'I'll tell Stalin, he wants the world', he said yesterday. But when he tried to open Roosevelt's eyes he seemed less convincing than when he spoke of the military situation. 'He is a great Tory', the President chuckled, though he was a little shocked by Winston's innocence of the modern world and by his imperialism. He would talk about the British Empire as if he was living in the reign of Queen Victoria. How could this crusted old diehard sympathise with the uprising of the Russian people? How could he understand the workings of Stalin's mind? There was something in this. Roosevelt, unlike Winston, had political intuition of the highest order. He knew that communism cannot be destroyed by invective. The President's mind was made up and only events themselves could have convinced him that he had lost touch with the facts; he died before he realised that he had invented a Russia which did not exist.

History may claim that Roosevelt not Churchill allowed Russia to get the bit in her mouth, or she may deal gently with them both, on the plain grounds that neither was in charge of events.

But in this tragic story of a good man in the grip of circumstances there is nothing mean or small, nor is it the first time that the voice of civilization has pleaded ineffectually with the barbarians at the gate . . . Roosevelt had it in his mind to dispel the deep rooted suspicion of the democracies which Stalin nursed by a great gesture of faith and trust, by an act of confidence in his friend

Stalin. It was Campbell Bannerman once again handing South Africa back to the Boer, but alas Roosevelt had omitted to satisfy himself that there were Bothas and Smuts in the Politburo. He could not know that there is no word in the Russian vocabulary corresponding to the generosity of spirit, which may be that it only grows in the soil of security. At any rate Stalin would only see in Roosevelt's attitude an opportunity to play him off against the Prime Minister of Great Britain.

Roosevelt was not afraid of Stalin but he feared his own people. Once before after a great war they had thrown over the old world. At the back of his mind was the persistent fear that it might happen again. It did not occur to him that what was needed was a blunt but precise expression of his country's intentions. America should say plainly what she wants, once said she should stick to this and she must convince Stalin that she means business. That, at any rate, Stalin would have understood. For Roosevelt's virtues were lost on him. To Stalin, it often seemed as if Roosevelt, who was haunted by moral issues, changed his principles like his clothes, to suit the climate. There were no anchored buoys which Stalin could see to chart the channel up which the President was leading his people.

As for Winston, he had been so preoccupied with winning the war that he had lost sight of what we were fighting for. While the threat of invasion hung over the shores of Southern England the issue had been simple and he was alone in his glory, fighting for the freedom of the world. 'I played,' he said to me after the war, 'a more important part in the first two years I was Prime Minister than I did later. Other countries began to play a big part in the war.' For a long time Russia and America had provided the great armies and England now needed something more than a great Minister of Defence. But he did not see into men's hearts as Roosevelt had done and now Roosevelt was dead he found himself at Potsdam without any policy, except the vague idea of smashing Germany and Japan into unconditional surrender.

*Potsdam, July, 1945*

In the autumn of 1914, when my hospital in London would not give me leave to join the Army, I had fretted that I should miss the march on Berlin; then I had gone without leave, and had crouched in a waterlogged trench in front of Armentières all winter; there was a milestone on the road, which cut through the trenches, marked 'Lille 8 kilometres.' And that was as near as we got to Berlin in my time with a battalion. Now, thirty-one years later, the Army is in Berlin, but youth has gone, and with it the illusions of youth; it is no longer an adventure, but just a business appointment.

The sun blazed down, and members of the Conference, who had been waiting for a long time on the airfield outside Berlin, looked hot and uncomfortable buttoned up in their uniforms. There were Russian soldiers everywhere, lining the road, behind bushes, knee deep in the corn. We drove to where a substantial stone house, which was said to have belonged to Schacht, the banker, had been reserved for the Prime Minister. I followed him through two bleak rooms with great chandeliers to the opposite side of the empty house, where french windows, that had not been cleaned for a long time, opened upon a balcony, and there, without removing his hat, Winston flopped into a garden chair, flanked by two great tubs of hydrangeas, blue, pink and white. He appeared too weary to move. Presently he looked up:

'Where is Sawyers?' He turned to Tommy Thompson. 'Get me a whisky.'

We sat in silence for a long time, looking at the lawn that sloped to a lake, into which, so it was said, the Russians had thrown some German soldiers who could not walk because of their wounds. Beyond the lake a field rose sharply to a wood. The only sign of life that we could see was a Russian sentry, who came out of the wood, looked round and disappeared again into the trees. When the light had gone a rifle shot, that seemed to come from the wood, broke the silence that had fallen on everything.

*July 16, 1945*

Alex called for me this morning; he wanted to see the sights of Berlin. The road was littered with German civilians; they all seemed to be looking at their feet as they trundled their belongings in box and barrow – anything on wheels. I wondered if they knew where they were going. The Russians had planted posts by the side of the road, bearing white placards, framed in a broad red band, with extracts from Stalin's speeches printed above his signature, which was engraved in large red letters. 'The teaching of history tells us that Hitlers come and go, but the German people and the German State remain.' The messages on the road to Berlin seem designed to persuade the German people that the Russians are really their friends, while the American and British are their enemies. Or perhaps the idea is that the Russian sector, though nominally independent, will presently become a puppet state of the Soviet Union. What are they up to? What are they thinking?

In Berlin itself we came across notices pitched in another key. Here the Russian authorities responsible for these posters have made no attempt to hide the primitive satisfaction they derive from frightening people. On one column of a great museum, that had been gutted, is printed: 'To forgive will never be possible. Don't go to Russia.' And on another pillar: 'For Stalingrad and Leningrad and all the ruined cities of Russia we bring back our hate to Germany.' A German, who was standing near, told us that the Russians had done a lot of damage deliberately.

On other boards the Russians have posted notices which, the interpreter explained, are to warn their own troops of the danger of loose talk: 'Remember when speaking on the telephone the enemy may be listening'; 'When moving from one sector to another don't stop and talk with anybody'; 'Don't talk to anyone, for it passes from ear to ear and is heard from one corner to another'; 'Whoever talks helps the enemy.' To the casual observer these restraints on the social proclivities of the Russians seem unnecessary. On another small board was written: 'Don't use captured food. It may be poisoned by the enemy.'

I stopped a German at the door of a ruined cathedral and asked him where he got his food. He produced his ration card. It is very difficult, the old man said. He came from the Rhine and wanted to get back there. With a gesture:

'There is nothing to do here.'

As we were leaving the porch three Russian officers came up the steps. We spoke to them. The Colonel, looking at the destruction before us, remarked:

'You sow a wind and reap a whirlwind.'

A number of Germans had gathered on the steps of the Reichstag and were busy bartering with Russian soldiers all kinds of articles for marks or cigarettes. I saw a Russian soldier carrying away what looked like a new pair of black boots. Some peddled their goods through the crowd, field-glasses for two thousand marks, fountain pens, a camera, a great mantelpiece clock, boots and slippers, dresses and handkerchiefs – every kind of garment; others sat on the wall with their particular possession in their laps, apparently waiting to be accosted.

As I watched this evisceration of their homes I felt a sense of nausea; it was like the first time I saw a surgeon open a belly and the intestines gushed out.

We climbed for a time about the rubble, but when we tried to enter the Chancellery a Russian sentry stopped us. Alex became very impatient.

'Do you know who I am?' he demanded, pausing for an answer, but the sentry's face remained impassive. 'I have not come all this way to be stopped like this.'

In the Chancellery the first room was carpeted a foot deep with papers and ribbons and Iron Crosses, and there was Hitler's upturned desk. Alex was rather horrified, a little stunned by it all; he seemed to feel as if he was gazing on a corpse for the first time. He does not really like this brutal humiliation of a proud people, beaten to their knees.

In the Sieges-Allee there had been hard fighting, and some of the statues were chipped by bullets. In front of the effigy of Albrecht der Bär was a garden seat with a notice: '*Nicht für Juden.*' Near the end of the avenue a cross marked the grave of two Soviet soldiers, one born in 1926, the other in 1908; a Russian inscription recorded that they 'perished in battle for their Soviet motherland.' How long will the Germans tolerate that alien sepulchre, planted in their victory avenue?

As we mused, a frieze of old men and women and children kept passing; they did not look at us. It made me think of an incident in the summer of 1915, after the Battle of Hooge, when some German prisoners were coming down the village street in front of Ypres; the Colonel of my battalion saw them approaching and stepped back into a house until they had passed.

On our way back we stopped the car to look at a board that was propped against a wall; it was plastered with bits of paper such as you might see in the window of a registry office advertising for domestic servants; they were stuck down with bits of gummed paper or drawing-pins. They all bore some offer. One German was anxious to barter some clothes for food; another was trying to go to Hamburg in a few days and was willing in return for food to take messages for anyone who had relatives in that city. While I watched, an old woman walked up and pinned up her offer. When she had gone a man approached the board and, taking out a pen, amended his previous offer.

When I told the P.M. about it, I saw that he was not listening; he had not come to Berlin to see the sights. However, this after-noon he announced that he would visit Berlin at four o'clock. I decided to go with him, for I was curious to see how he would react to this grim sight. I wondered, too, how German civilians would behave when they saw him. As we drove to Berlin no one on the road seemed to recognize him, until we came to the centre of the city, where a workman looked hard at us and pointed after the car. I had forgotten that the press and the cinema, which have made his face as familiar to the Canadian lumberman as to the Russian peasant, have in Germany by neglect brought him to earth and made him anonymous. We found a good many people at the Reichstag. The P.M. got out of the car and walked round what was left of the building – it did not seem a very safe performance. Some of the crowd looked away, others glanced at him with expressionless faces, one old man shook his fist, a few smiled.

As for the P.M., he said nothing. He did not seem greatly interested. His guide, a Russian soldier, led him across the courtyard outside the Chancellery to the dug-out where Hitler, like a wounded animal taking to its hole, is supposed to have died; the P.M. followed him down a flight of steps, but hearing there were two more flights, he gave up the idea of exploring the depths and slowly remounted the stairs. At the top he sat down on a gilt chair, mopping his brow.

'Hitler,' he said, 'must have come out here to get some air, and heard the guns getting nearer and nearer.'

I went back to the dug-out. Breathing the damp, acrid, foetid air, I felt my way down a lot of steps to another cell, strewn, as far as I could see by the light of a torch, with clothes and gas masks and every kind of litter. I picked up a burnt glove.

When I rejoined the P.M. we drove back in silence past the unending saluting Russian soldiers. His thoughts were elsewhere.

I talked to Winston while he undressed for bed.

'The Socialists say I shall have a majority over all other parties of thirty-two.'

I asked him if that was a working majority.

He replied: 'If my Government keeps being defeated I could resign. I should do so and have another election in the spring.'

This is a completely different tune from his demands during the election campaign that he would not tolerate anything but a majority that gave him real power. The truth is he is much less confident and, I think, would be content to win with any majority.

Before I put out the light I asked him what he had thought of Berlin. He answered with a smile:

'There was a reasonable amount of destruction.'

He asked me what I made of it. When I said I had picked up two Iron Crosses he asked to see them. I went to my room and brought them to him. All he said was, 'Poor devils.' Berlin did not seem to touch his imagination. It was not like that at Carthage when the P.M. found himself among the soldiers of the Eighth Army in the ruin of the Roman amphitheatre. Then, when he was about to speak to them, the associations of the place suddenly gripped him and for some time he dared not trust himself to speak.

I told him of Alex's reaction.

'I don't feel like that at all,' he replied.

I spoke about the vast, grandiose rooms of the Chancellery. For the first time he appeared to be interested.

'It was from here that Hitler planned to govern the world,' he mused. 'A good many have tried that; all failed.' He smiled. 'That is why England is where she is. I'll tell Stalin about this.'

The P.M. said he had looked very carefully at the children for signs of malnutrition, but they appeared much better fed than those he had seen at Hendaye. He spoke of Germany as a decomposing carcass and told me that he looked with terror at the coming winter.

As an historian the P.M. has been interested in the latest attempt to grab world power – he does not believe it is the last. As a practical politician his long experience of government gives reality to the difficulties of providing food and work for the Germans.

Mary was excited about the first meeting with President Truman:[1] 'Papa is relieved and confident. He likes the President immensely. He is sure he can work with him.'

*July 17, 1945*
The P.M. dined last night with General Marshall. Afterwards he said to me:

'That is the noblest Roman of them all. Congress always did what he advised. His work in training the American armies has been wonderful. I will pay tribute to it one day when occasion offers.'

---

[1] Harry Truman succeeded as President on April 12, 1945, on the death of President Roosevelt.

He gave out that he would go and see Sans Souci[1] at twelve-thirty. At one o'clock he emerged from his room and strode into his car. The Russians were told that he had just a quarter of an hour to go round. With quick, impatient strides, he hurried through the rooms, looking neither to the right nor the left; his eyes were fixed on the floor; his look was abstracted. His thoughts were far away in the coming Conference – or was he once more counting the votes?

The first meeting of the Big Three took place at five o'clock. I talked to the P.M. on his return, when he was changing. He was in good form. It was obvious that things had gone well and he felt relieved.

'Stalin was very amiable,' the P.M. began, 'but he is opening his mouth very wide.'

The P.M. stopped opposite me:

'He has started cigars. He says he prefers them to cigarettes. If he is photographed smoking a cigar with me everybody will say it is my influence. I said so to him.'

'What had Stalin to say?' I asked.

'Oh,' the P.M. answered, 'he doesn't care a damn about that sort of thing. I pulled Vyshinsky's[2] leg. He looks so mild and benevolent. I said I could not believe he could be fierce. He replied that he was only fierce when it was necessary. The other day he banged the door on the King of Roumania so that some of the pictures came down, and the monarch was left to pick them up. Now the Russians have given the King their highest decoration. He is doing what they want.'

The P.M. palpated his tummy. With a mischievous smile:

'I had some caviare and champagne. Can I take some of your medicine? I feel rather acid.'

As Winston was in a good humour, I asked him about Truman. Had he real ability? The P.M. stood over me. The white of his eyes showed above his pupils, his lips pouted. Looking down at me as

---

[1] The royal palace, built by Frederick II, near Potsdam.
[2] Andrei Vyshinsky, Vice-Commissar for Foreign Affairs.

if he were saying something he did not want to be repeated:

'I should think he has,' he said. 'At any rate, he is a man of immense determination. He takes no notice of delicate ground, he just plants his foot down firmly on it.'

And to illustrate this the P.M. jumped a little off the wooden floor and brought his bare feet down with a smack. Now comes Truman determined to get to the bottom of things and not content just to feed out of the P.M.'s hand. I think it is all to the good. Rowan complains he cannot get the P.M. to read important papers. And the same day Bridges said to me, 'A great deal depends on the Foreign Secretary just now. The P.M. isn't mastering his stuff. He has to be fed.' And Bob Dixon ended the dirge, 'Eden isn't really mastering his brief. He feels the strain of the meetings.' Poor devil. Between the death of his mother, the loss of his son, worry about his own health and anxiety over the election he isn't tuned up for this sort of ordeal.

*July 18, 1945*

Truman came here to lunch with the P.M. Half an hour before, fifty men of the Scots Guard had taken up their position in the strip of garden in front of the house; from my bedroom window I watched them being dressed in line. The band of the Royal Marines arrived and, at last, Truman. His strong, friendly face gives everyone a feeling that he is going to play a big part.

We all shook hands with the President in the anteroom; then he lunched alone with the P.M. Some hours later Winston said, 'You might be interested in our conversation,' and told one of the secretaries to give me a summary that he had dictated after the President left.[1] 'You can take it away,' he said, when I began reading it.

---

[1] Mr Churchill's account of this luncheon in *The Second World War*, Vol. VI, *Triumph and Tragedy*, is obviously taken from the same summary. Note what seems to him in retrospect worth quoting. He passes over the President's intention to 'Press with severity the need of the true independence of small States,' and his own concern at the time with the risks involved in enforcing unconditional surrender upon the Japanese, while he devoted a page to the advantages of American bases in England in time of peace.

'I dwelt on the tremendous cost in American life, and to a small extent in British life, which would be involved in enforcing unconditional surrender upon the Japanese. I had in mind saving their military honour and giving them some assurance of their national existence after they had complied with all the safeguards necessary for the conqueror. The President countered that the Japs had no longer any military honour after Pearl Harbour. He spoke of the terrible responsibility that rested on him in regard to the unlimited effusion of American blood. I left it at that. It was obviously in their minds, and they are thinking a good deal about it.'

Yet he has always refused to admit that the use of the words 'unconditional surrender' at Casablanca might have been a factor in prolonging German resistance. The President's kindly attention had led the P.M. frankly to unfold some of our difficulties.

'I spoke of the melancholy financial position of Great Britain. Half our foreign investments had been spent in the common cause when we stood alone. There is a great external debt of three thousand million pounds. We should require time to get on our feet again. The President listened closely, attentively and sympathetically. He spoke of the immense debt the Allies owed to Britain for that period when she fought alone. "If you had gone like France," he added, "we might well be fighting the Germans on the American coast at the present time."'

The summary ends with a passage which brings out the warm friendship and trust that has sprung up between the two men:

'He was good enough to say that this had been the most enjoyable lunch he had had for many years, and how earnestly he hoped the relations I had had with President Roosevelt would be continued between him and me. He invited personal friendship and comradeship and used many expressions at intervals in our discussion which I could not easily hear unmoved. He seems a man of exceptional charm and ability, with an outlook exactly along the lines of Anglo-American relationships as they have developed. He has direct methods of speech and a great deal of self-confidence and resolution.'

Winston has fallen for the President. Truman's modesty and

simple ways are certainly disarming. When he was on his way out, passing a piano in one of the rooms, he stopped and, pulling up a chair, played for a while.

Winston has twice spoken to me of the 'beginning of a fruitful partnership.' I would to God this had come earlier.

### July 19, 1945

No doubt Stalin came here greedy to get what he could, but he is too shrewd to miss the change of heart in the American camp; he must see by now that Truman and the P.M. are going to act together. Things are not going to be as easy for him as they were in Roosevelt's time. Stalin has learnt to be cautious in a hard school, and it was plain yesterday that he is not going to take unnecessary chances. It appears that he set out to reassure the P.M. when they dined together last night, and from what Winston told me this morning he has lost none of his cunning. His opening remarks were well chosen to put the P.M. in a good humour.

'The Marshal was very amiable.' (The P.M. has used this word three times.) 'I gave him a box of my cigars, the big ones, you know. He smoked one of them for three hours. I touched on some delicate matters without any clouds appearing in the sky. He takes a very sensible line about the monarchy.'

'In what way?'

'Oh, he sees it binds the Empire together. He seemed surprised that the King had not come to Berlin.'

There was a long pause.

'I think Stalin wants me to win the election.' Stalin suggested the P.M.'s majority would be about 80. He thought the Labour Party would have between 220 and 230 members in the new Parliament. If the P.M.'s majority was small Stalin predicted the Liberals and Labour would split. He was very well informed about political matters in England, whereas we do not even know who is his real second in command. The P.M. said he was not sure how the soldiers would vote but Stalin said an army preferred a strong government and would therefore vote for the Conservatives.

From the P.M.'s comments it seems that Stalin deliberately set out to convince the P.M. that his intentions are entirely straight-forward. Up to a point I think he has succeeded. They talked together for five hours. Winston does not allow things to be drawn out like that unless they are going well and he is pleased with life.

'Stalin gave me his word there will be free elections in the countries set free by his armies. You are sceptical, Charles? I don't see why. We must listen to these Russians. They mobilized twelve million men, and nearly half of them were killed or are missing. I told Stalin Russia has been like a giant with his nostrils pinched. I was thinking of the narrows from the Baltic and the Black Sea. If they want to be a sea power, why not?'

When the P.M. coins a phrase that he finds pleasing he keeps repeating it.

Things must have been going pretty well when the P.M. agreed with Stalin that the Germans have no mind of their own.

'When I said they were like sheep Stalin told me a story of two hundred German Communists who remained rooted to a station platform for two hours because there was no one at the barrier to take their tickets.' The P.M. grinned. 'They never got to their meeting.'

'Stalin said that people in the West wondered what would happen when he died. It had all been arranged; he had brought up good people, ready to step into his shoes. Russian policy would not be changed if he died.'

The P.M. gazed at the carpet for a time.

'I think,' he said, 'that Stalin is trying to be as helpful as it is in him to be.'

After the second conference at five o'clock this afternoon the P.M. said:

'We had a good wrangle for three hours. I don't think Stalin was offended at what I said. He doesn't mind straight speaking. I felt reassured. Stalin, at the end of the meeting, said he saw our difficulties.

'He pressed the case against Franco. When,' said Winston, 'you come to a stony place, you adjourn. You have a conversation, carry it a certain distance, and then drop it. Because we don't like the ways of a particular country, it is no reason for interfering in its internal affairs. Otherwise you get into no end of difficulties. How can you condemn a state in its absence? We didn't want to hold a court of enquiry.'

The P.M. rose and went to his room. Peck[1] turned to Rowan: 'Was Joe impressive at the Conference?'

Rowan: 'Yes, he speaks in a very low voice, but he is very certain of himself. On the whole, he is probably better briefed than we are. There was a spot of trouble over Austria. Joe ascribed the delay in working out zones for the Allies to the fact that General Alexander put his oar in: he was not in command of the Russians. The P.M. replied warmly that no complaint had ever been made of the general. He would like any complaint in writing, when it would receive consideration. Stalin interposed that he was not speaking as a public prosecutor. All this time the Americans remained silent, taking no part. The P.M. said later that he had the distinct impression that Stalin was in retreat and was sorry that he had brought up the matter.

'The P.M. rebuked the President for not supporting him. America and Britain are in the same boat. Truman said he was not quick and apologized to the P.M. Afterwards the P.M. said that the President was all right if he had had time to consider a question, but when something came up which he had not thought about he was rather at a loss. After all, he had little experience of these conferences. He was very conscientious, and, when he thought he had not dealt properly with something, he could not sleep.'

Truman was not the only one to come under criticism today. Stalin rose at the banquet given by the President, and said: 'There is one toast in particular I wish to propose. I drink to the American Navy.' This little pinprick evidently stung the P.M. He said that of the six hundred U-boats sunk in the German war, the British had accounted for a far larger number than the American Navy; the proportion was four or five to one.

---

[1] John Peck, Assistant Private Secretary to the Prime Minister.

*July 20, 1945*

When I went to the P.M. this morning he began at once:

'The Russians are being very difficult. They talk about the same things as we do, freedom and justice and that sort of thing, but prominent people are removed and are not seen again. We are not even allowed to enter Vienna.'

Last night about eighty of their security people took possession of the President's house before Stalin arrived for dinner, and surrounded it almost shoulder to shoulder. Two fat Security Generals came, not to dine but to see that the watch over Stalin's life was not relaxed for one second.

In Stalin's brute cunning there is not a tincture of the sagacity that is nurtured on the lessons of the past. He has been at pains to still Winston's suspicions, and then, like a mule, with one vicious kick, he has demolished the structure so carefully built up, brick by brick. Perhaps he does not care. He must know that he holds all the trump cards.

The P.M. stretched himself wearily.

'I shall be glad when this election business is over. It hovers over me like a vulture of uncertainty in the sky.'

For three days the P.M. has been certain that Truman's firmness has changed everything. Stalin has been very fair and reasonable. Now Winston is less certain about things.

On leaving the P.M. I drove with Colonel Peter Wilson, who is in the map room, to visit the 11th Hussars at Spandau. They have taken over a German military barracks. They found the Russians had been in it. They had been there for four or five weeks with no water, and everything was filthy. Their men had reared wherever the spirit moved them; there were no latrines. The stink of the place made some of our men vomit. Before the Russians left they had stripped the place of everything, and what they didn't take away they smashed. The Colonel told me that the voting papers of the 11th Hussars had been lost in some inexplicable way. When this was explained to them, they said they wanted to vote again. In the first instance they had voted for the Socialists, but since they had met the Russians and seen what they had done, they wanted to vote

Conservative. Another regiment did not vote at all. When asked why, they said that now that they knew something about the Russians, their views had altered.

The P.M. asked me to dine with him and the Edens. He warned me that Anthony had just had a telegram to say that his boy, who was missing, had been found dead by the wreckage of his plane. During dinner nothing was said of this. They talked until nearly midnight as if nothing had happened. I wondered if I could have behaved with the same quiet dignity immediately after hearing that my John had been killed.

*July 21, 1945*

I had gone to bed when a messenger knocked at the door: the P.M. would like to see me. I went down in a dressing-gown and found him with Anthony; they were standing with glasses of whisky in their hands, conducting a post-mortem into Stalin's dinner-party.

Winston: 'I thought the Russians were silent and not very forthcoming.'

Anthony: 'Oh, it went well, considering the row in the afternoon.[1] Anyway, I'm sure they were making an effort to be agreeable. This has been the President's best day so far.'

Winston, muttering: 'I thought the evening interminable.'

Last Wednesday Winston, dining alone with Stalin, was reluctant, after a five-hour sitting, to break up. 'Things,' he said, 'were really moving.' Tonight, however, was just part of the ritual; ceremony bores Winston, and unfortunately he shows it.

*July 22, 1945*

The P.M. woke in better form; his indigestion had gone. There was one moment when he complained that 'this bloody election'

---

[1] The fifth meeting of the conference on July 21 had developed into an acrimonious dispute over the western boundary of Poland. The Poles had taken possession of East Prussia (a quarter of Germany's arable land), displacing more than 8 million Germans, whom we should have to feed. Stalin kept reiterating that at Yalta nothing had been agreed about the western frontier.

hung like a veil over the future. I didn't exactly help matters by asking if all these estimates of the majority had any substance.

'They are not guesses, Charles, but the most careful estimates which come from each constituency – and,' he added irritably, 'you ought to know it doesn't help to tell me I can't attach any weight to these people's advice. Besides, they all agree I shall have a majority, Conservatives and Labour people alike.'

Later he said: 'I had a most fruitful hour with the President. We not only talk the same language, we think the same thoughts.'

He turned to Anthony and asked him how the meeting of the Foreign Secretaries had gone. Anthony replied that no progress had been made. The P.M. seemed put out. His feeling that things had gone wrong came back. He said no more.

Tonight after dinner the P.M. sent for Walter Monckton[1] and asked him his view of the Russian attitude on reparations.

'The idea of Germany as a single unit has vanished. Instead, we have Russian Germany divided from British Germany by a line drawn by God knows whom, on no economic or historic grounds. What do you think of that?' said the P.M.

Monckton answered that he did not like it, but what was the alternative?

'The Russians,' the P.M. continued, 'have stripped their zone and want a rake-off from the British and American sectors as well. They will grind their zone, there will be unimaginable cruelties. It is indefensible, except on one ground: that there is no alternative.'

His voice was very grave.

'I prayed the Americans on my knees not to hand over to the Russians such a great chunk of Germany, at least until after the Conference. It would have been a bargaining counter. But they would not listen. The President dug in. I shall ask Stalin, does he want the whole world?'

The bargaining counters have gone. But that was not all. The P.M.'s health has so far deteriorated that he has no energy left to

---

[1] Sir Walter Monckton, United Kingdom delegate, Allied Reparations Commission.

seize his opportunities. Bridges and Leslie Rowan tell me that a great deal depends here on Anthony, because the P.M. is not mastering his brief. He is too tired to prepare anything; he just deals with things as they come up. And he has, of course, quite a respectable excuse for dodging decisions. For he said at Hendaye that he would be only half a man until he knew the result of the election. In fact – he makes no bones about it – he intends to shelve the really big decisions until he knows what has happened at the poll. Moreover, I doubt if his heart is in this business. A profound study of the life of Marlborough has left him with a conviction that anything is better than discord among allies. Certainly at Moscow last year he seemed more concerned to keep Russia in step with the democracies than he was with the fate of the Poles.

Bridges agrees with me that the P.M.'s method of jocular bluntness is the right method of tackling Stalin. It is necessary to be rude in a measure. But when Winston has had the best of things in argument he sometimes does not seem to mind very much who gets the prize. Stalin's tenacity and obstinacy have no counterpart on our side. He knows exactly what he wants, and he does not mind how he gets it. He is very patient too and never loses his temper. Indeed, the Russians are courteous in conference. It is rather like a game of poker, with Joe trying to bring off a big bluff. Truman is like a Wesleyan minister who does not know anything about the game and is not very sure whether it is quite nice for him to play at all, but who is determined, if he does play, to make his full weight felt.

The P.M. predicted that the Germans in our zone will become increasingly pro-British; it will not so much be necessary to hold them down as to hold them back. Of course, we shall be charged with being pro-German.

'I am not frightened of that. The Labour Party won't mind; the Conservatives might, but I can deal with them. I am indispensable to them.'

*July 23, 1945*
When I went into the P.M.'s room this morning he was breakfasting. I found Sawyers mopping the table by the bed; the P.M.

had upset his pineapple juice. Sawyers took a long time and the P.M. got impatient.

'That will do, Sawyers; you can do that later.'

But Sawyers went on mopping. At last the P.M. burst out:

'Oh, leave it, Sawyers, leave it. Come back later.'

Immediately Sawyers had left the room the P.M. turned to me with great solemnity:

'I am going to tell you something you must not tell to any human being. We have split the atom. The report of the great experiment has just come in. A bomb was let off in some wild spot in New Mexico. It was only a thirteen-pound bomb, but it made a crater half a mile across. People ten miles away lay with their feet towards the bomb; when it went off they rolled over and tried to look at the sky. But even with the darkest glasses it was impossible. It was the middle of the night, but it was as if seven suns had lit the earth; two hundred miles away the light could be seen. The bomb sent up smoke into the stratosphere.'

'It is H. G. Wells stuff,' I put in.

'Exactly,' the P.M. agreed. 'It is the Second Coming. The secret has been wrested from nature. The Americans spent £400 million on it. They built two cities. Not a soul knew what they were working at. All scientists have been busy with it. I have been very worried. We put the Americans on the bomb. We fired them by suggesting that it could be used in this war. We have an agreement with them. It gives the Americans the power to mould the world. It may displace fuel; a fragment gives 800 horse-power. If the Russians had got it, it would have been the end of civilization. Dropped on London, it would remove the City. It is to be used in Japan, on cities, not on armies. We thought it would be indecent to use it in Japan without telling the Russians, so they are to be told today. It has just come in time to save the world.'[1]

---

[1] Moran later pointed out that Churchill had written prophetically about the atomic bomb back in 1925. 'Might not a bomb no bigger than an orange be found to possess a secret power to destroy a whole block of buildings – nay, to concentrate the force of a thousand tons of cordite and blast a township at a stroke?'

I asked what would happen if the Russians got the idea and caught up. The P.M. replied that it was possible, but they wouldn't be able to do it for three years, and we must fix things up in that time. The Americans and ourselves, he said, were the only nations with principles.

I asked what would happen if Germany gets on to it. The P.M. said:

'They were working on it during the war, but—' with a smile, 'you can't produce this overnight; we shall find out their preparations. Fire was the first discovery; this is the second.'

I own I was deeply shocked by this ruthless decision to use the bomb on Japan. I knew I was hopelessly illogical. From bows and arrows to bullets, and shells, and gas-shells, and gas, to a torpedo which might send a thousand men to the bottom of the sea; and finally, to an atomic bomb; there could be no one point when the process of destruction becomes immoral. It was all to no purpose. There had been no moment in the whole war when things looked to me so black and desperate, and the future so hopeless. I knew enough of science to grasp that this was only the beginning, like the little bomb which fell outside my hut in the woods near Poperinghe in 1915, and made a hole in the ground the size of a wash-basin. It was not so much the morality of the thing, it was simply that the lynch-pin that had been underpinning the world had been half wrenched out. I thought of my boys.

Rowan came into the room and I found myself listening to his conversation with the P.M. as one hears the voices around when going under an anaesthetic, voices very far off and not like real people. I went out and wandered through empty rooms. I once slept in a house where there had been a murder. I feel like that here.

All day, preparations have gone on for the dinner tonight. The P.M. feels that he has discharged his duty as host if he provides plain good fare and gives his guests plenty of elbow room to get at it. The sappers have made a great table to seat twenty-eight, but how, he demands, do they know how many it will take? He will not, he insists, have more guests than the table will seat comfortably, even if he has to cancel some of the invitations already sent out; so six of us rather self-consciously sat in the chairs – Tommy was Stalin, and I stood for Pavlov – until at last the P.M. was satisfied that there was plenty of room for all. As it is, two Ministers, Lord Leathers and Lord Cherwell, not to mention the Solicitor General, Sir Walter Monckton, have been sacrificed to give elbow room to the rest.

Half an hour before the appointed hour fifteen of the OGPU[1] marched through the gate in single file, carrying their tommy-guns as if they were about to use them. They vanished to take up positions behind the house. And then came the three national leaders with their captains, who had survived the miscalculations of six years of world war.

I sat next to Admiral King.[2] By contrast with Marshall, who has been a steadfast friend of England, King has always been very critical of us. His war is in the Pacific, and the conflict with Germany has been to him only a tiresome distraction. However, he made himself very pleasant to everyone and agreed that Britain and America were the only Powers in the world capable of disinterested action.

Innumerable speeches, as usual, punctuated the meal. The P.M. spoke of Truman in a happy little speech, and the President, in his reply, said that when he found himself chairman without any experience of these conferences he was almost overwhelmed. He felt very timid, but he hoped he had been fair, and he would try to be so in the future. When he sat down, Stalin got up at once and extolled Truman's modesty. This is an old trick of Stalin's to divide the democracies. He will not learn that the P.M. is jealous of no man, and that his generous temper is one of the graces of our time. While the P.M. was praising Truman, King whispered to me:

'Watch the President. This is all new to him, but he can take it. He is a more typical American than Roosevelt, and he will do a good job, not only for the United States but for the whole world.'

---

[1] The Russian organization for the investigation and combat of counter-revolutionary activities. Founded, 1922.
[2] Chief of American Naval Operations, 1942–5.

As the night went on the P.M. became more and more carefree, and it was in the most glowing terms that he spoke of Stalin, ending, as at Teheran, by calling him Stalin the Great. Then Stalin got up, and with a few perfunctory words of thanks – even in Russian his words rasped out as if he were impatient and rather contemptuous of this smooth stuff – went on to speak of Japan. He has usually got something at the back of his head, and tonight it was clear that it was Japan. Stalin said it would not be right to allow Britain and America to shed their blood there without help from the Soviet Union. When Stalin sat down the P.M. rose to propose a toast, but he did not refer to Stalin's speech. Rowan tells me that the P.M. is not really keen on Russia coming into the war with Japan because of the demands she will make on China; anyway, he isn't going to seem pressing.

At the end of dinner I noticed Stalin on his feet with a menu in his hand, collecting signatures. Winston growled, 'This means signing twenty-eight menus,' but for some reason all these hardened, sophisticated, wandering men began to take their menus round, and the P.M. himself sent Sawyers round with his. There was a shortage of fountain pens, and the consequent borrowing and general movement seemed to break the ice of formality and to generate a very friendly spirit. Brooke brought his card to me:

'You must sign when we have travelled together so many times.'

From anyone else that would mean little, but it is very unlike Brooke's reserved nature, with his dislike of gush, to make an observation of this kind. Anyway, his friendliness gave me pleasure, for as the years have passed I have come to respect his character, his complete integrity, his contempt for flattery, his indifference alike to praise and blame, and his great longing for peace. He said to me tonight:

'I have felt that every day of this war was taking off a month of my life.'

Stalin took his own menu around. At first he had been a little sticky; now he was smiling and most amiable. More than once he got up and walked into the next room, where the band of the Air Force was playing, and stood listening. 'Could they play something light?' he asked.

The P.M. put through a call to Max tonight and asked whether he still took the same view of the result of the election. Max replied that minor corrections might be necessary. The figure of a hundred was not sacrosanct, but, broadly speaking, he had not altered his estimate. The P.M. would have a comfortable majority. Winston invited Max to come to Downing Street on Thursday morning, when the results would be coming out, and to stay to lunch; Brendan was coming.

*July 24, 1945*
The P.M. went to visit the President in his tropical Air Force uniform, but the wind had gone round to the east, and he came back very cold and out of humour.

'I'm sick of the bloody Poles. I don't want to see them. Why can't Anthony talk to them? If I have to see them I shall tell them there is no support in western Europe for a puppet Polish state, the tool of Russia.

'Tommy,' the P.M. burst out irritably, 'I really think General Montgomery ought to do something about our water.'

(Since the main was torn by a falling tree we have had no water.)

'Can't they bring a water cart and fill the boiler from it by a hose?'

Tommy hadn't thought of this. The devilled chicken, too, was wrong; the P.M. doesn't like chicken 'messed about.'

Two very stiff whiskies and a brandy dispersed the black clouds, and at the end of luncheon he was all quips and smiles. 'Charles, will you transfer your services to Attlee?' I was driven to protest, but he held out his hand affectionately: 'Ah, my dear, I was only joking.' Presently he began to nod; it was more apparent to him than ever that it was Anthony's job to see the Poles. I pressed him to rest before the conference, which had been fixed for five o'clock. He asked if he might take a 'red.'

'I feel quite different,' the P.M. said when he awoke after a short sleep. Sawyers kept looking at his watch. 'You're going to be late, sir.'

After the conference I dined with Rowan; he was full of the

P.M.'s tussle with Stalin. There had been a real set-to, and the P.M. had been superb. All the petulance and irritation, to which we are accustomed when the bath water is cold or the food is not to his liking, are shed when he comes to play a part in public. Like the boxer, he has learnt what happens when he loses his temper; long experience has taught him a kind of self-discipline in debate. He does not just blurt out the first thing that comes into his head.

Truman was firm, too. The Russians could not introduce their particular form of government into countries liberated directly or indirectly by all the Allies and then expect America and Britain to recognize those governments. This was his view today. It would be his view tomorrow. The P.M. said that in one country our representatives were restricted and shut in; it really amounted to internment. Stalin retorted that the P.M. was indulging in fairy-tales. The P.M. at once replied that it was one way of conducting a debate, to represent what the other side said as just a fairy-tale. Rowan said Vyshinsky was perspiring freely and was plainly unhappy. Birse, the interpreter, was sure that Vyshinsky was in for a real dressing-down from Stalin. The Russians were having a bad day. Stalin saw that they were getting nowhere, and said that their points of view were so different that the discussion must be adjourned for private debate.

Rowan said that the P.M. had asked him afterwards whether he had been too rough with the Russians.

'I told him he wasn't rough enough with them, at any rate when they talked about the Turks.'

In one afternoon the Russians had asked for a say in Algiers, a colony in North Africa and for the Dardanelles.

The P.M. has been helped by the atmosphere of this Conference, which is quite different from that of Teheran and of Yalta. There, Stalin was at pains to secure Roosevelt's backing. The President, without a word to the Prime Minister, would declare that the Russian case was most reasonable, and that it would have his support. What could Churchill do? But here, at Potsdam, it was soon plain that Roosevelt's death had changed everything. Truman is very blunt; he means business. His method is not to deploy an argument, but to state his conclusions. It reminds me of 'Wully' Robertson in the First War – 'I've 'eard different.' The President is not going to be content to feed out of anyone's hand: he intends to get to the bottom of things, and when Stalin gets tough Truman at once makes it plain that he, too, can hand out the rough stuff. The Allies are not in the mood to do all the giving. It is even possible to speak critically of the Russians.

And the P.M., Rowan says, rubs his eyes to make sure that he is not dreaming, chortles, looks very pleased and is quick to give President Truman vigorous and measured support. And how adroit he is!

Tonight, when he was full of Truman's praises, the P.M. said:

'If only this had happened at Yalta.' There was a long pause. 'It is too late now,' he said sadly. He knows that the time to settle frontiers has gone. The Red Army is spreading over Europe. It will remain.

### July 25, 1945

Winston told me this morning that he had had an unpleasant dream:

'I dreamed that life was over. I saw – it was very vivid – my dead body under a white sheet on a table in an empty room. I recognized my bare feet projecting from under the sheet. It was very life-like.' He mused: 'Perhaps this is the end.'

### London, July 26, 1945

Today as I walked along Pall Mall to the College of Physicians, where I was lunching, I met Jock Colville. He said there had been a landslide 'like 1906.' Brendan, Harold Macmillan and other Ministers were out.

After the Comitia, when Fellows were having tea in the hall of the College, Dorothy brought me the three-o'clock results given on the wireless, which I read to them. They were so taken aback they stood there in complete silence. One Fellow so far forgot where he was as to emit a low whistle. A little later the four-o'clock results confirmed the rout.

I walked down to the Annexe. The P.M. was with Alan Lascelles;

I wrote him a note. He sent out a message that he would like to see me. He was sitting in the small room next to the secretaries', where I had never seen him before, doing nothing. He was lost in a brown study. He looked up. 'Well, you know what has happened?' I spoke of the ingratitude of the people. 'Oh, no,' he answered at once, 'I wouldn't call it that. They have had a very hard time.'

I expressed my fears that it might end in Stalin's being given too much of his own way. But the P.M. replied that Attlee and Bevin would stand up to Stalin: 'I do not feel down at all. I'm not certain the Conservative Party could have dealt with the labour troubles that are coming. It will be said Max brought me down,' he mused, 'but I shall never say that. He is far harder hit by this result than any of us.'

I said what I could to comfort him: that there was great unrest in the country; that demobilization, housing and unemployment would add to it; and that it was inevitable that the Government in power would get the blame. I said that I had dreaded the next two years for him. I think this brought him a little comfort, but he said nothing. At last he spoke. 'The public will be staggered when they hear tonight at nine o'clock that I've resigned. Labour will be in for four years at least. They may make it difficult for the Conservatives to come in again. But I think the financial consequences of their policy will be their undoing. This is not necessarily the end.'

I said that if he went abroad for health or other purpose I would like to go with him as I had done during the war, and that I should be hurt if he did not make use of me. He rose and thanked me for what I had done for him. 'If it hadn't been for you I might not be here now,' he said with tears in his eyes.

He blamed no one. He was very sad as he talked quietly about what had happened. I left him, for I did not want to add to his distress by showing my own feelings. For some time I have had a growing disquiet that he has lost touch with the way people are thinking; but I was not prepared for this debacle. I was so sure that we should return to Berlin that I left my luggage there. Now I must arrange for its recovery.

*July 27, 1945*

This morning, calling at the Annexe at 9.45, I found everything strangely quiet. The place seemed deserted. Sawyers told me before I went to his bedroom that Winston had been giddy before retiring. But when I went in he said at once: 'I'm very well.' He spoke very quietly; he was sad but quite composed. He had been 'stunned by the result.' He felt there was 'some disgrace in the size of the majority.' If it had been thirty or forty it would have been different. The soldiers had been noticeably cool when he opened the 'Winston Club' in Berlin. They had been told to cheer, but it was obvious that they had voted against him. The Army, he went on, had had a big say in these events. At his age there could be no question of a come-back. I asked him if he was going to take a holiday.

'There is no difficulty about holidays now,' he said with a wistful smile. 'The rest of my life will be holidays. It will be worse in three days, like a wound; I shall then realize what it means. What I shall miss is this' – pointing to the red box full of papers. 'It is a strange feeling, all power gone,' he mused. 'I had made all my plans; I feel I could have dealt with things better than anyone else. This is Labour's opportunity to bring in socialism, and they will take it. They will go very far.'

# Appendices

Appendices

# Appendix 1

List of hitherto unpublished material included in this new edition.

1. January 9, 1942
New notes on Singapore, Rudolph Hess's flight to Scotland, von Ribbentrop, Lord Beaverbrook and Churchill's health have been added, from Box 59 – PP/CMW/K.4/1.
2. August 7, 1942
New note on the P.M. and remarks by General Alexander, from Box 59 – PP/CMW/K.4/1.
3. August 14, 1942
New note on Sir Alexander Cadogan, from Box 59 – PP/CMW/K.4/1.
4. August 15, 1942
New note on John Reed and remarks by the P.M., from Box 59 – PP/CMW/K.4/1.
5. January 16, 1943
New remarks by Lord Moran on Casablanca, from Box 59 – PP/CMW/K.4/1.
6. January 30, 1943
New footnote on the P.M. and the Turks, from Box 59 – PP/CMW/K.4/1.
7. February 3, 1943
New note about Tripoli and the Italians, from Box 59 – PP/CMW/K.4/1.
8. August 11, 1943
New note about Clemmie (Mrs Churchill) being difficult, from Box 59 – PP/CMW/K.4/1.
9. August 21, 1943
New notes about General George Marshall and Mountbatten, from Box 59 – PP/CMW/K.4/1.
10. August 22, 1943
New note on people's opinions of Mountbatten, from Box 59 – PP/CMW/K.4/1.

11. August 23, 1943

New note on General Sir Hastings ('Pug') Ismay, from Box 59 –
PP/CMW/K.4/1.

12. September 2, 1943

New note on Churchill's thoughts on war, from Box 59 – PP/CMW/K.4/1.

13. September 14, 1943

Signal from Churchill to General Alexander giving advice, from Box 59 –
PP/CMW/K.4/1.

14. November 16, 1943

New note on Moran's thoughts on Winant and others, from Box 59 –
PP/CMW/K.4/1.

15. November 18, 1943

New note on a conversation with John Martin, Churchill's P.P.S., from Box
59 – PP/CMW/K.4/1.

16. December 1, 1943

New note on an argument between Moran and Churchill, including a
disagreement over the imprisonment of Oswald Mosley, from Box 59 –
PP/CMW/K.4/1.

17. August 17, 1944

New notes on Moran's thoughts on the Italian campaign, from Box 59 –
PP/CMW/K.4/1.

18. August 20, 1944

New note on Moran's assessment of General Alexander, from Box 59 –
PP/CMW/K.4/1.

19. September 13, 1944

New note on Churchill's remarks on the war and the future, from Box 59 –
PP/CMW/K.4/1.

20. September 13, 1944

Addition to footnote about Churchill's role in 1940, from Box 58 –
PP/CMW/K.3/3/3.

21. Chapter 22

New note on Roosevelt and Russia, from Box 59 – PP/CMW/K.4/1.

22. October 11, 1944

New note on Moran sightseeing with the C.I.G.S., from Box 59 –
PP/CMW/K.4/1.

23. October 20, 1944

New footnote – Churchill's opinion that England wanted nothing from the
war, from Box 59 –
PP/CMW/K.4/1/1

24. February 4, 1945

New note on Stalin and an observation on Sir Alexander Cadogan by
Moran, from Box 59 – PP/CMW/K.4/2.

25. February 11, 1945

New footnote on Roosevelt's ineptitude over Poland at Yalta, from Box 58 –
PP/CMW/K.3/6/1.

26. March 1 1945
New note on the views of the P.M., Basil Brooke and Herbert Morrison on
Ulster and the Home Office, from Box 59 –
PP/CMW/K.4/1/1.
27. July 12, 1945
New footnote on Indo-China, from Box 59 – PP/CMW/K.4/2.
28. Chapter 27
New note on Roosevelt shortly after his death, from Box 59 –
PP/CMW/K.4/1/3.
29. July 17, 1945
New note on Truman and Eden, from Box 60 – PP/CMW/K.4/2.
30. July 19, 1945
New note on Stalin's views of political matters in England, from Box 60 –
PP/CMW/K.4/2.
31. July 23, 1945
New footnote on Churchill's prophecy of the atom bomb in 1925, from Box
58 – PP/CMW/K.3/6/1.

# Appendix 2

*Letter from Sir Charles Wilson to Lord Beaverbrook.*

18<sup>th</sup> April 1941.

Dear Lord Beaverbrook,

I find this in my war diary:

> Last Monday when we were in the trenches a man reported sick and I sent him back to duty. The following day he came again and again I sent him back. But the day after he was still there among the morning sick. 'It's no good, Sir,' he said, 'I can't stick it no longer.' Once more I thoroughly overhauled him; there was nothing wrong with him physically and he was sane enough. He was simply tired; but so were others. Once more I sent him back. Next day he was killed. Unable or unwilling? This man festers in my mind. I see his face weak and sulky, and watch him slouching back reluctantly to the trenches. I see him return on a stretcher, his head all swathed in bloody bandages, a yellow froth around his gaping mouth. I hear his breathing almost stop, and then rise gradually to a great heaving gasp; and this regular rise and fall goes on till there is a pause when nothing follows and after a little I know that he is dead.

That sort of thing is always happening in war; it eats into the mind. It would be intolerable if the lives of those of us past fighting were not at the disposal of the country. We do not count; our lives are nearly over. I read the brief obituary notices of those boys who go out in the air; their story has hardly begun, but you get enough to see they were the leaders of their small community, school or university. It drives one to work that this business may come to an end before all these lads are gone; every minute seems to count. Those who have reflected on war come to admire not the gaudy act performed on the spur of the moment but rather the steady resolve to see the thing through. I remember a man at Ypres whose nerve had gone, and I sent him sick, but when he got to the casualty clearing station and the war for him was over he got out of the ambulance and asked to be sent back to the Battalion. That seemed to me real courage.

That your boy – when he had done enough in the air to satisfy his conscience in doing a ground job – should of his own free will return to night fighting is a superb gesture; this is the real stuff of leadership. I know what it must mean to you. I watch my own lad, now 16½, and determined to join the Air Force when he can, grow older; if he went out the meaning of life would be gone. I feel no thrill, no sense of achievement in being President, only a chance of doing something in my small field to make the machine go more smoothly, for the Ministry of Health is of more moment in a war than many think.

You say your job is finished. Surely it has only just begun. It is not numbers of aircraft that will win the war in the air. It is, of course, quality. We have to harness science to the job, and that is as yet only done in a small way. No other nation has a body like the Royal Society. Men who have creative minds, who invent and plan new things. Dale, the President of the Royal, has creative talent and yet is a man of affairs – a rare combination. I'd like you to talk with him and get to know him. Your job finishes when the war finishes. To leave it now before a solution is found to the night bomber, when things look black, is unthinkable. Scientific men of real creative genius are individualists and kittle kettle to control. I want you to go down as the man who was unconventional enough to break through convention and bring these men to the rescue. We can't win in any other way. Humour them, like racehorses, they are all nerves, anybody can scrap with them, only you could get the best out of them. Patience was the faculty which the historian put first in Marlborough's equipment of war. Think of the effect just now of the resignation of a member of the War Cabinet on the public when it is going to get a good many hard knocks; the inevitable suggestion of divided counsels. How often is it necessary for anyone engaged on a long job of work among uncomprehending people to resist resignation as an easy, emotional and impulsive escape from a tangle of difficulties and uncertainties. Your real task is not to get the better of the Bosche but of your temperament.

I'd like to see you get away from your desk at times, among the workers of the aircraft factories. They would respond. The relations between employer and workers are as you know governed not by wages but by emotions; it is a question of psychology (cf. Rootes of Coventry). We might have even in war a new era in which this great industry was held up after the war as an example of how men can work all out and yet be content. I'll be your welfare officer if you haven't one. I remember going on a night trench raid without stretcher bearers on the theory that the men would bring back their own killed and wounded if they were satisfied that the Medical Officer was willing to take the same risks as they were. It was looked on as a mad scheme, but it worked, and they brought back nine killed and thirty-nine wounded out of a party of a hundred and ten. It will always work. Where labour is restive it can only be reassured in like fashion. I'd like to live among them in a bad area and get my wife to work among their women.

I entreat you not to be angry with this didactic letter. What you do now may save the life of your boy and mine and the lads of thousands of others; more, it may win the war. That is why I have written and because I like you very much. I broke the rule of a lifetime in talking to the Prime Minister about you, not because he was Prime Minister but because I wanted him to be clear there was no health reason why you should not go on doing your job.

Be strong enough to be idle at times, even when Rome seems to burn.

Yours sincerely,

*Letter from Lord Beaverbrook to Sir Charles Wilson.*

19th April 1941.

My dear Wilson,

You are as good a letter-writer as you are an orator.

But it is not possible for me to continue in office.

There are three reasons that stand in the way –

(1) Influenza in March.
(2) An operation to my eye.
(3) The removal of six polypi, as a result of which I am still bleeding.

And even if I were willing to stay, I would be of no value to the Prime Minister. He does not ask my advice, nor does he need it.

As for my special responsibility, there are more aircraft than the Air Ministry can use.

And when I criticize the Air Ministry, the Prime Minister looks upon me as a quarrelsome fellow. The rumour has been circulated everywhere among my colleagues that I have a bad temper.

I can do more good outside the Government than inside. I will support them in the Lords and in the newspapers.

I admit that there is one reason, although only one, why I should not go. It would prevail if I were not sick.

In addition to being sick I am tough. The Prime Minister needs tough men around him. I hope he will always give the tough men he has got encouragement in their tough courses.

I would like very much to see Dale. I was at a dinner the other night and looked all about for him. But he was not there.

It is quite unnecessary of you to hope that I will not be angry with you for writing me this letter. On the contrary I find it a most charming and splendid letter.

Yours ever,

# Appendix 3

Churchill's 'Iron Curtain' telegram.

*Prime Minister to President Truman*

12 May 45.

I am profoundly concerned about the European situation. I learn that half the American Air Force in Europe has already begun to move to the Pacific theatre. The newspapers are full of the great movements of the American armies out of Europe. Our armies also are, under previous arrangements, likely to undergo a marked reduction. The Canadian Army will certainly leave. The French are weak and difficult to deal with. Anyone can see that in a very short space of time our armed power on the Continent will have vanished except for moderate forces to hold down Germany.

2. Meanwhile what is to happen about Russia? I have always worked for friendship with Russia, but, like you, I feel deep anxiety because of their misinterpretation of the Yalta decisions, their attitude towards Poland, their overwhelming influence in the Balkans, excepting Greece, the difficulties they make about Vienna, the combination of Russian power and the territories under their control or occupied, coupled with the Communist technique in so many other countries, and above all their power to maintain very large armies in the field for a long time. What will be the position in a year or two, when the British and American Armies have melted and the French has not yet formed on any major scale, when we may have a handful of divisions, mostly French, and when Russia may choose to keep two or three hundred on active service?

3. An iron curtain is drawn down upon their front. We do not know what is going on behind. There seems little doubt that the whole of the regions east of the line Lübeck–Trieste–Corfu will soon be completely in their hands. To this must be added the further enormous area conquered by the American armies between Eisenach and the Elbe, which will, I suppose, in a few weeks be occupied, when the Americans retreat, by the Russian power. All kinds of

arrangements will have to be made by General Eisenhower to prevent another immense flight of the German population westward as this enormous Muscovite advance into the centre of Europe takes place. And then the curtain will descend again to a very large extent, if not entirely. Thus a broad band of many hundreds of miles of Russian-occupied territory will isolate us from Poland.

4. Meanwhile the attention of our peoples will be occupied in inflicting severities upon Germany, which is ruined and prostrate, and it would be open to the Russians in a very short time to advance if they chose to the waters of the North Sea and the Atlantic.

5. Surely it is vital now to come to an understanding with Russia, or see where we are with her, before we weaken our armies mortally or retire to the zones of occupation. This can only be done by a personal meeting. I should be most grateful for your opinion and advice. Of course we may take the view that Russia will behave impeccably, and no doubt that offers the most convenient solution. To sum up, this issue of a settlement with Russia before our strength has gone seems to me to dwarf all others.

# Index

Photo opposite: Sir Charles Wilson (Lord Moran) supplied by his son John, the present Lord Moran (privately owned).